TALKING OF MICHELANGELO
AN AUTOBIOGRAPHY

TALKING OF MICHELANGELO

AN AUTOBIOGRAPHY

Meditations on doubt, struggle and fulfilment

JOHN HARRY

Copyright © John Harry 2025
First published by Hembury Books in 2025
hemburybooks.com.au
info@hemburybooks.com
Paperback ISBN 9781923517127
Hardback 9781923517134
Ebook ISBN 9781923517110

The moral right of the author has been asserted.
All rights reserved. No portion of this book may be reproduced
in any form without permission from the author and publisher,
except as permitted by Australian copyright law.

 A catalogue record for this book is available from the National Library of Australia

Dedication

For Donna Harry, my wife: a woman blessed with beauty,
empathy, kindness, energy, joie de vie and will;
who has guarded and rescued me
and made me trust and believe again.

Contents

Preface	ix
Beginnings	1
Family	29
The Storm and the Calm	45
Extended Family	53
Wine	61
Parents	73
Ralph – His Life	79
Dorothy – Her Life	91
Sport	107
Some Philosophy	141
Harry Family History	149
Switzerland	159
Singapore	175
Melbourne	185
Out Into the Wide World	217
Law School and Trinity College	225
The Sixties	235
Intermission	241
The Big, Bad World	245
The Law	247
The Rio Tinto Years	255
The University of Virginia	281
New York	291
Photography	293
Edging Away from Law	303
Wanderings	331
Epilogue	353
Scribblings	355
Acknowledgements	399
About the Author	401

Preface

I'm not sure why, one day, I decided to write a life story. You would have thought I'd know because a decision to spend five years of my afternoon light at my Mac Air ought not to have been taken lightly.

I know now.

It's to thank the universe for having allowed me the privilege of life. I'm the beneficiary of the cataclysmic moment of creation, the formation in the stars of the elements of which I'm made, billions of years of evolution involving the extinction of uncountable species that struggled to maintain a foothold on the earth but failed; and my membership of the human race, with its ability to perceive itself and its powers and the nature and destiny of the universe, and to form its future.

It's been a final accounting with myself as well, of course. Life is like a puff of white smoke in a wind: here and gone. For a man to want to anchor a picture of himself somewhere in the deluge of time is understandable, even though the photo might be grainy and faded.

My father taught me that the way to virtue and acceptance was through compliance, discipline, compromise, convention – a combination of qualities that were the opposite of those I was born with. My life was a war and constant questions: Who am I? Why have I felt unresolved and anxious? Why have I made such poor decisions at such important times? How can I find balance and peace?

It's not hard to see why many of my friends and family have seen me as a puzzle. A man at war with himself is like that.

I had an eye operation not long ago. It's been life-changing. My vision is now sharp and bright, textures and contrasts are now visible, colours are unclouded and true. White is white, not sepia. The world looks fresh and inviting and everything I see brings joy: from the brilliance of a flower to the star fire in the night sky.

Just as I lacked the ability to see the world as it was, I now understand that my upbringing didn't give me the emotional tools I needed to see the world of people as it was.

This volume is a tale of my long journey towards understanding, and of the many kind and patient people who've reached out to help me along the way. It's been like climbing down a deep valley and up the other side. At the bottom, a magnificent person, my wife Donna, took my hand and led me upward.

I don't want to mislead you. Many of the contradictions and puzzles in my life have no easy answers, or perhaps no answers at all, but I think contemplating them seriously as I've grown older has brought a measure of calm and satisfaction.

As well as searching, I'm trying to say: this is who I really was and now really am; I hope you can now understand and, finally, we can see each other. There's adventure, success, failure and regret. Each experience has taught me something. I'm happy about the failures and regrets, because out of them have come knowledge, gratitude and the vulnerability that makes us tolerable.

Like all humans, my heart is part-dark and part-light. I'm not sure what this volume will show; dusk maybe. I acknowledge the dark, but some of the dark things I leave for you to guess. After all, my children will read this. I hope they now understand that they're reading the truth. If they don't believe me, then they'll have missed one of the main purposes of this work. And they will have failed to understand that parents have no choice but to allow their children to understand them slowly.

All of us reach a tipping point where ageing can no longer be contested. I have, and that itself has concentrated and balanced my thinking.

I began by assuming this would be easy. Just list your memories in some sort of order and all will be well. Most people see me as an achiever, as larger than life, as a visionary, as a builder, as a maker of things, who should find it easy to tell a good story.

I was wrong, of course. I had no idea it would be so hard.

I thought my door would open more easily for you if this story took the form of a quiet conversation between me and a much-loved boyhood mate. That way, it would be more human, more honest, more real.

My old mate is Jimmy Marr. Jimmy was one of the few people who cared for me when I was young, and who was happy to spend any amount of time talking to me freely about anything.

I loved my time with Jimmy. I hope you enjoy meeting him too.

You might be wondering about the title to this volume. It's a phrase from the great poem "The Love Song of J. Alfred Prufrock" by T.S. Eliot in which Prufrock, alienated, impotent and anxious, overhears women speaking amongst themselves of Michelangelo in a conversation he feels he can never be part of. I named the first book of photographs I made years ago as "Outside In", because then I was the same kind of man. Now, I feel I can join and feel welcome in that conversation. It's taken such a long time.

JH

Beginnings

My farmhouse sits in the foothills of an ancient mountain range just east of Melbourne.

We're at the southern end of the Great Dividing Range, on the edge of the wildlands that run north to the Snowy Mountains of New South Wales. It's been a home to miners, loggers, fringe Christians, Buddhists and hippies since the 1850s.

My bluestone gravel driveway runs away steeply from our house and divides a small lake, alive with ducks and lilies, from my silver winery shed. It's early spring and the flower beds are a sparkling sea of daffodils, jonquils, tulips and irises. The quality of light is bright and precise but not yet the searing, hard radiation of summer, so the colours are soft and deep. Summer is coming. So might be bushfires. So is my hard vineyard work.

I'm sitting at the top of the drive, finishing a coffee, looking out for my old friend Jim Marr. I saw him after a long break only a couple of weeks ago and invited him up to see the farm. I thought I might talk to him about a life story I'm writing because he's known me since I was a boy and he tells the truth.

His smart Audi crunches to a stop a couple of minutes later. He steps out of the car looking old and uncertain. He's not the man I knew, but I'll always love him. We're both in our seventies now, but I'm not as worn as he is.

"Jim, great to see you, come on in."

"Good to be here, Johnnie. What a lovely part of the world," he says, smiling, looking up at Mount Victoria to the west. "You look fit!"

I don't, but I accept the compliment. Men say that to each other out of respect, like shaking hands.

Johnnie or Jack were the names my school and uni mates called me, but it's been a while since anyone's used them.

"How are you?" he asks.

"Not bad," I say. "It's been too long, no excuses. I should have been in touch."

I try to keep up with old mates, but lots of them are in bad shape now, and I'm wary of being drawn into lives I can't help. So, I keep to myself a bit these days.

Jim steps into the kitchen. Our wood fire's burning even though it's October. Winter leaves these mountains late. There's comfort and friendship in a fire; it's a warm spirit that winds through the house when you light it and retreats silently when it dies. Like many of the things I find myself drawn to, it's an ancient and communal thing that has gathered and protected mankind for millennia.

Donna and I have been living here for twelve years, and we wouldn't move to the city now.

Jimmy was a lot like me when we were young, except that we were different sizes. We lived in a different lane, not like the conformist, headed-for-prefect sucks there were so many of. We had an edge, a sense that other boys couldn't resolve – me probably because my size was a threat and I could be unforgiving and sarcastic, and Jimmy because he didn't buy the Toorak booze and blondes routine.

He was quiet and settled and just wanted to surf. In the early '60s the culture was tight, and to be in, you had to be an athlete, have the right body shape, shut your trap and obey the rules. Jim was a beautiful skier as well. He was always in trouble for wearing surfie shoes or bumfreezer suit jackets, sneaking off to a nearby pub for a couple of pots at lunchtimes, or smoking in the dunnies.

In winter he used to take me out of boarding school to Lorne for weekends and push me into the bitter green surf on a patched malibu, wearing budgie smugglers and an old woolly jumper. The winter beach was always deserted apart from idiots like us.

Jimmy thought that I should surf because I could ski. He would cut a precise and loving path through that ocean chaos; I would fall and fall and fall, but when I stayed on a wave, it was shouting, mad joy. In winter the sun would slant and soften and turn the waves into translucent, shifting jade prisms, not the blinding white slabs of January. Because I was a rower, I couldn't surf in summer. I would love to have had more of that gypsy life.

When we got thawed out we'd have a couple of hamburgers with the lot on the esplanade and walk past the crashing surf down to Ron Todd's Pacific Hotel bar after six p.m. closing time. We were maybe fifteen, but I was well over six feet then. We'd knock on the door and a little hatch would open, Ronny's tired eye would appear and look us up and down, then he'd let us into the bar full of rowdy local farmers and tradies. I don't know how Jim and Ron got to know each other.

After many pots, we'd buy a bottle of port and go back to Jimmy's parents' house and sit on the high terrace wrapped in blankets, looking out at the beach through the dim streetlights. More often than not we'd wake up on the terrace with the warm gold of morning in our eyes. Sometimes we'd talk all night. Sometimes we'd just sit there for hours quietly soaking in the briny wind. Then, anything seemed possible.

Ron Todd was, by the way, a famous Collingwood full forward but he got hit a lot in his footy days and didn't age all that well. But he told us some great stories.

Jimmy was slim with a high forehead and close-cropped curly chestnut hair, a weathered brown, round face, and he didn't talk unless there was something to say. He had a way of making people feel easy and liked. His face would crumple when he laughed. He made big money as a stockbroker then retired when he was thirty-something to sail a yacht in the Mediterranean with his family. He developed a serious alcohol habit and it was plain that he'd come to grief one day. Sometimes he'd come back to ski at Mount Buller because he liked our ski club. I saw him there and we went out together a lot. But I could never get up the mountain early enough on Fridays to beat him to the bar – he was usually into his second bottle of Ouzo when I arrived, and out of reach.

So, I decided Jimmy and I should just start a conversation and let it run. He won't worry about a bibliography or an index. He's a rare bloke who mostly asks questions. He was interested in me in my early years and understood a lot of my life and what a grim prison boarding school was. A rebel with quick eyes and a good heart. He thought he could turn me into someone interesting. He was ambitious, because back then most people would have said it was a waste of time.

"Come and grab a seat, Jimmy. Donna's away for the night so we have some time. Would you like a glass of something?"

"Very kind of you."

"Chardy?"

"Perfect."

I grab a bottle from the fridge.

"Is this your wine?" Jim asks.

"It is."

"I knew you were a wine lover, but I had no idea you'd got so deep into it."

"One day that door opened. I've been captivated by everything about it since I was a kid. I love caring for the vines as the summer rolls on, the tension of harvest and the hope for each barrel. And seeing the wines through their growing up. It's been hard work but lots of fun. But I'm tired of it now so I've decided to pull the vines out at the end of this season."

"Never thought you'd surrender to age!" Jim says.

"Nor did I. I'm happy with the decision though, and anyway, I've got more than I can ever drink so it's not all bad. And I'm not going to be tied to the vineyard from September to May any longer."

We chat back and forth about different people we know. He mentions someone I used to think of as my best mate, called Peter.

"Do you see much of Peter these days?" he asks.

I'm slow to answer. He married a young and beautiful girl called Savannah, who turned on me after my first marriage ended. I always thought she was soft and liked me, but she spat me out without a thought and so Peter faded away as well. I was sad to lose him – we had some great times. His mum was mad but loved me. Maybe I owed the friendship to her. She was one of the first adults who offered me respect and kindness and showed me her soul.

"Don't worry, mate. It happens. I always thought he crossed too many boundaries. No great loss to you, I reckon."

Jim's right. Pete was charming but naughty. He tried for years to set me up with one open-minded girl or another, but I was too gauche to appeal to any of them. Being a boarder was the kiss of death because it usually meant country rough. He became a courier for a kids' bus touring company in Europe after he left school, which gave him many opportunities, but I've never questioned him about that period.

"Anyway," Jim says, "let's talk about the book. You want me to turn you upside down and give you a good shake to see what comes out. Can I ask anything? Do I have to stick to a timeline? I'm looking forward to this because you never were someone to share secrets."

"No rules," I say. "You ask, I'll answer."

"So, why me?" Jim says, with a look stranded somewhere between doubt and gratitude.

"Because you know me and you're smart. There's something kind of doubtful about anyone writing a book about themselves. A look-at-me, dictatorial feel about it. Everyone's going to suspect me of lying."

"OK," Jim says, nosing the chardy and glancing at the bottle to see how much is left. He looks so happy and comfortable now. I think he likes the wine. "I reckon there might be more of this somewhere," he says, looking at me with a trace of a smile, but a trace of sadness too.

"Plenty enough even for you, son."

We laugh.

I suggest making a roadmap we can follow for our conversation, one with regular rest stops and permission to turn down interesting lanes.

"No!" Jim barks. "Let's just start and see where the road goes."

Sounds like he has more of a plan than I do. "And you can stay over?" I ask.

"No problem, I'll enjoy it. You can show me the winery and the cellar if you like. I'd love to take a look."

Jimmy sits back on the big pale tan sofa we're on, looking out the high windows to the east, toward the Yarra, through a plantation of high Chinese elms covered in new, shining leaves.

So, Johnnie, how much of the story have you written?

I've got a kind of first draft now, but I think of something else to add or change every day. I did a lot of work on it while Donna and I were in Syros last winter.

Can I try to get a picture of what you're aiming at with the book? That might help me?

Fair question, Jimmy, but I'm not sure I really know. Maybe, when it's done, I will.

Wouldn't it be better just to slide away silently like an actor leaving the stage and hope you're thought of in a good way?

Not me. You know I always rush in where angels fear to tread.

I remember. Our headmaster went on forever about how we needed to have integrity. What he really meant was that we should always obey orders and that if we did, we'd be thought of as reliable and responsible. You were famous for kicking against the wind and no one really envied the jams you got into.

You could agree with Oscar Wilde that it was better to be talked about than not talked about, but you know I was embarrassed and guilty about my indiscipline and stupidity. I feel as though I'm talking about a different man now, but I still look back on that time with sadness, with a sense of missed opportunity, of isolation and confrontation. I felt as though everyone I knew stood back and warmed their hands happily on the fires I lit and relished the idea that I was making a mess of my life and they weren't.

Can you be sure, do you reckon, that what you put out there in this book is really you?

No idea. All of us have inbuilt reflexes, prejudices, rule structures that cage us and stop us being what we would have preferred to be, or were destined to be had we had a clear shot.

And anyone's story's doubtful because it's always built from scraps and shadows or innocent fiction. Nothing I say or do means much in the end, I know, but even so, I need to leave a keepsake, a token, some paper and print that no one else could. Maybe it's that no one wants to go through the sweat and agony of being here without asking himself what he'd done and what kind of person he was?

I understand the thought. But most people wouldn't have had the will and energy to make it happen. I have the feeling that you're going to have a lot of people make a lot of noise about things you say, but it's admirable that you're willing to take that risk.

Before I started writing I hadn't thought much about me and my life. I have now. I can see that a lot has changed. I've decided I like myself more.

One Sunday morning a while ago I thought, well, maybe the way to test whether you do actually like yourself is to ask whether there's anyone else you know that you'd sooner be. I ran through the many people I'd known in my life and there wasn't one that I'd change places with. You can't believe how relieved I felt. Despite all of that, there are still moments when I feel as though my jigsaw's missing a piece or two.

Have you thought about what might make a good man? That's something you're thinking about, isn't it?

There aren't any benchmarks, Jimmy. It's just the fickle opinion of others. I've had a fair amount of undeserved criticism in my life and have been let down by many people I trusted, so now, my judgement is the only judgement that matters. It always disappoints me to hear people judge others as they were decades ago, without a second thought.

I've always tried to look at the ethical compass to see where I'm going. I've taken some detours, as we all do. But the last thing I'd try is to carve a monument to my goodness.

I want to make sure the facts are checked and recorded; to thank people who helped me in important ways; to celebrate my luck in being Australian and privileged; to provide a record for my family.

The Chinese think your key duty is to look after the generations that follow. I'm not going to leave my kids and grandkids wealthy, nor would I want to, but to give them a family record that they can feel is full and honest, and which connects them to their history, seems right. It might give them a sense of continuity, of roots, of belonging more securely to their family and background.

I know what you mean. But do you think the effort's going to be worth it?

I hope so. When the credits roll down the screen after a movie, it always makes me sad to see names appear at the top and roll off the bottom so quickly; such a short recognition for such hard work. The reception for this will be as short, but that doesn't matter to me; at least it will exist for longer than I do.

I have to ask you this – is your memory still OK? I don't mean that I've noticed any problem, but people like you are good at masking stuff like that.

I don't have looming Alzheimer's, if that's the question. But you're right. We need to understand memory if we plan to say anything about the past.

Janet Malcolm, a brilliant American biographer and critic, said something like this: The glitter of memory is deceptive. The past is a country that issues no visas. We can only enter it illegally.

Remembering is pulling together the fragments we've packed and reconstructing them; the result is hostage to how many fragments we recall, how many we've repressed or recast, our hopes, our prejudices, our fears, and how we look at the world. And everyone has multiple personas that we jump between, like in my case the sportsman, the adventurer, the wise man, the lawyer, the winemaker, the know-it-all, the deceiver, the dutiful husband. Who knows why we wake up as one and not the other?

And what about research?

The basics, yes. I've been doing bits and pieces for a while now. I might do a bit more digging when the draft's finished. I'd like to run through all my father's old films and diaries to see what that brings forth.

If you're expecting something scholarly, move on.

So, are there any guiding themes?

Yes. Honesty, and not offending anyone unless I can't tell the story otherwise. And the truth is that no matter what I say, there'll be some people who choose to get cranky.

There's an obvious issue around my former wife Mary. She has been unfriendly toward me and Donna since our separation which was twenty-three years ago, and as sad as that is, I have no intention of revisiting old battlefields. What I will do, though, is be frank about the origins of our difference.

I also need to weigh what I say about my father Ralph. His interest in my life was limited and somewhat reluctant, so we weren't mates. It would be easy for a son who didn't command much of his father's attention to be unfair in his judgements. But he gave me life and much other than attention, for which I'm in his debt, and I admire him for giving as much as he did to his country at high personal expense.

My children have been a deep joy and a fundamental commitment around which a large part of my life has revolved. They are actors in this drama, but their stories are theirs to tell, not mine, and just as when I die, they will be treated absolutely equally, I will tell each of them here, briefly, what they mean to me.

Do you worry that this won't capture anyone's interest?

Of course. But what else should I expect?

Will people be interested in the way you write, do you think?

I can only hope. I sometimes think of my background and wonder whether that could ever give birth to writing that's memorable.

Look at Paris in the '20s: a more cosmopolitan, diverse or productive society is hard to find; it brought together a galaxy of genius. Stein, Cocteau, Picasso, Stravinsky, Diaghilev, Proust, Hemingway, Chanel and on and on.

Read the magnificent autobiography of Margot Asquith, which draws a vivid picture of London society and politics in the 1890s and early twentieth century. Her pictures of Gladstone, Lord Randolph Churchill, Balfour and Chamberlain are unmissable portraits of those great minds. What must life have been like in that circle.

Few people have lived in societies like that, certainly not me, but I've been on the outside, challenged the rules, lived life with energy and will. I've been happy to step into new lives and take on things that most people don't. And thanks to my father, I was able to meet many great Australians who visited our family in different parts of the world, which lit my ambition and gave me my sense of possibility.

Are there any other individuals you've found inspirational?

You know about Alexei Navalny, the Russian opposition figure. We know that after recovering in Germany from Putin's poisoning attempt he went back to Russia only to be arrested and thrown into prison, but we don't understand that this man's life has been one assault after another, that he has constructed a Russian opposition on his own from nothing and with brilliance amidst great danger. His decision to return to Russia demanded extreme courage and persistence – what a man and what a life. He stands head and shoulders above most other mortals. And now Putin has killed him.

And what about Sinéad O'Connor? Not many people understand her history as a battered child and committed fighter for the independence of both women and men from the grip of the government, the Catholic Church and the press. She was a beautiful, intelligent and loving woman who underwent rape by media, which destroyed her happiness, her health and her journey as one of the most inspired vocal artists of her age. But her courage in battle was sustained and magnificent.

I discovered some years ago the abuse of children by men in a charitable Catholic order I worked for, unaware of their criminal habits. My response was decisive, but polite compared to Sinéad's. If we have time, Jim, I'll tell you that story. That she was a hero and a kind of saint is beyond doubt. If only I could say I'd had as much courage and defiance.

I realised years ago that men are what they do, and that the rest doesn't count. The truly commendable ones do things that are dangerous but necessary.

They ignore the tin gods of success and celebrity.

If only more of us did that.
So how have your kids reacted to the project?

They're aware of my work. One of them looked at me in a frightened kind of way when I was discussing my progress and asked if I meant to have it published. Was it that publication would disgrace the family because of incompetence? Yawns? Scandal? It was a funny moment. I didn't answer. Overall, though, they've supported me and they're keen to see how it turns out.

So has all this thinking about the past dug into the concrete of your assumptions about yourself? It sounds as though you've been your own psychoanalyst.

Yes. I've found it hard work. I've been left in tears many times. I've mourned many things and places and people, and the simplicity and eternity of childhood. I would love to have played more music with friends. I deflected my creative impulses for many years, believing that they were wasteful or somehow inappropriate. But that happened to men like me more often than not in those days.

Remembering has generated thoughts and connections that seem like rewiring to a long-past time – I'm looking at an image and suddenly there's déjà vu, more like déjà felt, actually. I'm taken back emotionally to the time and place where something happened. I'm looking for music on Spotify and a wisp of memory about what it was like for me to look at a picture of the Beatles for the first time quietly creeps in. The agony of envy, love, invitation, hope, hopelessness. Like being whipped along a wormhole. I thought all of that had long died, that the husk I was turning into was incapable of it.

New eyes can open; what I thought would be predictable and dry might not be after all; jumps in time can happen, learning can continue; spinning myself around on an imaginary lazy Susan might expose possibilities I had never imagined.

We'll be left with literary tweed, not silk, I know, but that's not such a bad thing.

You know I love quotes. For me, they're like a Buddhist bell ringing: sharp, clear, indisputable and necessary. They open doors and remind me of how much knowledge I'll never have, and how many brilliant people I'll never meet.

I know. It's depressing to read the sayings of great thinkers: while you love them and they're like finding the last number in a sudoku,

they make me realise how different and slow I am compared to them, and somehow that brings existential darkness closer.

We're brothers in that.

Anyway, you seem to be anxious about getting your story done. Do you have a reason to be worried?

No, but it has to be soon. I dread losing capability to old age and I know that phase isn't too far away. It turns the gas up a bit.

My sainted mum had Alzheimer's, so genetics are against me. Time was a gentle breeze for me at twenty; now it's a cyclone that wants to blow me off the world. I feel that wind every time I get out of bed. I continue to write despite those winds. Now I've come this far, the job has to be finished.

Charles de Gaulle said that ageing is a shipwreck. I know what he means: it's unexpected, it's fast and it's unpleasant.

Do you know Margaret Atwood?

I know she wrote The Handmaid's Tale, but that's it.

She published a collection of essays in 2022 called *Burning Questions*, which is full of intelligence and curiosity. At one point she quotes the Polish author Kapuściński as saying that we stand in darkness, surrounded by light.

That's how I've felt for a lot of my life: looking for connection, meaning and integration. Like being on a raft: always in motion, never able to rely absolutely on where I was, with no god, no pastor and no ease. Part of my problem of course was the curse of Aussie males: never admit sadness, never confide deep feelings in anyone especially family or friends, lest you be seen as weak.

So this is what you might call a Chautauqua? You remember the book called Zen and the Art of Motorcycle Maintenance? It became a cult classic in the '70s. It was a word Robert M. Pirsig

used to describe events where people met to discuss moral and philosophical subjects, and where learning came from lectures, concerts, performance and the general group energy.

Yes. I'm asking, who am I? and what have I done with my life? and does that feel acceptable? Say I try to be agreeable. Is that just an affectation? Put another way, is it me, or something cultivated and deceptive? I have no idea. It's also about confronting the reality of what my talents and disposition are. Do I have the ability to assess my life clearly and decisively, or am I producing nonsense?

Aren't you likely to find that there's no bottom, or reliable happiness or meaning? The sadness none of us can escape, isn't that because of the insoluble conflict between our search for meaning and significance, and the random nature of the universe?

I'm not ready to believe that life's absurd in that way. We can have faith; we can love; we can impress our intelligence and our creativity on the universe; we can be proud. We're in a precarious position but we can work and give and hope.

There's a verse in the Bhagavad Gita that says man is made of faith, and he is his faith. What's yours?

That's the central question I'm asking. Even if there isn't an answer, the quest is as important as the destination. There's the old Buddhist riddle: what's the sound of one hand clapping? Who will ever know, but the Buddhists believe that contemplation is an essential step on the road to enlightenment.

In the end, who am I and what do you see when you take the clothes off? What happened to me? Why? Was it good or evil, lucky or cursed, happy or unhappy? How did I respond to disaster, temptation, corruptibility? Was I empathetic or did I deliver high-sounding judgements I had no right to? Did I understand the power and importance of fantasy? Did I open spaces in my life for the contemplative and the spiritual?

I often wonder, Jimmy, about you and your life. I owe you so much for giving me respect and belief when we were young. It was a kind of loyalty and kindness I can never repay, and yet, what do we really know about each other? And why do we part ways for such long spaces when there is so much we could have enjoyed together?

I feel sad about that too. I think mostly it's because of my decision to part company with my Australian life. And I'll be honest, you know the grog got me and I can't shake it no matter what I do. That shrinks your world so much so that you don't notice time go by. Just the next marina and the next bar and the next vodka, day in day out. Life without alcohol looks too steep a mountain for me to climb now.

Let me know if I can ever help you with that.

It wouldn't be time well spent. So, what form will this take?

A printed book, because books get passed down; digital files get put on hard drives that corrupt or fail or get thrown out. And I want to include some photos, some letters and speeches, and maybe other graphic things, so it's better in a physical form.

I have a big library as you can see over there. I adore the texture and weight of books, the turning of pages, the fact that they wait so patiently for someone to pick them up. The experience of standing in the presence of so much wisdom and endeavour has a clear spiritual quality for me. When my father Ralph died, I had to cull his library, by which I mean I threw most of it out. It was in those moments that I realised by how large a margin my life had missed his and despite that, how much my culling felt like a violation. That process did more than anything to teach me about mortality.

There were some works I kept, but his books were mostly superseded volumes of *Who's Who*, reference works, treatises on foreign policy, all of not much use. I would have been pleased if I'd discovered a cache of crime novels, not out of malice, but relief.

It's unbearable to think that one day someone will pick over my collection as I did with his, but I hope a recognisable core is inherited by someone sensible.

Did you ever think about having a professional writer involved?

No. I'm better off being the witness to my life. But an editor, yes. Someone to look at the pattern in the kaleidoscope and say, one more turn please.

Having you here, Jimmy, I know is going to make me remember more, keep me on track and maybe help me understand and accept some of the less happy bits. I can be forbidding and challenging sometimes, so I need someone who's not worried by that and who doesn't mind using the crowbar.

So, do you see your life as important?

No. It's been full, and at times I've done good and helpful and even unusual things, but it hasn't been like Navalny or O'Connor. And I don't see it as being more valuable than anyone else's. The whole idea of some lives being superior and some not, or more virtuous, is OK in the case of Bach or Einstein for example, but not for the mass of humans like me.

I dislike hierarchies, which are always abusive. I haven't tried to become a master in anything. I've often wondered whether I should have settled on, say, music, and dedicated myself to that, but I think I'm much happier being a jack-of-all-trades. It's made it easier for me to take up new things, and to think myself capable of anything. Jack-of-all-tradery gives me many doors to open if the black dog attacks.

Is that really fair, I wonder? You've done much more with your life than most people, and you should be proud of it. There's value in people who challenge, who sink themselves in life and hope things catch fire.

Maybe.

Jimmy, do you know the Japanese practice called shokunin, which looks at how to judge accomplishment? The idea is that it doesn't matter what you seek mastery of – it can be sushi-making, or nursing, or sweeping, or being the emperor. What's important is your respect for the task, your humility, your perseverance and your desire to improve. There are things I try to be good at where I take a shokunin-like approach, so to say I'm just a jack-of-all-trades maybe isn't completely right.

I believe in this kind of value. I don't believe in likes or posts or good luck or parentage or celebrity or victory in politics or business.

Do you take the same approach to learning as you do to doing? I mean a broad kind of investigation of the intellectual and creative universe?

Yes. I have a strong general memory, but I don't seem to have a talent for remembering verse or speeches or other collections of words. My mate Peter Newman learned a lot of poetry as he was growing up. It's a comfort to him, as well as marvellous entertainment for his friends when he's in a reciting mood.

You probably know Clive James, an Aussie who went to London in the '50s to seek his fortune, like Germaine Greer and Barry Humphries. He wrote a book a few years ago called *Cultural Amnesia*, which is a collection of a hundred or so essays about the lives and thoughts of the men and women he believed were the outstanding cultural figures of the twentieth century. Clive was a brilliant man, although wayward in his relationships with women and other things too. He was blessed with wit and a sense of humour and the ridiculous, so much so that establishment intellectuals wondered who he really was and tended to treat him as on the fringe. He didn't receive an *Economist* obit. I went back to *Cultural Amnesia* recently and felt better about all my quotes: the book is essentially nothing but quotations.

He called himself a humanist: he believed in the idea that there was a unifying thread among his cast of characters that consisted of the creative, good, patient, independent and persistent.

I've followed the James model, and I'd describe myself as a humanist. My age hasn't blunted my curiosity. I still buy books and music, and of course wine constantly, and I adore trying to understand things I can't, like cosmology, astronomy and philosophy.

You said you were sometimes unhappy, but I didn't realise that you had serious black dog moments. You were never a carefree person, but you never seemed to be down much.

I've always had them.

There was a time in my late thirties when my life imploded. I was in a bar in Queensland with some of my law partners after a long conference day when a young woman with wild fair hair and lightning in her eyes plunged into the shout that I was in, grabbed me by the arm and dragged me onto the dance floor. I had never sought the company of any woman other than Mary in the seventeen years since we had married. I tried to resist but my assailant refused to give up and I spent the rest of a very long night in her company. This was Donna. I'll come back to the story of how it was we finished up where we now are, as a happy couple with a farm, fruit trees and a dog.

Donna tore my walls down. I never thought this would happen to me. The experience was like falling into the sun: searing, explosive, utterly beyond my ability to stop.

We ended our relationship within weeks because she was only twenty-one and not nearly ready for a permanent and demanding life with me. I didn't want the family to break up; I wanted my children to finish their education before I made any decision about my marriage. But I said to Donna that although neither of us knew where life would take us, if I became free, I would let her know. If she was committed at that point, no more need be done, but if not, then perhaps there would be a future.

I guess Mary realised what had happened before too long?

Of course. I had left some photographs of Donna in my briefcase. I don't think it was just stupidity. The subconscious is a powerful thing and I'm sure I wanted to be found out. Every friend and family member was informed and I was consigned to permanent disgrace.

I began to have panic attacks at work, and I was prescribed medication that helped up to a point, but when I decided to come off it I fell into a terrifying spiral. I remember visiting Thailand just after this happened, and when I arrived at my hotel I was incapable of doing anything other than sitting in a chair and looking out over the city, weeping. I'd heard of depression, and I thought I'd experienced it before, but this was like a slow death.

Our GP suggested that I should seek counselling and referred me to, no kidding, an orthodox Viennese Freudian psychiatrist for treatment, which I subjected myself to four days a week for almost three years. I ended the program without having become much happier, but it was informative and the existence of a non-judgemental listener was comforting. I learned about the massive power of our minds and how little agency in life we really have.

It became clear that I suffered from entrenched anxiety that plagued me for the next thirty years. It only improved under Donna's influence.

I was invited in the late '70s to address a conference of the Australian Mining and Petroleum Law Association, a super-formal and stuffy organisation, on a topic I knew well, the law of international seabed mining. A panic attack started in the early morning and despite consuming much Xanax and wandering the streets of Perth for hours, I arrived at the podium exhausted and incapable of doing anything other than stumbling through my words, incapacitated for all to see as I went.

I was in New York on a business trip a couple of years later representing the big mining company Rio Tinto. We had hired a very bright partner from a fine city law firm called Debevoise & Plimpton to help us look after a joint venture problem.

He invited me to his smart Manhattan apartment for drinks one evening with his social laser wife and some of his friends. I had a panic attack because these people were all wealthy and from old New York families, and I felt well and truly outgunned. Everyone could see that was distressed but, God bless them, they lent a hand to right my ship.

I still have odd bad days, but the downs are much less deep than they used to be. I can now speak in public much more easily.

So you had a troubled marriage, a tough workplace and an anxiety disorder. It must have been hard to manage?

It was. I was working out on a rowing machine in Tattersalls Club in Sydney one day in 2005 when I felt my heart go spectacularly out of rhythm. It didn't seem like a heart attack or any major malfunction, but I decided to get it looked at pronto and I was referred to Professor Michael Fennelly, who was then head of cardiology at St Vincent's Hospital.

I was tested thoroughly, and the professor, a lovely and brilliant man, informed me as gently as he could that I had cardiomyopathy. This meant that my heart had been overstressed too often for too long and had lost part of its pumping capacity. It was devastating for a former athlete to hear.

Luckily, my condition stabilised and I was fortunate to have had Donna to help me through the emotional and physical recovery. I'm OK now, more or less. Not many people are aware of this history.

How is the black dog now?

I walked up Mount Victoria, which you can see behind the vineyard over there, with our two dogs a few days ago, and when I turned to come down again, an easterly storm front was coming in. Alive and majestic, shining white, dove-grey and charcoal clouds rearing and folding. It reminded me of some of the skyscapes of a photographer hero, Ansel Adams. When I'm down I find it hard to absorb and celebrate experiences like that, but I stopped and asked the dogs out loud to look up and wonder. That must be a good sign.

Do you think people understand you?

A few. Most people now tend to look at the surface and dismiss everything else.

I've made a lot of new and firm friends in my recent life; that isn't meant to happen to someone over fifty. And there are lots of women in that group. This is Donna's work. She believes that we have the right to whatever friendships we choose. All of these new friends see me afresh. I feel much more confident in their assessments of me than people from earlier times.

So would you describe your childhood as happy?

Some happiness and some sadness.

You know my father and mother were conservative, closed people who didn't show their love easily.

My father was not well-suited to mentor a curious and energetic boy growing up. It's taken me a long time to admit this, but despite his extraordinary professional achievements, he was more interested in his career than my emotional upbringing. He investigated me for talent and I think found me wanting because he could see that I was never to be a great mathematician, chess player, linguist, bridge expert, historian or bureaucrat. He was there, like a distant lighthouse flashing now and then, but didn't give me the calm, frank and patient induction to adult life that I needed.

There were a few special successes like sporting wins later in my school career when I felt like I'd finally been issued an entry ticket to life and acceptance. I'd always expected my father to be with me when I walked through those doors but he never was. I was always looking over my shoulder, waiting for him to arrive.

So I grew up believing I was second-class, not helped by the fact that I was well overweight and copped a lot of sledging for that until testosterone intervened. I had no other male role models, so of course I wanted to be like Ralph. An adolescent trying to behave like a senior diplomat didn't impress many people.

People saw aggression, ambition, sarcasm, recklessness, aloofness, unreliability. That made me bad company. I've spent decades trying to cut that knot, and I might be down to the last threads now.

Sounds like that's been your defining journey?

It's taken almost all my life to change into someone who's somewhat aware, who listens, who sees the value of empathy, who's forgiven himself, who has an idea what love means. I've worked every day to understand and change. The process has been exhausting – like melting yourself down in a furnace and pouring your elements into a new mould.

If only I'd learned early that human interaction is a deeply subtle process and that the emotional signals people send can be imperceptible and need concentration and practice to understand. It's much more complex than just listening. It involves body, expression, voice, language – everything. Humans are built to be on the lookout for danger, and convincing them you're not a threat needs experience and sensitivity. I had no idea; many people would have found my emotional clumsiness a challenge.

I had a lot of different talents, like you, which added another layer of problems, because people found it hard to grasp the contradiction between sporting or academic ability and waywardness, or musical ability and aggression. But most of my old mates have been patient and understanding of my behaviour and helped my emotional coming out.

You don't carry any anger or resentment about how people see you?

No. How could I – the ones who are neutral are better at seeing me than I am. The folks who don't see me as worthwhile can believe what they want. I'll never get rid of the formal lawyer logical/careful/controlled thing – it's just part of me but usually people don't see it as a fault; they often see it as a benefit, especially when they want me to look at a contract, or see Centrelink for them, or help them with a divorce settlement. My successes, such as they are, have been a great surprise. Maybe that's why I don't feel the need to bore others with my résumé.

Living with Donna, and also living on a farm, has made me broader, deeper and more resilient. She's got no patience for chaff. You get her views between the eyes and even though it stings sometimes, you know it's good for you. With her, there's no time for moping around.

How did the locals see you when you moved to the Yarra Valley?

Most of the people around us at Warburton are salt of the earth; capable, practical, unpretentious.

I think they thought we were citified, not very useful and a bit devious when we arrived, because our life was different and we were interested in things they thought were a waste of time. Now they see a successful little agricultural operation and people who can fix things, pay their bills on time and dish out lamb and wine, so we're accepted, like provisional members of the Melbourne Cricket Club where the waiting list's forty years. So in Warburton we have a junior membership, but we're not allowed to go to the grand final just yet.

When my contractors arrived to start the vineyard installation, all the neighbours turned up to see what was happening – they're a curious lot. They told me that I was wasting my money and that I'd never get a crop ripe because of the altitude and the rain. They didn't know much about global warming.

I always thought you might get into politics. A lot of people saw you as the MP from Central Casting because you had a presence – maybe also a threat – about you and you were a partner in a powerful law firm, which intimidates people sometimes.

Never. I'm interested in policy but not in telling people what to do.

Power means nothing to me, although I gathered it here and there as I got older. It just never suited my personality or my anxiety. I didn't like

Beginnings « 23

being on stage, I hated putting myself out there for evaluation, I hated the perversity and dishonour of politics.

My father respected politicians because they had the final call, but he treated them with caution. He was responsible for many advances in the relationship between Australia and other countries, but some of his initiatives were sidelined, he was sent to odd places for no good reason, he was not always in the loop. The only indiscreet stories he ever told about his career involved errant parliamentarians. Andrew Peacock would create a circus when he came to New York for the summer sessions of the United Nations General Assembly while Ralph was UN Ambassador there. He was forever being rescued from the clutches of Shirley MacLaine or some other celeb lover while an uneasy cover-up was hatched, or asking for reservations at impossible restaurants, or offending the representatives of less privileged nations.

Would you say you started out with a vision of how you wanted your life to be and worked toward that persistently?

Absolutely not. I had plenty of ambition, but it wasn't always accompanied by thought or organisation, or common sense for that matter.

Did you always want to be a lawyer?

No. My Year 12 results came in when I was on summer holiday in Canberra. All good honours but no Top of the States, so Dad was, I know, disappointed. I asked him what he thought I should do after school and he told me I'd be doing law. What he actually said was something like, "Well, son, I've always believed that public service or politics is a wonderful path through life and one I'd like to see you on. If you agree, then it should be law, because it's a wonderful preparation for either." Game over.

Even though law provided well for my family and was a somewhat respected profession then, it was a hard and constricting life, which I disliked. I said to my children that law was the only job I would discourage them from. In the end, they all did unexpected and wonderful non-legal things in their careers.

Do you think you did the best you could with your talents?

There are a lot of ifs here, Jimmy. If I'd had no children, there would have been more room for accomplishment but less for the fulfilment that children bring. If I'd chosen politics or a corporate life, opportunities would have been richer but the family would have suffered. If I'd had no sporting ability, there would have been time for greater devotion to the law reports. If I'd chosen not to become a winemaker, I might have read more broadly.

My talents could have taken me further in management, government or politics if I'd had the courage, if I'd been willing to sacrifice the family and if I hadn't suffered from anxiety. I was also slow to recognise the natural advantages I had in being tall, athletic, presentable and male. I'd be standing there wondering why something wasn't working for me, and would often just watch the door to that opportunity close in front of my eyes.

What I ask myself is whether I engaged fully in life, whether I was awed by the universe and existence, whether I asked where we came from, where we've been and where we may be going. I did. My life has been complicated and difficult and I've survived OK. But I can never say I've led a pure life, or dedicated my life to a higher cause, or been a good citizen or satisfied any of the many other standards that people invent. I have as many flaws as the next man. I was in the game, I have no resentments or enemies, I'll die kicking and screaming but content and will probably be remembered as unusual and able and a reasonable bloke. That's enough.

If you had the chance, would you live the same life again?

Who would? Not me – it's been hard yakka. Most humans find life tough and uncertain, with scattered moments of joy and fulfilment; the universe becomes more mysterious as every discovery is made, and the theoretical possibilities seem to have become more and more alien to our senses and expectations. So, the existential mystery continues to grow.

Do you have any regrets about things you should have done more of?
I spent thousands of humdrum hours in law, where one is forever the bridesmaid and not the bride, and was forced to live with partners 24/7 who were brilliant but often judgemental and pedantic. I'd like to have some of that huge tract of time back.

I retired from rowing at the age of twenty-six when most careers were in full flight. I'd love to have done more. But by then we had three young children, so Mary's expectation that I give it up was understandable.

I do regret – a lot – not spending enough time on music. While I was at university, I had the chance to join a band that was moderately successful, but one member blew his eardrums out and turned deaf, and another almost died from drug and alcohol addiction, and it would have wrecked my rowing career, so I figure I dodged a bullet there.

My anxiety problem did prevent me, at least in mid-career, from doing interesting things that involved public exposure, like radio and TV, which I was often asked into, and acting.

A good friend of mine was one of the barristers who represented Eddie Mabo in the High Court when he decided to ask it to recognise native title. So I was familiar with the issues, and because I had many mining companies as clients at the time, I appeared as a speaker at one of the earliest Mabo conferences, which led to widespread press. Then I was chased by all the networks to join panel discussions into the meaning of Mabo, but I refused them because I was so terrified that I'd melt down.

Do you sometimes regret not having had a public career and what our American friends call a profile?
Not for a second. I can't think of many people I met having that kind of

public recognition who weren't self-promoters, narcissists, arrogant or just plain unhappy.

During my law career I was often chased by head-hunters trying to persuade me to work in other firms or organisations. I turned all these offers down for similar reasons. I thought that the firm's pension plan was valuable and would offer retirement security. How wrong I was – when the firm went national the plan was emasculated. Then I had to cope with an expensive divorce settlement. I left the law from boredom to found a new business. By great luck and with the help of my new colleagues, it worked and I recovered my capital and was able to retire, if not magnificently, then at least in comfort.

Have you ever wondered what you might have done if you'd decided not to do law?

I've had plenty of daydreams. Music, politics, writing, sports administration. The real opportunity missed was my career in Rio Tinto, which I ended to return to the profession. Had I been more astute and politically deft there would have been a pathway to leadership in the group, which then was one of the leading and most ambitious business conglomerates in the world. But although working as a lawyer was repetitive and not tremendously satisfying, it did provide security, predictability and high cashflow, which, with a wife and four children to provide for, I needed.

Family

Should we take a look at your family now?

Sure.

The Harry family came from Cornwall to South Australia in the 1850s, only fifteen years or so after the state was founded by Captain John Hindmarsh in 1836. I am a fifth-generation Australian. Over the years, most of the family moved away to other states. I have copies of the many family trees that earlier generations created, but I've made no contribution to their modernisation.

Mary and I met at the age of twenty-one and married at twenty-three.

How did you get together?

I was introduced to her in 1968 at the King's Cup rowing regatta in Penrith. She was then the girlfriend of David Douglas, who was a fellow crew member. I met her again at David's twenty-first birthday party at his parents' house in Glenferrie Road, Hawthorn. David was headed in the direction of another girl with whom he thought he had better prospects, and Mary signalled that she was interested in a relationship with me. Not long after this she invited me to be her partner at her sister Ann's debutante ball and then to her own twenty-first birthday party. It wasn't long before we were as a couple and went to most things together.

We were very happy in each other's company and I became fond of her parents and sisters. Mary helped me with the drudgery of college life, and many a tray of delicious slices and baskets of fragrant washing came my way when we were courting. It seemed to me that she would be a good life partner and mother, and that she and I would blend and find happiness and peace; our engagement was announced to the great delight of Mary's family.

Unfortunately, the seeds of difference were there to see.

What do you mean by that?

I was young and inexperienced and Mary was my first partner. All my friends were marrying around me; Mary's family was welcoming and made no secret of their wish that we would settle down.

But Mary shared few of my interests. She was quiet and reserved and many people doubted that we were sufficiently compatible for a long life together.

I received letters from members of my family warning me of the need to be sure about the long-term, partly because the McKenzie family was Catholic, which in those days was seen as a difficulty, but mostly because they believed that our differences of temperament and interest would separate us sooner or later.

I took offence at this counselling and told my family in clear terms to keep their noses out of my business.

I know that in those days, your relationship would have been called a mixed marriage?

There were some hurdles to jump.

The McKenzie family assumed control of all of the wedding preparations from the beginning, and I was informed of decisions much more often than I was consulted. At the time, for someone like me who was fond of indolence, this was welcome, but I did feel like a prize bull being led into the judging ring at times.

It was decided that we would be married in a Catholic church despite my making it clear that I would prefer an ecumenical service – a '60s thing to do. I was also required to undertake instruction with a Catholic priest before we would be allowed to marry in a Catholic church. In my first session, I told the priest that I had no time for denominational hair splitting or conversion, that my family had been Protestant since the Reformation and that we would do far better if we just shared cups of tea and discussed politics. That is what we did.

Mary's mother Bridie tried to sell me the idea of conversion and how much easier it would make our lives. I found this disrespectful.

I was informed by Bridie on one of our early visits to the McKenzie's home town of Echuca that I was expected to attend mass on Sundays. Their local church comprised priests and brothers from the order of Missionaries of the Sacred Heart, who at that time were predominantly Irish. My first attendances were unpleasant. It was as though the sermons were being delivered from seventeenth century Dublin: dripping with anger and threat, uncompromising and dark. It also happened that Bridie was not a skilled cook; our post-mass lunches were often problematic. So I proposed a deal to Bridie: I would retire from mass and would assist her in the kitchen in return. Luckily, the problem was mostly avoided because we usually had barbecues, which were presided over more successfully by Mary's father Ken McKenzie. Nonetheless, my relationship with Bridie was respectful and warm: she was a great supporter.

Tell me about the wedding.

It was on 14 December 1970 at St Carthage's Church in Royal Parade, only a few steps from Naughtons Hotel. I insisted on my friend and Anglican priest Peter Hughes being present at the ceremony, but he was shuffled into a dark corner and given almost no role.

The reception was a white tie event at the Windsor Hotel.

Most of my family on Dad's side were teetotal, being Methodist, although not my parents, who did enjoy a drink from time to time. So all of them were quarantined into one area of the function room and the drink waiters were able to circulate outside the invisible barrier all night with no evident disturbance. We were all much relieved.

So did the Protestant/Catholic thing get in the way of your family or your relationship with Mary?

No. Even though there were bitter battles between me and Mary's parents about schooling, the girls were eventually settled into Merton Hall after a rough experience at their first Catholic school, Sacré Cœur Convent in Malvern. We also warred over christenings; I lost – the girls were all christened Catholic but Michael was christened Anglican because I wanted him to attend an Anglican school. To her credit, Mary never pushed the Catholic cause against the interests of the family, so that wasn't any kind of influence in our parting.

Would you say that Mary was a good mother?

In most ways yes.

She was devoted to our children when they were growing up, and was as careful and attentive as any mother could have been. It wasn't easy for her. We had four children in the end, and fast: Sarah, Pip, Nicola and Michael. In those early years, she accepted that because of the demands of my legal career and rowing, I wouldn't be able to contribute as much as she did to the household. I remain grateful to her for that decision.

As the kids grew into teenagers and began to assert their independence, she managed less well. She liked clear-cut control, and this coupled with her Irish stubbornness made for some spectacular disciplinary stand-offs. When Pip was fifteen or so, her relationship with Mary was so angry that, fearing a physical confrontation, I asked the Merton Hall headmistress to admit her to the boarding house for a term to see if that would cool things down. As it turned out, she enjoyed the break, and her close relationship with the head, who mentored her faithfully throughout, was the circuit breaker I had hoped for. Pip came home a changed person and thereafter, peace reigned.

Mary found it hard to migrate her relationship with the children from the dominance of childhood to the more respectful and less demanding approach that would have suited them best as adults. But now that the kids are all in midlife and successful in their own right, their relationship works well.

But overall, family life as the kids grew up was warm, happy and productive.

It sounds as though things were getting worse and you didn't have a history of being able to manage your differences?

Right. As time went on, life between Mary and me became more complicated and serious cracks emerged. When the children began leaving home, of course, the parenting glue began to fail and as I was contemplating retirement, our differences about our future life became more and more pronounced, while at the same time we became less and less able to discuss them. Having been yoked to my law work for such a long time, my vision of retirement did not match Mary's, and I was left with no doubt that life for us would become steadily less happy and that if I decided I had to leave it should be sooner rather than later.

We tried counselling several times but Mary treated the process as a trial rather than as truth and reconciliation, so it never worked.

I decided under the shower one morning that we would each be better off in a new life. It was obvious that her anger about Donna was incurable and that my presence in her life could only do us further damage. I had just returned from a visit to the US where I had again been unfaithful to her, which she discovered. I make no excuse for that. One thing was clear: Mary did not deserve to live with someone who was capable of such betrayals, whatever the reason was, or to live with someone so emotionally confused.

And so out I walked on a sunny St Patrick's day in 2002, making perhaps the first decision of my life that was entirely mine, and knowing that hellfire was about to pour down on me. And it assuredly did. But it changed my life. A few weeks after leaving home, by an unbelievable stroke of luck, David Douglas, the very person who had delivered Mary into my arms, by chance ran across Donna, who then owned a bar in

Melbourne with a partner; she was childless, unhappy and ready to leave her relationship. Six weeks later she moved into my apartment in South Yarra.

I've never had to deal with a family separation even though things have been very tense at times. I always thought it was the worst thing that could happen to anyone.

Our divorce was brutal, Jim. Mary's advisers launched an expensive all-out war over two full years. She has carried the full force of her anger and disappointment about our divorce and about Donna since it happened over two decades ago, which has made our lives difficult since. I've tried to show her that I'm interested in a better way and I've suggested to her that a more kindly relationship might benefit all of us but it hasn't resulted in any change. I continue to hope that we can find a more generous and forgiving relationship one day.

I will always be grateful to Mary for the many good times we did have, for her hard work in raising our children, for her tolerance of me and my eccentricities and for her care and support.

Mary, and others I'm sure, concluded that I had maintained a relationship with Donna between 1987 and 2002, when I left home. There is no truth in it. Observers can believe or not, as they choose.

I have now been living with Donna for twenty-three years. We're happy and content, and our loyalty to one another has been unbroken. At the beginning, almost no one predicted that our relationship would be durable. Despite the age difference of twenty years, Donna has been a kind, friendly, imaginative and hard-working companion who has had the success of our marriage uppermost. She is intelligent and funny and has been tireless in anticipating and looking after my interests, and she has a moral compass that's firm and uncompromised.

She's charming except when provoked, when you get what you deserve. She treats the world with tenderness and empathy, always looking first to see whose lives she can help. Her smile is radiant and frank and she takes every care to see that her friends and guests are comfortable and happy. She was brought up in a family that accepted no pretence or laziness, and served others first, and those qualities shine in her. Her house is always full of flowers and empty of dust and disorder and is immediately welcoming to all who enter.

She has been the architect of my emotional recovery from the abrasion and unhappiness of my former life. She has given and sacrificed much, and I will always bless her willingness to be my partner.

Do you think you did an acceptable job as a parent?

I hope my children would think so.

Naturally, I would like to have spent more time with them. I committed, with many misgivings, to a career in law because I thought it would allow me to provide my family with the best, and to keep them in the one place, which meant accepting a heavy professional burden, but I was there at the most important times. Complete commitment was expected in my day in important law firms, and I doubt that much has changed. What could I have done to alter that, and would the alternative have been preferable? An impossible question to answer.

I think my children would say that despite my career demands and my driven and somewhat one-track personality, I gave them security, love, opportunity and an exposure to the world that not many of their peers received. But maybe they would see those comments as vivid evidence of my inability to empathise, and maybe there are issues they have had with me that I'm not aware of.

When I think about the task young people face as parents these days, it scares me. I decided to homeschool my son Flynn while we lived in France and that worked extra well for a number of years, but eventually we could see that he needed to go back into a conventional environment in his last couple of years to get him into the system.

No doubt about it, ideas about what it means to be a good parent are all over the place.

It's a complicated question, especially at a time when the notion of masculinity and femininity and how they should be expressed and handed down is being torn apart. The rudder we used to have has fallen off and we're nowhere near putting it back.

I also have to recognise that my divorce from Mary was a big problem. There's no question that for my children it was a deep shock, and that inevitably, they blamed me for destabilising their lives and were quick to see me as traitorous, ungrateful and deceptive. They also directed much undeserved anger and criticism at Donna when we became partners. Mary co-opted them as warriors in her cause after our separation, and they, understandably, gave her strong support and encouragement in her darkest time.

So, the restoration of good relations with my children has taken time and the experience has left a shadow on our lives. I knew this would be one of the costs of rupture; they did not deserve the dislocation. They were in every sense innocent and it has always, and will always, trouble me that this had to happen.

Is there anything you think you should say to your children individually? They were a big part of your life and you were a big part of theirs.

I should, Jimmy. They were the centre of our lives for decades. We tried hard to provide them with love, safety, comfort, loyalty and all the things they needed to come into the modern world with a decent shot at happiness and success. They didn't see much of the conflict between Mary and me because we worked hard to shield them from it, which is one reason, I believe, they were so upset when we parted.

All the blame was placed at my feet, and I fell in their estimation, as you would expect. I was black and Mary was white. However, I think that as the years have passed and as they have had to accommodate ups and downs in their own partnerships, they understand that life isn't so simple and that humans aren't necessarily required to live unhappy lives, and sometimes a long-term relationship has to end. We have a way together that's now respectful and caring and I see them all as good, friendly and distinguished in their lives, which is deeply satisfying.

If you asked them, they would probably say that there were many things Mary and I as parents did or didn't do that they disliked, but they would recognise, I hope, that we did our best and put aside many of our own desires in their interests.

I know that your daughter Sarah died a couple of years ago. That must have left you in a state of permanent grief. Do you feel like saying anything about that?

I should, yes. No day goes by without Sarah and her tragedy coming to my mind.

She was our eldest, a brilliant individual, but she was fiercely ambitious and determined to win the battle of life almost at any cost. She was a natural carer and healer, skilled financially, capable of being funny and wry and a powerful advocate and media performer, but she could never satisfy herself, either that she was good or that her many pursuits were sufficiently successful. She was, in short, unable to be happy or content with what she had.

Sarah went into the fashion business post-university and developed a serious eating disorder trying to be slim. We were aware of this early on but she underwent therapy and we thought she had things under control. She approached us after several years to say that she was still unable to master the problem and sought our help to requalify as a psychologist. She came back to live with us and gained her psychology qualification, then established a vibrant practice in eating disorder management. I was never sure, though, whether she eventually beat her problem.

She was unfortunate to inherit a combination of genes (I suspect mainly from me) that disposed her to weight gain, which she never conquered.

Her response was to become a plus-size advocate and a warrior against plus-size bias. As a counsellor and media performer she was outstanding and helped many sufferers back to health.

Sarah was diagnosed with a serious degenerative brain disorder in around 2015 and died at the age of forty-eight on the night of 27 March 2021.

My relationship with Sarah was difficult. She wasn't happy with me, although I was never sure why. I was devastated not just by her death, but also by the realisation that we would never have the opportunity to understand one another.

Sarah married an Englishman called Simon Fletcher and there were two children, Max and Charlie. Simon is a well-meaning and decent person but not long after he and Sarah married, he was diagnosed with depression and bi-polar disease. That, and their sharp personal differences, led to early separation and divorce. Sarah took custody of the two boys and was a fiercely committed and successful mother to them. The boys now live with Simon and have established a way of living with him that's been happy and productive, and has allowed them to adjust to being without their mother. Mary as their grandmother has also worked hard to help their recovery, as have Donna and I.

I respect and honour Sarah's life, her courage, her commitment and the great good she did for so many other people. In another world at another time, she could have been or done anything.

I think you said that your second daughter is a writer?

Yes. That's Pip. As a child she was strong, determined, attractive and rebellious. She was a talented swimmer and oarswoman and the fact that sport meant so much to me made us great mates. But she was always deliberate, thoughtful and resilient, and I often wondered what she'd become. When she graduated from university she took off for Sydney with number three daughter Nicola. This was their declaration of independence. She then launched a career in journalism but I knew that her real ambition was to become a published author. She worked away quietly and consistently for around ten years, creating manuscripts, talking to agents and publishers, and finally was taken up by the University of Queensland Press when she wrote her first young adult novel *I'll Tell You Mine*, which was published in 2012.

She's now published by Hachette and has produced a further five novels in the young adult genre. More recently, she's developed a collaboration with two illustrators and has produced two books for young children that have been well-received. She won the 2020 Children's Book Council of Australia book of the year for younger readers, which has put her on the publishing map as one of Australia's most respected and successful authors. She was nominated for the same award in 2023, and subsequently won a separate best book prize voted for by students, which she may have been even prouder of.

I know you're probably a committed fan, but can you say something about Pip's writing?

Yes. Pip writes with clarity, simplicity, compassion and shape. When I say shape, I'm borrowing from my photographic experience. If you take an image with a camera that has a good, but not excellent, lens, the picture's sharp and informative. But when you take it with a high-quality lens, say a Leica, you see a plasticity and solidity in your image that's of another dimension. Pip is a writer with a Leica lens: she writes with a shape that's unmissable.

The other quality that's distinguished her has been her ability just to get down in front of her screen and get stuff done. Putting many thousands of words together in a novel, much less the tedium of editing, rewriting and polishing, is a lonely and demanding process and Pip has had the endurance and commitment to do it.

And does she have a family?

She does. Her husband is a delightful IT expert, Dale Buck, and she has one daughter, Sophie, who is bright, artistic and wise. Pip's a great mum, a lovely woman and is fiercely committed to Sophie, who has every bit of the promise her mother showed all those years ago.

And daughter number three?

That's Nicola. She lives in Sydney and has committed her life to raising her two children, Olivia and James. Her family is united and successful largely due to her patience, foresight and hard work. Her husband Damien is a hard-working and successful accountant and a great bloke. He's been a committed dad and he and I have always had a close and understanding relationship.

Nicola developed a keen interest in cosmetics and make-up design and worked successfully at a high level with the Napoleon Perdis organisation. At one stage she went to live in Los Angeles to do stage and movie make-up, but I think she became homesick so came back to Australia. Then she set up her own make-up business which ran profitably for several years. Now she works part-time with Mecca.

Was she sporty as well?

She was never interested in sport like Pip but was kind, mature, smart and very musical. She learned the clarinet at school and I used to listen in awe to her practising in her bedroom at night. If she'd been interested, she could have been a player of orchestral quality, but she decided to drop it.

Being the third child and last daughter, she learned how to fit into the family unit without fuss and was always quiet and helpful. She has always been kind to me and was the first to reach out after I left Mary. On the first Father's Day following our separation, she was the only one of my kids to call me. I owe her for her understanding and willingness to see past the propaganda and realise that for any story there are always two sides.

And her family?

She has two children, Olivia and James. Olivia is a determined, vibrant and aware eighteen-year-old who, when she matures, will open many doors and achieve much; James is an intelligent, curious and happy boy who is becoming a talented mathematician and wants to understand the universe, and one day will advance the state of human knowledge. I've been delighted to see James take up the guitar. I've played a bit and I can see that he has real talent, so I've done what I can to encourage him.

I have the greatest respect for Nicola's kindness, her persistence, her loyalty and her get-on-with-it attitude.

And your son? I know Michael, because he and my son Flynn were boarders at Melbourne Grammar together after my family came back to Australia from France. Michael helped him settle into traditional schooling after our homeschooling period.

Like Pip and Nicola, Michael has great personal presence, determination and intelligence. He's tall and good-looking, and is always smartly dressed, easy to get along with and amusing. I was fulfilled completely when he was born, because while three lovely daughters had come along in succession, the statistical prospects of Mary having a boy at that late stage were next to zero. So his birth was a wonderful surprise, and in its way, miraculous.

Mary and I were living in Singapore, where I had been posted by Rio Tinto. She had been after me for a while to have a vasectomy. I duly visited a Chinese surgeon who asked me to sign a disappointingly long disclaimer form indemnifying him against any liability resulting from the operation. After I had reluctantly signed, he looked at his watch and said, "Well, Mr Harry, we have just enough time before lunch. Please get onto the couch and we'll get it over and done with." I thought this was a preliminary consultation and was quite unprepared for the event itself. So, I said, "Mr Chee, I'm sorry, but I need more time to prepare! I'll have to make an appointment to come back." Michael was conceived around two weeks later. Mary took a bit of adjusting to the idea of a fourth child but soon enough we were looking forward to the birth with great excitement. Perhaps Michael was always meant to be.

So, how was Michael's growing up?

It was clear to me from an early age that Michael wasn't your typical Aussie boy. He was much closer to his mother than to me and seemed to lead an internal life that I couldn't decode. I decided when he was seven or so to take him to what was then called Auskick, an AFL induction program. I bought him all the necessary kit plus a good ball and we drove down to the local oval to sign up. Michael refused point blank to take part. We spent ten embarrassed minutes on the boundary until I realised footy was a lost cause and we drove slowly and a bit quietly home.

He was a good student and was much liked by his masters and peers. Later in his school career he blossomed as an oarsman and rowed in the school first crew, as well as being in the Rugby First XV. After our footy experience years before, it was a delight to see him involved in sport at a high level. He had a self-confidence and reliability that attracted comment and missed being made school captain narrowly in favour of another boy who, as it turned out, was unsuited to the role. But he became captain of his house, which I was nowhere close to achieving at his age. His housemaster in his final year parents' debriefing hinted to us that Michael would need to confront some issues in his life, by which I know he meant Michael's sexuality.

I know Michael is gay?

I told Mary when Michael was in his early teens that I thought he was probably gay, but she wouldn't believe it. He came out in his first year of university. I did my best to convince him that he had my support and that my pride in him and my love for him were not affected in any way. I think he still has doubts as to my sincerity, because he saw me, and probably still does, as an unchangeable social conservative. Well, Michael, if you ever read this, I assure you that nothing has ever affected my respect and love for you and never will.

Michael became a journalist, and after a few stops along the way he became the Australian editor of the successful and prestigious Broadsheet, the sharpest and highest-quality online lifestyle magazine in the country. He is now freelancing and I think enjoying the more independent environment. He has an innate and precise feeling for the Zeitgeist and where things are headed so he's in just the right place. His knowledge and judgements in the world of lifestyle and fashion are widely respected in his profession. He is also a talented writer who could easily have a career as an author but so far that's not something he's been able to fit into his life.

We are friends but not brothers. He has a life large parts of which quite naturally I'm excluded from, much as I would wish otherwise. But he's young and still quite firm in his opinions; and as you would expect, his views of me are to an extent shaped by Mary, so I have to hope that as later adulthood arrives, he'll see that he is much loved and will make a bit more space for me in his life. He is now happily partnered to Brett Simmonds, an accomplished architect.

I guess a question all parents ask themselves is whether it was all worth it?

Without a doubt. It was hard, emotionally testing, expensive, time-consuming and frustrating, but to have had four smart, balanced, hard-working, honest and kind children is a joy that those without children will never understand. Yes, there are times when you wish, say, the phone would ring for no reason, but the fulfilment of having raised a group of delightful and competent kids who have been outstanding citizens of this country is immense.

Jimmy, I do struggle with Sarah not being here. It's as though the fabric of my life and all my assumptions about how things should be have been broken. The shape and balance of the universe has shifted and will always feel unsteady. I hoped I'd be easier with it by now but clearly, I'll need to wait a while for that to happen.

I have an idea of what you mean. When I realised alcohol was no friend, I knew I had no chance of escaping, that my life had

changed to grey, to compromise, to humiliation, and that I would always be at one remove.

I have some ideas about that, Jimmy. But later, I think.

The Storm and the Calm

Where were we? I was asking you some questions about your approach to life. You were saying that you'd always felt hostage to events. Does that mean you just followed life wherever it went?

No. There was some thinking involved. But life for me on the whole has felt anything but planned. Whatever calm and vision others may have seen in me, I've felt like I was in the centre of a tsunami most of the time. The only common element has been that I always seem to have taken the road less travelled when a decision presented itself. And that road would usually be strewn with nails and rocks.

One time I exercised good judgement about one of those roads was when I was asked to work for John Howard as his private secretary, when he was treasurer in the late '70s. I just said no and shut the door tight on that possibility. Politics is alluring but I know of no political career that didn't end in unhappiness, just as I've never known anyone seriously rich who was content.

I remember being flown to Canberra, driven to John's office in an official car and shown into his office at Parliament House with John Hewson in attendance. His first question was, "So John, what are your opinions on the state of the Australian economy?"

I was as nervous as hell and battled my way through an answer, expecting to be shown the exit, but the conversation settled and went on to Rio Tinto, the press, the structure of the PM's office. I wasn't made an offer then but in a couple of days the chief of staff called to say they would like to have me. I declined.

I have no regrets because I've always thought there was something mad about it. If someone like Donald Trump can be president or Boris Johnson prime minister, what's the point? Politicians are like jockeys: astride an unruly country scared to death and in no way really in control. Why would anyone want to be in the news or on social media all day every day? That seems to me the distillation of madness.

A smart call I reckon. So what about the new millennium? I've been grateful to grow up in these times. It just seems to have been a good place to be. Do you feel that way?

No question. My lifespan of the late 1940s to now has seen huge change for both good and bad. In science and technology, in space, in medicine, in international relations. Who could have imagined that China would evolve from a poor, peasant country into a world superpower in a generation? Who could have anticipated the discovery of the genome and gene reconstruction, which promises the evolution of tailored human beings and indefinite life? Who could have imagined instant, freely available, global social media communications? And what about seeing Neil Armstrong on live TV take our race's first steps on another planet? Or ChatGPT?

On the other hand, look at climate change, rogue viruses, terrorism, pervasive dictatorship, social media tyranny and human rights abuses. Or the autocrat Trump, denying the concept of truth? Or that arch-criminal Putin? We've grown some wonderful tools but as always, the question is, can we use them to the advantage of humankind?

It sure is a world battling to find itself morally and ethically, and losing, where ideas like decency, respect and tolerance sound clapped out and almost naïve, don't you think?

I agree completely. We have to get used to a world where no one is made to account for anything anymore. Honour went down the drain with the First World War when all the old rules of civility shattered. Now, the media will say anything for ratings, politicians of all colours lie, vile social media behaviour is never apologised for or punished, no one's dignity or reputation means anything. The modern world is brilliant, but so hard, so amoral and so disappointing. Should we have traded truth for technical mastery? I guess it just happened, but what's going to replace it? Maybe dishonour is a kind of mutation that favours the adopters, which is what allows cultures and social norms to be torn down and replaced by what we see today.

I was watching a Netflix series on the Viking invasions of Britain the other night and my response was to say, there was a civilisation out of control, where torture, killing and dispossession was the accepted way of life, and by contrast, look how far we've progressed as a civilisation. I'm not so sure about that anymore. Nowadays it's mostly words cast from one political party or woke group or identity club at another but they carry as much brutality, deception and cruelty as any Viking pillage.

You could say that the world has always been the same, with good and evil always present and opposed, with the balance just altering now and again. I have the feeling that what we are seeing now is a permanent shift. How else to explain the monstrosity of Trump and the contemporary Republican Party in the US? Or Syria? Or Putin?

It used to be the case that the leading nations would see a problem and solve it by consensus, as in Versailles, or the creation of the State of Israel, or the reconstruction of Germany and Japan post-World War Two. Now those international mechanisms are failing everywhere, Israel–Palestine being the best example. No one expects consensus on a solution to emerge from anywhere at any time. The body that might have been a positive influence, the UN, has done nothing but inflame, complicate and obscure. In fact, this experience shows again that in many ways the world might be better off without it.

I wonder about ethics, don't you? About what the word means and whether there's any way of working out not just what the principles are but how they should be applied?

That question is the sub-text of everything. I'm not really as educated in that field as I should be. Ethics is studied much less at schools and universities now and few students now complete their courses having taken an ethics component. I know that apart from a small course in legal professional standards, I've had no exposure to formal ethics instruction. I now see that as a gap in my education.

Ethics has core aims including the development of an awareness of ethical responsibility, the development of critical thinking and the consideration of ethical norms. Whereas, say, in the early twentieth century one of the roles in parenting would have included exposing children to ethical norms and problems, and ensuring that schools did the same, today's parents have vacated that ground to schools and to social media. In so doing, they've got what they deserved.

Even though you and I were bored senseless by our headmaster on the question of integrity and our duty to serve society, I think we did emerge with a kind of moral platform buried somewhere in our subconscious – that there was such a thing as truth, that honesty was important, that moral norms were indivisible; that a qualified or conditional norm wasn't a norm.

Our old school may still transmit that message, but in general I think educators are less clear about moral norms today. All those values seem to be presented in a relativistic way now. In the culture wars, it seems that the means have become justified by the ends: if your team is leftie and woke, for example, it's OK to de-platform a conservative without due process, and even to manipulate the evidence; it's OK to run media campaigns that are pure sledges about someone's character to build social bias for electoral reasons; it's OK to hint that the dreadful October 2023 Hamas attack killing 1,300 Israeli men, women and children was somehow excusable because of the previous experiences of the Palestinians. These are all moral failures that, if they become accepted techniques of social discourse, drip acid on our social structure and compact.

I agree.

The structure of the educational establishment has changed in disappointing ways, hasn't it? Universities seem to see themselves nowadays as primarily champions and prosecutors of their version of diversity, equal opportunity and racial equality rather than merit, scholarship, free speech, tolerance and independent inquiry. They have positioned themselves as political actors that take political positions on social subjects where they have traditionally had no place.

The Harvard of even twenty years ago would never have tried to protect Claudine Gay as president from dismissal even though she was an acknowledged plagiarist and had equivocated in Congress about whether or not antisemitism on campus should be condemned. At just the time that Harvard should have been most resolute, it failed. The crash of a mighty oak falling has been heard around the world. If not Harvard, then whom?

The same can be said resoundingly of the equivocal and fence-sitting approach of our vice-chancellors to the Israel–Palestine disaster and the malignant growth of campus antisemitism in the form of tent villages condoned, uncertainty on the use of abusive expressions such as "From the river to the sea" and "intifada" in protests described by the timid professors as contextual, whatever that means, and the bullying of Israeli counter-protesters and students.

There are examples everywhere you look of ethical failures in other public institutions, in business, in politics. Think of Qantas selling seats on already-cancelled flights to raise cash and not refunding flight credits; think of the compromise of the right to fair trial by the media and the errant behaviour of state prosecutors.

And not one of the guilty resigns.

So, Johnnie, do you think you know yourself and life generally better now? Another way of asking that is whether you think you've gathered at least some wisdom?

You would have hoped so. As a young man I had no emotional intelligence.

Now, I have some. I know what upsets people. I try not to do that, but there are times when I know I still do. I also know that because of my genes and maybe mainly because of my upbringing, I find it hard to trust other people, and I think that means it's been tougher for me to empathise and love quickly and easily, but living with Donna has turned the tide a bit.

Life sure is a mystery – intense and rich and sad. I have a glimmering of what death might mean and how I might approach it. The universe gives life, and takes it away, when it feels the time is right. My atomic composition will return to the air and sea and sky, so in that sense I live on. My children and grandchildren will represent me up to a point as genetic carriers. Everyone hates to leave a good party, and so will I, but I have nothing to complain about, so I hope I'll go with a measure of peace and acceptance. I'm more tolerant and maybe realistic than I was, so that's progress, but I'll leave the deep philosophising to my friends – there's too little time to waste it on questions that you're 99.999% certain don't have an answer. I know I won't die of boredom or loneliness, which I think Dad did. That would be the worst fate possible.

Jim, another splash?

Yep, I will. Love the wine, what's the story?

It's made from chardonnay that grows just up the hill behind us here. The clone is called Mendoza, from Argentina. The soil up the hill is deep and old red loam over clay soil that seems to produce more dense but refined characters than many traditional areas. This one was an instant hit: lively, powerful but not overblown, taut and energetic. It won our first show gold medal in 2019. How a little backyard operation beat the big guys is a mystery but we were happy.

You're lucky. Jumping headlong into something every day like you do isn't something that many people do. Most lives are just a collection of habits, especially at our age when you want to surrender, to stop being curious and energetic.

I guess that's one way of looking at it, but against that you could see all my interests as having deflected me from other achievements; being me, of course, I sometimes feel that way but as we were saying earlier, why? I think I really am happier knowing, say, how to make wine, ride motorbikes, ski, sail, explore and cook than if I had been an international expert in patent law.

Do you ever wonder about what truth is and whether you're telling it?

Of course. That's the permanent theme of most of literature and art. I know that when people talk about themselves, they're fallible. They hold views sometimes without any idea where they come from, or because their mates do, or their political heroes do. Lots of people wouldn't know the truth if they fell over it, and many memoir writers are just propagandists. Is the self-vision we create consistent with the facts of our lives? Has everything that's relevant to a life been drawn out?

I wonder whether we can ever know what motivates us to do this or that. It's like atomic physics. No one understands what lies at the bottom of the hierarchy of particles we've discovered. The best explanation we have so far is that the universe, and we, are made up of quantum field perturbations. Quantum mechanics tells us that certain things are unknowable and that paradox is everywhere. So when we ask what kind of man stands in front of us, or whether a memoir is authentic, who can know, and what is the purpose of the question? It might be that we decide something is true because we like the man or the writing, and who knows why we do?

Extended Family

Tell me something about your sisters.

My sister Virginia is two years older than me. Her life has been a success. She is tall, dark, poised, and throughout her life, has been acknowledged as intelligent, beautiful, tasteful, tactful and a shrewd manager of people and organisations. She founded and ran the leading arts and artist management business in Australia, earned the respect and friendship of the arts community and became a board member of Opera Australia, the Sydney International Piano Competition and NIDA – you know, the National Institute of Dramatic Art – among others, and is still much sought-after as an arts consultant.

She and I have always been close. Her support and loyalty to me through some hard times has been exemplary.

She married at twenty to Martin Braden, but divorced around ten years later. He was a ministerial staffer and the demands of his career made their life together unsustainable. She then met and married the brilliant architect Ken Woolley, who sadly died in 2015. He and I were good mates. I took a portrait photo of him relaxing at their house at Palm Beach north of Sydney, and one of my great satisfactions as a photographer was knowing that he loved it.

Virginia was never able to have children of her own because of an early and traumatic ectopic pregnancy, although she's very close to Ken's kids.

I can't think of anyone other than Donna who has influenced my life more for the better, or who has delivered that influence in a more wise and gentle way.

The relationship between me and my younger sister Penny was badly affected by my divorce, when she became an advocate of Mary's. I'm not sure why that happened, but our contacts now are mostly formal and infrequent. I hope they can be revived but I'm not optimistic.

Her husband is a conservative and blunt American, whom Penny met in Saigon during the Vietnam war when my father was posted there as Australian Ambassador. He and I find it hard to agree on much but he's been a good husband to Penny and a generous and kind father to his children, for which I respect him.

Have other members of your family written memoirs?

Here and there, yes. Family record-keeping used to be a genteel pursuit that men and women with leisure pursued on Sunday afternoons. I'm not sure whether that happened in your family. Having aspirations to gentility, the older Harrys created their share of family trees, memoirs and photographs, but Ralph's generation was less good at it, and my generation has been quite slack. Maybe because Ancestry.com can do it for me.

My grandfather Arthur Hartley Harry on my dad's side wrote a memoir late in his life, and my grandmother left some recollections as well, which I've kept in my library. Arthur's volume was called *Green Flash at Sunset*. He was a quiet but brilliant and determined classics master at Launceston Grammar School. I like the idea of having that volume in my library, but I can't say I look at it much. I know Arthur was much loved by his students and was sadly farewelled when he retired. He affected many young men for the better.

The chances are he had a quite different view of his responsibility as a teacher than some have today. Maybe I'm wrong, but the idea of teachers striking, for example, makes me furious. And the adoption of curriculum fads like the elimination of phonics for reading has been disastrous for many young kids. Now all that's being changed I see. And the promotion of political agendas in the classroom.

Arthur would have had something to say about all that. But in his quiet moments he wrote poetry and was a keen amateur photographer. I'm sure he was a good gardener and handyman around the house; at that time you had no option because no schoolteacher had the money to hire tradesmen. His poems are in the classical style as you'd expect from a man who read and wrote Greek and Latin, but even though they're often stilted to our ears and make references to people and events that almost no one today would be familiar with, they show his concern for beauty and his respect for creation. His photos are beautiful but most of the negatives have been lost. The loss was an act of family vandalism that I find hard to forgive.

I have some of Dad's diaries, and also his home movies, slides and audio tapes, so there's a fair amount of material if someone wanted to do the work.

Has the process you're going through here unlocked any hidden memories?

Yes, of course. As I was saying about you, Jimmy, I hadn't realised how much I regretted the fact that we'd drifted apart for such a long time, and how I had missed you. There have been lots of memory jolts like that.

While in one sense my growing up was rich with travel, challenge and experiences, I was forced to fend for myself most of the time.

Also, the family culture was conservative and over-careful. Sex was never discussed, much less things like homosexuality. Art was something you read about in books. I recall no time when I was taken to a gallery for the sake of it, or invited to discuss what art might mean or what inspired it. Most discussion around the family dining table was politics or current affairs; no stories, fables, personal disasters, ambitions. Safety lay in the banal.

Have you stayed in touch with your father's family?

No. The broader Harry family hasn't survived as any kind of community. Mum's family didn't exist as far as I and my sisters were concerned. I'll come back to this as well, but she wasn't Australian-born and for reasons I think I now understand, it seems she wanted her family history buried.

My father's siblings scattered after growing up in South Australia and Tasmania. As kids we never formed friendships with our cousins, because I don't think Mum was keen on them. My sister Penny's kids have also been spread around the world. Her family hasn't shown any interest in mine, although there is occasional contact with my kids and grandkids, and my sister Virginia of course.

I've spent some time trying to keep track of my cousins on Dad's side, but maybe half of them have died already, and the survivors don't seem too keen to have a relationship with us.

The McKenzie (Mary's) family on the other hand does have a kind of unity and they do communicate and look for chances to gather.

But you stay in touch with Donna's family?

Constantly. Donna's family in Warrnambool is a living and dynamic tribe: there are scores of members, reunions, gatherings at notable times like 90th birthdays and a camaraderie and goodwill that is touching and comfortable. I've been co-opted wholesale into this lovely team and I'm better for it. I contribute to it whenever I can, and that engagement makes me happy.

One character in the team needs to be identified and thanked, although there are many others. She is Jenny Farrell, a cousin of Donna's living in Sydney. When I turned up in Sydney for the first time after Donna and I had begun to live together, she demanded to have lunch with me so she could look me over, much as cowboys in the Wild West would inspect a horse for soundness. Like many of Donna's mates at the time, she was worried that a relationship with an ageing ex-lawyer might not be in Donna's best interests. Well, I managed to pass the audition, and Jenny became a huge friend and eased my way into acceptance from all Donna's family and close friends. I'll never cease to be grateful to her for that, for her unconditional love and for herself: a tireless worker, a keeper of the best of the Aussie spirit in all she does and a person of consummate loyalty and energy.

I thought your father would have produced a memoir given his achievements?

My old man was a committed record keeper, and he wanted a good legacy, so yes, you would have thought he would produce memoirs, but he never did. Maybe he figured that despite a long and respected career he hadn't achieved enough to warrant the exercise. Maybe he didn't think anyone would be interested. And a book about his professional life as an intelligence operative could not have been written. Maybe he expected me to do the job! But the National Library of Australia did establish an archive for him. After he died I organised and catalogued his personal papers and diaries and put them in the archive, which can be accessed by the family.

Ralph did contribute to the *Australian Dictionary of Biography* by writing short summaries of the lives and careers of some of the important Australians he knew. He also wrote and published *No Man is a Hero: Pioneers of Australian Diplomacy* in 1997, outlining the lives of the prominent Australian diplomats he had met during his career, and *The Diplomat Who Laughed* in 1983, a collection of jokes and anecdotes about the lives and foibles of members of the diplomatic profession. He was also a translator of works into and out of Esperanto, and a revered lexicographer of English and Esperanto.

Have you ever written anything about his life?

I wrote his long obituary for the Fairfax papers. It was a hard task for me, especially when grieving, but it was the only full and sympathetic testament to his amazing life that had, and has, ever been published. I then used that as a base for a Wikipedia article about him, which I presume will be around for a long time. So I feel that some justice has been done to his memory.

I'll turn over my family records, such as they are, to my children and hope that one of them will bring them up to date. I'll be lucky if I finish this memoir, scan and catalogue my photos, organise my library and music collection, and do everything else I need to do in order to make an orderly exit!

I pause, looking for a break. "Jim, I appreciate you giving up your time to go down this road."

"It's a pleasure," says Jim, turning on the million-watt smile. "And interesting. You've always been a reticent bugger and I like this kind of thing. It's the stuff of life."

I stretch and close my eyes, and Jim goes quiet for a minute or two.

You know, Johnnie, just thinking, it's already clear you've had some big issues in your emotional life. I always thought I wasn't seeing the whole you and I'm convinced that's the case. I'm not sure there's any man alive who hasn't been sad or lonely or disappointed but it's how you adapt, isn't it. One thing I know is that your head was always above the pack and there are lots of people who want to kick it for absolutely no reason. When that happens you always blame yourself. I might be telling you what you already know but the only voice and the only belief you can rely on is yours.

We're on common ground there, Jim, aren't we. You're right, I used to think I was some kind of freak who could never command friendship but it's a language you have to learn. In a way it's like talking to a waiter in a Paris restaurant: you can't expect any grace or friendship from anyone unless you can speak their language, be it French or friendship.

"I tell you what. Let's listen to some music for a while and let the minds wander," I suggest.

Jim nods.

I set up a vinyl of Thomas Tallis in the HiFi. It's gorgeous. Calm, textured, surprising, old but modern. Recorded music has always been important to me, and being who I am, I never stop buying this or that bit of gear to improve the set-up.

Jim's been asleep for a while so I have to give him a gentle shake. He wakes, smiling and rueful.

"I needed that, mate," he says, stretching. "Soul fuel."

"Ready again?"

"OK."

Wine

Johnnie, why don't we take a turn off here for a bit. This chardy we're drinking is lovely, and I'm looking straight into the vineyard, so what about wine?

Excellent.

Wine moved from being mildly interesting in my youth to a full-blown amateur commitment, and now to a serious business involvement in Wild Fire Wines, and a big consumer of my time.

It's funny that I should have become a wine person because both my grandmother and great grandmother on Ralph's side and Ralph's sister Millicent were teetotallers and became presidents of the World Assembly of the Women's Christian Temperance Union. My mother and father drank occasionally at home, and at formal diplomatic occasions, but I can't remember a time Ralph poured me a beer or a glass of wine, or took me to a pub or bar for no reason, just for the companionship of it.

There are times that I feel that I've let the family down, although as soon as the cork pops out of the bottle at night, the feeling goes away.

What lit the fuse?

It all started with my mad Polish uncle when I was around ten or eleven.

Ralph's sister Marjorie moved to Canberra as a government librarian a few years after my father had arrived. She was forty-ish and had never had a partnership with a man. She and Jan Dabrowski, who was a Polish World War Two refugee, met and married soon after she arrived in Canberra, when he decided to settle down after years of manual work on the Snowy Scheme. He'd qualified as a lawyer in Poland but couldn't practise in Australia without re-qualification, which was beyond him then.

He was a homeopathic medicine nut, and every corner of their house was full of jars of impaled insects, bottles of smoking crystals and packets of violet and green powders from which he mixed his remedies. You can imagine what my sceptical mother thought of him. I loved him from the start because he was out there on the edge with me and he listened to what I said.

He was a regular consumer of plum brandy, which he distilled from fruit grown in his orchard. He would always offer my parents a glass when we infrequently arrived to visit, and they would wrinkle their noses but not me. He always found a way of getting me a sip or two.

Did he ever invite you to watch him distilling?

Yes, but my parents always found an excuse to keep me from going. He did describe the process to me of course so I knew roughly what to do. So, I decided to go into the booze business myself. We had some plum and apricot trees and a good supply of Fowlers Vacola jars at home, so I stole a supply of fruit, sugar and yeast, and shazam! A fermentation started in my jars, hidden in my mother's laundry, which I was mesmerised by, until one night a jar exploded and covered the entire interior of the laundry with a sticky, red, glassy mess.

My liberty and my dignity were taken away for quite a time as a result, and my reputation for instability grew yet greater. But an itch to make liquor was permanently planted.

So how did the winemaking start?

Industrial-scale alcohol production began at university college, when a mate of mine and I were driven by our poverty to buy a beer kit and started supplying our fellow students. It was drinkable and it worked wonderfully as a business until a snitch sold us out to the authorities and that was that.

Then a bit later, a member of one of my rowing crews from an Italian family, Bruno Romanin, invited me to his place for lunch just before vintage time. His old man, Andy Romanin, a rheumy, short but jolly Piedmontese, poured me a glass of his wine, which every Italian family used to make in those days along with passata and pork products like salami, prosciutto and sausages.

The wine was good. Andy could see I was interested, so he invited me to come back the following weekend to take part in the family vintage. There were no vines on Andy's property, but the family would go to the Victoria market at dawn on the chosen Saturday morning to meet the grape trucks coming in from Adelaide. I didn't realise that thousands of migrant families around Melbourne would turn up at the market when the fruit was ripe for their annual grape supplies and that pop-up wineries would clank and hiss into action all around Carlton, Footscray, Richmond and Coburg.

When I arrived at Andy's place, waiting for me was a small barrel and a couple of boxes of shiraz for me to make my own brew. The process was ancient and simple. You just emptied your grapes into your barrel and squashed them by foot, then threw an old tea towel over the open end and waited. Eventually, a wild yeast ferment would start; when that was finished, the raw wine would be siphoned into glass demijohns with airlocks and left for the winter to mature. No sterilisation, no filtration, no preservatives, no nothing. Then in spring when the moon was in the right phase and dogs were barking just so, the demijohns would be bottled in long neck beer bottles with a crown seal.

How was your first wine?

To me it was nectar but the truth is it wasn't great – oxidised and a bit volatile, but that was the way it had been made forever. I felt privileged to have been admitted to the traditional family winemaking weekend and to have been made part of an activity that man would have begun many thousands of years before the birth of Christ. It was honourable, traditional and sociable. Thank goodness for Australia's migrants, without whom we would still not have decent bread, oils, coffee, salamis, risottos, pastas, restaurants, bars, pastries and so many other wonderful things.

And did you decide to continue?

Of course, but tragedy intervened and Andy died about six months later of cirrhosis, and because the family was still in mourning the following summer, I set up a winery in the garage of another Italian friend, also now dead, called Armando "Ted" Sorani, a beautiful Florentine with large blue eyes and a soft soul. He loved my kids to death.

Tell me some more about Ted.

He worked for the federal scientific research organisation, CSIRO, as an instrument maker and there was no piece of kit that our winery was ever without. Ted had been forced to scavenge for his displaced family in Italy immediately after World War Two and had never lost his enthusiasm for small-scale "collection", which was fortunate for our partnership, if unfortunate for CSIRO. We introduced more modern winemaking techniques and before long our products were delicious and sought after.

Then Ted's son became addicted to heroin and Ted was forced to leave our partnership to look after his son's health.

So what happened then?

I moved operations home to my first house at 24 The Grange, East Malvern, then into the carport of our neighbours at The Grange, Jean and Max Lindsey, then to their retirement property near Merricks on the Mornington Peninsula, which involved my first planting of grape vines. We named our wine "Maxwelton" after the name of the property, which had previously been a large Mornington Peninsula estate but had been cut down in size as family deaths occurred. It was very good.

Max was diagnosed with early-onset Alzheimer's a few years later and I made my final move, to this place, where we planted a vineyard in 2013 and built a small modern winery and wine store.

I have to say a few words about Max in memoriam. He was for years a man I loved, respected and defended. He was a kind, softly spoken and courteous English doctor who fell in love with a nurse at his London hospital. Being already married, and on the receiving end of a grim social pile-on, he had no choice but to migrate to Australia with his lover to escape the hypocritical noise.

Max was a beautiful golfer, rugby player and skier, a bon vivant, wine lover and a magnificent host. He proposed me for membership at the Royal Melbourne Golf Club. He and I played as partners in the Quirk intraclub championship often but didn't win. He was the ideal member – skilled, patient and able to let the politics and pretension of that kind of place run off him easily. I was less happy with it and resigned after his death. But I'll always recall the easy and unflashy way he could construct a beautiful round, his patience with me and his endless good humour.

His second wife, Jeannie, was a kind but determined and somewhat impatient woman who persecuted Max too often for this or that minor transgression. Jeannie did not treat Max well after he contracted Alzheimer's and I thought the less of her because of it. He, however, was an inspiration and a joy to know, and when finally I realised that he was drifting away, I knew it was the end of a unique friendship.

So the last stop was installing a vineyard here?

Yes. After ten or so years in Sydney, Donna and I decided to come back to Victoria. This farm belonged to a friend who wanted to sell. We visited one winter weekend and fell in love with the place and a couple of months later we moved in. It didn't take me long to plant a vineyard. After that, I founded Wild Fire Wines with my old and cherished friend Peter Newman in 2015, which has proved modestly successful financially and has produced wines of great quality. We were joined as partners first by Donna and then by Geofrey Shenfield, who has worked tirelessly to broaden and improve the business. The advent of Wild Fire was hastened because once Max was gone, Jeannie started to make decisions about our vine management and winemaking without consulting me, which I found unsettling since I was still in Sydney. I didn't want to continue with her – it was just too much for me to manage – so we parted company.

So, have you collected much wine over the years?

I have. I've always been a collector as well as a maker. I have many bottles. Variety in wine is the appeal for me, because it allows me to believe that I can identify unique wine characters and fill in the jigsaw puzzle of the wheres and the whats better than other people. Arrogance of course, but it's a world every bit as rich, diverse, beautiful and challenging as any other.

A lovely human pastime is browsing in wine shops or visiting wineries, buying what appeals to you and then carefully laying your bottles down in their bin in your cellar. It's like any other form of collecting, but you can't open a stamp or a piece of silver up after ten years of slumber and drink it. Wine is, if you choose it well, alive, beautiful, complex and of ancient and noble origin. It also generates celebration: any meal with friends around the table and with fine wine is a memorable notch you can carve in the belt of your life: the bottle, and the occasion, will never come again, so it is to be cherished and then recalled often.

I know I'll die with a full cellar, which Donna and my friends and family will love, and I hope there will be bitter battles fought over who gets what, but what a wonderful way to be remembered. I'm now making wine as carefully as I know how so that my final vintages will last for the lifetimes of Donna and my children. Now, there's a way to keep a family thinking of you, and itself.

Good single malt whisky has always been a favourite. I bought two 60-gallon casks of Springbank, a famous distillery just north of the Mull of Kintyre, in the 90s which I matured for fifteen years and then bottled and imported. I find my remaining stores of this luminous substance a great joy. I'm not sure where my enthusiasm for Scotch came from, but it may have been triggered many years ago. Dad was a protégé of Richard Casey, later Lord Casey, the then head of the Department of Foreign Affairs. One evening in Canberra in the 60s he invited Casey home for a drink and I was given the task of pouring him a scotch and water. He seemed to enjoy it in his patrician way and Dad was pleased that his plan had gone without incident. Perhaps that small victory was responsible.

Dan Robinson was my best mate at my school boarding house. I'll say a few things about him later on, but his old man Sos Robinson was a sociable and hard-drinking individual, and when he brought Dan's family to Melbourne during my last couple of years of school, I spent many weekends at his house. There I gained my first introduction to the glories of flagon chablis and shiraz from Jimmy Watson's Carlton cellars. Saturday lunches with Dan and Sos were epic always, and taught me that wine was meant for good food, good company and bad philosophy.

So how did the wine collection thing start?

Ralph introduced me to fine European wines during my visits to the family in Brussels in the late 1960s. He would keep partly drunk bottles from his diplomatic functions, mostly burgundies, and bring them out in the days following. So, I was able to taste Clos de Vougeot, Nuits-Saint-Georges, Chambertin, Palmer and Léoville. The gulf between these wines and 1960s hot Aussie shiraz and cabernet was wide. It's what made me decide to build a cellar and fill it with the best wines I could afford.

I began my collection in 1970 just after my marriage to Mary when, following the custom of the time, a gift preference list was published for invitees a couple of months before the ceremony and I made sure that wine was on it. So, something like ten cases were installed in a cupboard in our first apartment, the beginning of a lifetime interest. None of it was especially fine, but it was treasured.

Have you spent much time looking around the wine areas of the world?

Yes! Everywhere. All over Australia, Canada, the US, Germany, France, Eastern Europe, Greece, the Balkans, Italy, Austria, Russia, Japan, China, Spain, Portugal and on and on.

Donna and I took a long lease of a house in the small Burgundian village of Nicey, about forty kilometres north of Chablis, from 1995 to 2000. We lived there happily for several European summers. It was a fabulous learning experience not only because of village life, but because we travelled widely, improved our French, made many good French friends and in a way, completed our wine education. We visited most of the wine areas of northern and western France, important as well as modest. We bought widely and managed to repatriate most of our purchases to Australia. I find it a great pleasure nowadays to look up the prices of some of our acquisitions: my best investment by far. The Nicey period was full of fun and multitudes of guests, some welcome and some not. There are many stories that I could tell about that period, but the word count is getting the better of me quickly so, next volume perhaps.

So, Johnnie, can you mention a few of the wines that have stayed in your memory as special?

My favourites over my lifetime so far? I'll mention a few. The tip of a big iceberg.

Wynn Coonawarra Black Label Cabernet Sauvignon has been a constant: fine, long lived, reasonably priced and, when from a good vintage and well-cellared, distinctive and delicious.

Bowen Estate Coonawarra Chardonnay and Shiraz have also been fine and reliable since young Doug left Lindemans in 1972 to set up his own business.

Yarra Yarra Dixons Creek wines generally. The owner and winemaker Ian McLean has been a friend and wine counsellor for many years. Quality has been variable recently owing to some tough issues in Ian's life, but when he's on song, the wine's as good as anything you could buy anywhere.

Tarraford Vineyard wines from Healesville, now made by Giant Steps. Owned by another great mate Chris Long, Tarraford Chardonnay has been magnificent in many years.

Funder & Diamond Wandin Vineyard wines, primarily the chardonnay made by Oakridge, have been outstanding, as has the cabernet. I was lucky to receive John Funder's small crop of pinot noir for several vintages, which has proven exceptional as well.

Bordeaux, both Right and Left Bank, has been a focus, as well as *Vouvray* and *Beaune*. One of the happy developments for Australia has been the development of pinot noir growing and vinification. Twenty-five years ago almost none of our pinot was worth drinking; today it is, at the upper levels, the equal of anything anywhere other than pinnacle wines like Domaine de la Romani Conti.

Crawford River Riesling from John and Belinda Thompson. There is none better in Australia and few better anywhere.

Sauternes, of course. The classics, but Chateau Raymond Lafon, re-established by Pierre Meslier who was then the manager of d'Yquem in the neighbouring property, is hard to pick from d'Yquem and a fraction of the price.

Champagne. When Donna and I had our house in Burgundy, we were 19 kilometres south of the border of the Champagne appellation and bought a lot of stock from around the town of Les Riceys, some of which is still drinking beautifully. It's made for ageing: bright, clear, lovely floral and citrus aromas with a life-giving acid backbone. And cheap.

Chablis. We would visit the Chablis markets most Saturdays, and always look for good chardonnays to buy. We still have a good stock of Premier and Grand Crus, mostly from Regnard, going back to 2000, that we treasure.

From *New Zealand*, mainly pinots from Central Otago: Mt Difficulty, Felton Road and Gibbston Valley.

I've steered clear for the most part of the Hunter Valley and Napa/Sonoma, in the latter case mainly on the grounds of value for money. I have some Barolos and Barbarescos from Italy, but I find them slow to develop and some of them can be unforgiving and hard to my taste for their entire lives.

I've not collected many Penfolds wines; some are excellent but made to a style that in general I don't like. I find Grange too expensive and now too extracted and powerful for my palate.

Pinots from Pooley in Tasmania, Kooyong Estate, Paringa Estate, Moorooduc Estate and particularly the Robinson Estate Moorooduc pinots.

That's enough of a sample, Jim. My beneficiaries can explore my cellar more fully when the time comes.

Has your interest in wine brought you closer to other people?

Definitely. I belong to several wine-oriented groups, some all-male and some mixed, that meet to celebrate wine in different ways. One group, composed of ex-Rio Tinto employees, has the motto "Often wrong, but never in doubt." These are honest and compassionate people who have been my friends since the '70s and who, unfortunately, are dying off too fast.

I also have a group of friends from the industry, customers of Wild Fire, suppliers, storemen, show representatives, distributors and others whom I see regularly and happily. It's a kind of guild, for the most part honest and respectful, that I love because such people are so rare. Like the people who help me in the vineyard, for example. Rob Walker, the comprador of Iona, has been a magnificent worker and friend; we have stood beside each other for ten vintages now and we understand each other and the needs of the vineyard completely. The same is true of Toni Sampson, who has become the shoot trainer during the season and wrapper after pruning, which takes imagination, patience and softer hands than I have.

Why did you name the property "Iona"?

We chose the name "Iona" for two reasons: first because the island of Iona, off the West coast of Scotland near Mull, was the place that the monk Columba fled to with twelve other monks after being exiled from Ireland. He turned the tiny island into one of the most important centres in the Celtic Christian world, which preserved many of the most important classical and Christian texts of the time in its library and created and illuminated many beautiful manuscripts including the Book of Kells. I thought it would be right to show respect to this beacon of hope and civilisation. The other reason was that Donna's paternal grandmother was named Iona.

And how have you found the process of becoming a grape-grower and a wine maker?

Being a grape-grower is just another branch of farming where you battle seasons, weather, mildews and parasites and sometimes you have amazing crops and sometimes you don't. Viticulture has been a great teacher. To stop and observe; to wait; to predict; to organise. Executing a spraying regime is a bit like performing music; in our case, the music is the complex lattice of dozens of compounds we use for the fight, observing the weather, scouting for disease outbreaks and keeping our hardware ready for action 24/7; the performance is getting the spray mixed and on at the right time, in the right concentrations, avoiding chemistry clashes, judging sprayer speeds. Not for the slapdash.

How do you feel about the Melbourne restaurant scene? Do you visit them often?

Yes, I do. There are some restaurants that genuinely cherish their role as cathedrals of food and wine appreciation, with none of the attitude, hype, discrimination and snobbery of many culinary establishments. My favourite by far is (in Melbourne) Scopri in Nicholson Street, which serves fine Italian food with grace and conviviality and will allow you to bring your own wine for a ridiculously low corkage fee. Why would you want to go anywhere else? I now know the waiters, who never change and are all accomplished, friendly and warm people, and I'm welcomed and helped generously every time.

Another great association is the Australian Club, where I belong to the wine committee, naturally a sought-after membership. It's responsible not only for what is in reality a magnificent in-house wine retail business, but also all wine-related social functions. It also hosts an annual committee dinner, which is the stuff of legend.

There's a collection of wine blogs I wrote for different people, one of which is annexed to this volume. I thought they might lift our sales. I was entirely wrong about that, but they'll give you a better sense of why I did what I did in wine.

It's really been a second life, in a way. No matter how black the world seems, you can always visit your vines or pat your casks and drift away from the daily grind.

Absolutely. It's so much part of my life and in a way my identity now that I'd be bereft without it. I know the end is coming. But what a grand journey.

Parents

Sorry, Johnnie, but I need to drag you back onto the path a bit. Blokes like you avoid saying too much about their parents and family background. I don't know why, because kids are who they are because of their parents, so how can someone be understood without that history?

I agree. It's an important ingredient for the family, though less so for the casual reader. My mother's family was a forbidden subject. And all I know about Ralph's family comes from dusty family trees and kindly but anodyne notes of what was done when and by whom. The old photos are the same – they don't say much to me. There's no lore, no treasured family stories of loves, wins, losses or glittering night sky arcs.

In those days, people who were socially conscious kept hand-written books of quotations where they would inscribe literary excerpts to remind themselves that they were educated, good and superior. These people were not really true to themselves. That's a problem that affects most of us today, but less, I suspect. Respectability meant you had to hide any part of your life that might be seen as questionable, meaning ambition, wealth, creativity, talent, self-promotion, any interest in the demimonde, and especially alcohol.

You also had to be frugal: you scraped butter wrappers, folded Christmas paper away for next year, kept old string, made glue, boiled jam and grew vegetables. Otherwise you'd be found extravagant or wasteful, probably the worst of sins.

This was the life I grew up in: I can still hear a voice telling me I'm bad when I spend anything on myself, drink too much or overeat, or feel angry or jealous, or waste something. The voice is a bit quieter now.

And, being a member of a financially modest family, which all public service families were in those days, was limiting. Having friends with smarter cars, fancier clothes, better experiences and the entitlement of the wealthy was no fun.

Do you remember the social scramble when the Beatles came to Melbourne in 1964?

I sure do. Most of my privileged mates found tickets but the best I could do was listen in on my transistor radio. I still remember the bitterness of that night.

It might explain why I find myself giving so much to other people, and being indulgent with myself. I can't imagine what my parents would have thought of me buying a Maserati supercar at my age – they would have found it incomprehensible.

I hadn't heard about that one!

No? I had a friend who was car mad and he suggested I buy a Maserati 3200 GT because it was cheap and fabulous to drive. I was lucky – the one I bought was in great shape and was quite a magnificent animal. It had a sweet Ferrari V8 engine and was lethally fast. During Covid I secured a permit to travel to Warrnambool to look after Winsome and Tommy Brittain, Donna's mother and father, and once I escaped all the roadblocks there was literally no one on the road for 300 kilometres, so down went the foot. It was a time that won't come again. A couple of years ago I sold it for a smart profit to a Melbourne Mafia boss whose father had owned it. That transaction was a story on its own.

So, you think you didn't have the depth of support kids need to develop emotional stability?

I didn't, certainly not during those formative years when I was in boarding school. I say that as a fact, not in self-pity. My parents had my back but there was only so much they could do remotely. They missed most of the signature events in my youth – sporting events, plays, musical performances, exams, graduations – that I expected they would be there for. I realised that this was going to be my life.

Let's start with Ralph.

OK. Our relationship over a lifetime was distant and tentative. At no time do I remember him looking me in the eye and saying, tell me your troubles, let me share my thoughts about life and people with you. Our conversations were a bit like a garden party where everyone speaks about the weather. Ralph had a superlative intellect; he was a loyal and dedicated servant of the Australian Government; he was widely acknowledged as a fine diplomat; his reputation meant that our family was always respected; he provided for the family without complaint, he educated me and my sisters well and opened the door to learning and understanding that would not have been available otherwise. For that there will never be enough gratitude.

But he was a serious, contained and reticent man. When I was growing up he was an imposing figure. He always returned home late from work in the evenings and was often away, and at weekends he would work on projects that he enjoyed, like his orchard, his garden, his diaries and crosswords, or playing board games with my sister Penny, who loved them as well.

The Canberra hierarchy suited him because he respected rank, although he sometimes seemed to be intimidated by it.

He wasn't a storyteller either, and didn't have an easy way of amusing people. In conversation he usually talked about what he was doing, not what you were doing. I can't remember him asking me things like, How are you feeling? What do you think about? How do you find your school masters, friends, experiences? What would you really like to do with your life?

I didn't know his landscape: I would have found it impossible to ask, Who are your mates? What do you really love? Who do you really love? You know, why did you think you should come to a tiny Canberra with a family when it was just snakes and paddocks? How did you feel about being away from the family so often?

His one-to-one encounters with other men didn't flow, he had no drinking buddies, no one to call for no reason at weekends; he had a Christmas card book where every receipt and dispatch was recorded. I won't forget the Novembers when the book would come out and another batch of no-repliers would be blue-pencilled out. He allowed (to me, anyway) no paradox, no fantasy, no excitement and no entry.

A kid feels sad when a parent's struggling, especially emotionally. It's as though you're looking at them naked on a beach. I'm sure that made you feel guilty as well. As a kid you probably thought that if only you'd been normal, other parents might have been more welcoming to Ralph?

I did. Ralph would sometimes ask me to caddy for him when he formed a golf playing group, always related to work. I would stand behind him nervously on the first tee and pray that his drive would go well; it would often be hooked into the bush. His frustration was visible to the other players, which disturbed the harmony of the occasion. During drinks after a round, he would find it hard not to talk about what interested him rather than trying to establish conversational safe spaces with his companions.

I was speaking to my daughter Pip the other day who suggested that these days he might well have been diagnosed as being somewhere on the autism spectrum. I had never considered the possibility and it seems to me quite plausible.

So how did you feel about him?

I respected him as my father, as someone of enormous ability and importance, and someone who had the family's best interests at heart. But I felt he wasn't really interested in me, and of course, as you say, I blamed myself for that and never gave up trying to please him. I've accepted that he and I weren't mates and that he didn't want to involve himself in my life all that much. No traditional activities like kicking the footy, or fishing, or camping, or hiking.

So I just went my own way. I never learned the unspoken but fundamental social rules that exist between men and men, much less men and women. Of course, this meant confusion about how I would ever be embraced or be seen as desirable, or bonded with anyone or any group. I needed the knowledge that there was someone who had my back and acted like it for no other reason than it was me.

How did that affect you?

I looked for attention, naturally, and collected the emotional uncertainty you know about, which compounded as time went on. My parents saw me as difficult, impetuous and irresponsible, and didn't conceal their disappointment.

My father's mind and mine were different. I didn't realise that for a long time. To him, if you weren't good at symbolic logic – math – you weren't intelligent and had a second-class mind. If you didn't have every grammatical rule at your fingertips, if you hadn't read a respectable list of classics, if you weren't interested in puzzles, crosswords and riddles, you weren't educated. That sort of view chucks out most of life – the drama, politics, ambition, mateship, betrayal, lust, fascination, satisfaction and complexity of being human. It wasn't that I was so bad at those things, in fact I was quite good at most of them, but I just didn't see the point. I was much happier building something, say, than trying to solve a crossword clue. Ralph's outlook was, at a family level, hard to change, just at the time when society was changing faster than at any time in its history.

Ralph – His Life

We have to get down some biographical detail about Ralph here, don't we?

I think we have to. Those who'd prefer to escape the detail, flip the next few pages.

Ralph was born in Geelong on 10 March 1917.

His father, Arthur Hartley Harry, was then a classics master at the Geelong College, having moved there from Prince Alfred College in Adelaide in 1904, and became vice principal in 1917.

Arthur was the first student at the University of Adelaide to achieve first-class honours in both classics and philology.

His wife, Ethel Roby Harry, was a scholar, having been the first female Master of Arts graduate from Adelaide University. She had become a significant figure in the temperance movement early in her life and worked long and hard for many civic and community causes.

Her father, my great-grandfather, was Sir Frederick Holder KCMG, a premier of South Australia and also the first speaker of the first federal parliament of Australia in 1901. Fred famously died in the Federal House of Representatives (then located in Victoria's parliament buildings in Spring Street) in 1909 during a heated late-night debate and was given a South Australian State funeral.

Fred was one of Ralph's heroes and we were proud of his history. We were often taken to see the famous 1903 painting by Tom Roberts of the opening of the first Federal Parliament on 9 May 1901, my birthdate, at the Melbourne Exhibition buildings, in which Fred figured prominently. The picture is now hung in Parliament House in Canberra.

So, how long did Ralph's family stay in Geelong?

Arthur moved to Tasmania in 1922 from Geelong College where he became the head of the classics department at Launceston Grammar School. Ralph grew up in Launceston and went to the Grammar School. Arthur retired in 1948.

Ralph must have had a tough time being the son of a senior school master?

I think so. He was challenged as he was growing up. He was expected to top, and did top, every class, play in every senior sporting team, debate, be a church worker, and take on a large share of the labour around a household that had slim resources and was unsupported by few modern conveniences. All his cash prizes were contributed to the family.

Only when he was six or seven did his parents realise that he had problems with his sight, because he seemed to be having trouble reading. He was tested and found to be badly short-sighted. That he managed to function at all up to that point was remarkable. His struggle to keep up without being able to see probably developed his memory, grit and ambition. It's easy to see how he became the person he was.

He left Launceston Grammar as dux, received a first-class honours degree in law from the University of Tasmania and was a Rhodes Scholar for Tasmania in 1938. He worked his way to the UK on a small cargo ship, and completed a politics, philosophy and economics degree at Oxford immediately before the outbreak of the Second World War. I remember being told that he tried to enlist in the British Army in England at the outbreak of the war while still in the UK but was rejected because of his bad eyesight. I don't know if that's true.

He joined the Department of External Affairs briefly when he came back from England in 1940, and then enlisted in the army as a military intelligence officer after Pearl Harbour and was posted to Papua New Guinea. He was recalled to the Department in 1943.

What are the earliest memories you have of him?

My first memory is seeing him in the early Canberra mornings, with his back to me, putting on his shirt and tie and fiddling with his radio to get it tuned to the ABC news.

I remember being hugged by him at bedtime; I remember him trying to teach me chess; more clearly, I remember feeling tested and examined for talent. But he always seemed lofty and important in a way I felt I never could be.

When he took up golf, he didn't take me to the driving range or have me taught by a professional even though I was keen and somewhat talented. We continued to play together now and then, which I enjoyed because it was one of the few times I had his undivided attention.

Do you remember him teaching you about how you should behave, about ethics, about society?

No. Ralph was brought up during the Depression when academic achievement, professional skills and government service were paramount. Those values were a given in our family. So, my environment was no tolerance of anything less than a brilliant school and university record and a fully respectable career. He believed that a good academic record would solve any problem.

But there was no teaching in the central importance of getting on with people, of society and how it organised itself, of how society was stratified, of how people would ignore almost anything if they liked you. This is odd, isn't it, for a man whose livelihood was in being an advocate for his country, and who did that job well.

One of the things I remember about you was finding out that Ralph had been the director of ASIS – the Aussie equivalent of

the CIA – and had been at the centre of the Australian intelligence community.

I didn't find out about that until a book was published in the '80s, well after Ralph retired, by an Australian journalist called Brian Toohey, which named him as a former ASIS director. By long tradition the directors' identities had been concealed from the public. You can understand what a shock it was to find out that way.

Early in his career he had been drawn into, and then never left, the intelligence community. Because the Department of External Affairs was so small at the beginning, he acted as the departmental cipher clerk and would have been involved with establishing the military precursor of ASIS, which was a joint UK/US/Australian wartime intelligence group located in the army barracks in St Kilda Road, Melbourne. The American OSS would have been one of the drivers of the unit. He would have been involved in liaison between the unit and the Australian Government, and probably also in intelligence operations. From that point on, there was probably no time in his career when he wasn't involved in some intelligence activities.

Once he entered into the community, parenting would become even more difficult, because he would never have the time, and he would never find the process of parenting as magnetic as running a portfolio of agents, briefing cabinets and always keeping more secrets than anyone else.

Have you ever thought about the ethical issues around his intelligence work?

The first thing to say about my father and his intelligence life was that not once as I was growing up did he say or do anything that suggested that he was an intelligence operative, or anything about any of his intelligence activities. He was a blank wall. So if you ask me about what he did, my answers will be speculative but, I believe, likely to have been true.
His work would almost certainly have involved what are referred to today as black ops. Assessing the merit of his work in ethical or any other terms

isn't possible, but that he led a double life and that his life was brutally contained by his secrecy commitments was beyond doubt.

He was a key player in the Australian support for the attack coordinated by the Indonesian military on the Indonesian communist party, PKI, following the failed communist coup in 1965 during Sukarno's presidency. This led to the deaths of more than 500,000 Indonesians in 1965 and 1966 and the destruction of the PKI and Sukarno. Australian intelligence concerning the identity of key PKI operatives would probably have been made available by ASIS to the Indonesians, leading in many cases to their deaths.

Following Indonesia's annexation of East Timor, he was a leading participant in the controversial Australian and Indonesian negotiations about where the maritime boundary between Indonesia and Australia would fall. That boundary would regulate who would be entitled to the revenues from natural resource exploitation of the area. This provided Australia with a large prospective share of the resources rights in the gap area, where the maritime boundary between Indonesia and East Timor could not be agreed because of Portugal's withdrawal from the administration of East Timor. No provision was made for sharing by the Timorese. This outcome effectively acknowledged Indonesian sovereignty to East Timor and constituted an annexation of revenue rights that in equity belonged to the East Timorese. When East Timor became independent in 2002, the United Nations encouraged a process by which the commercial elements of the previous gap treaty were adjusted in favour of East Timor.

And he was Australia's ambassador to South Vietnam during the war from 1968 till 1970. His experience as an intelligence analyst and his contacts within the CIA and other elements of the US intelligence apparatus meant that he would have been fully involved in the Allied intelligence effort, including such things as the development of the brutal covert Phoenix assassination operations that so ravaged the South Vietnamese people and led to the collapse of the US's moral authority.

You should read Neil Sheehan's *A Bright Shining Lie*, a history of the war based on the life of US soldier John Paul Vann. Anyone interested in the origins and calamitous outcome of the US and Australian war involvement will find Neil's book essential because of its completeness and quality. I was too young and gullible, and too cowed by my father's strong support of the US war policy, to have developed a reasoned anti-war stance in the late '60s, although, because I associated with anti-war people at university at the time, and it was fashionable, I was drawn into the public demonstrations and general anti-war sentiment.

Do you wonder how he was attracted to intelligence and a covert life?

Yes, often. Adam Sisman's *John le Carré: The Biography* claims that le Carré was recruited by associates at Lincoln College in Oxford, which was the college Ralph attended just before World War Two. It's possible that MI6 sympathisers in the college and in Oxford spotted him as a prospective intelligence recruit for Australia, which then led to his engagement with army intelligence during the Pacific war.

We've also wondered what drove him to make that commitment. Sisman quotes le Carré as saying that spying "opened a door to a world beyond good and evil, and that it felt like betrayal but it had a voluptuous quality. This was a necessary sacrifice of morality and that is a very important component of what makes people spy, what attracts them."

For someone like Ralph, who had been raised in an orthodox, Victorian moral universe where everything was regulated and constrained, an offer of the romantic, exciting, intellectually challenging and wicked world of intelligence, dressed up as heroic national service, would have been irresistible.

Whether the lies, compromises and brutalities of his trade were justified is something I'll never be sure of. I'll never know, despite the hard work, reticence and courage he needed, what he really achieved for the good of Australia.

I can see how your father would have applied spy tradecraft to unglue you, to see what your bits looked like, to predict what you might do and what trajectory your life might take.

No question about that. I realise now that these tricks were used on me routinely. There was no place to hide, no document that would have been unread, no phone call unobserved, no lie undetected, no bluff unpenetrated. I have a memory of him finding in my personal stuff a copy of *Man* magazine, an early and tame tabloid that featured a few photos of what would today be regarded as too proper for page three. I had hidden this somewhere I thought was unreachable and yet there he was, waving this thing at me, accusing me of moral failure and so on and so forth. How times have changed.

I just would have preferred to be his friend.

It sounds as though there wasn't much whimsy or sympathy in Ralph's character?

He was a searching observer and analyst, but there wasn't much poetry or song that he ever revealed to me. I never saw him drunk or frivolous or abandoned. He collected jokes like stamps. When he heard one, he filed it in a card index. He appreciated wit but was not a naturally funny man.

In his last years he destroyed all the personal or controversial parts of his papers and correspondence, and refused any discussion with me that would disturb the shape of the life he wanted to be left behind. He left those sanitised papers to me in his will, me, the one who most wanted him to reveal himself. This was a wonderful irony. I suppose he thought that after the censorship, it wouldn't matter much who they went to. He was happy for us to have his curriculum vitae, but not himself.

He can't have been a particularly happy man?

I'm not sure. His approach to people was structured rather than instinctive, and the opposite of mine, which for decades was pure improvisation. He believed that he needed to shield himself from the possibility of unwise contacts that might compromise his work, which restricted his friendships. His life did provide him with recognition and satisfaction, but the fact that he didn't enjoy mateships with many other men might have isolated him at times. I often had the feeling that he was sad about that but because he was who he was, I will never know.

But would you say that on the whole he was a good person?

He was, at least in his non-intelligence life, as far as I know anyway, entirely honest, honourable and hard-working. He was also competent, imaginative and sceptical. This was a combination of qualities that suited him for the bureaucracy perfectly, and that endeared him to his bosses, up to a point, all his life.

He believed in merit. Although he knew what personal background meant, he would never have been a party to an appointment or promotion unless it was for the right reasons.

He accepted his formal family responsibilities and sacrificed many personal desires in the interests of our education and maintenance. In his distant way he did love us and wanted the best for us. He was fair, patient and, sometimes, generous. But he rarely stopped to ask whether what he wanted for us was what we might want.

He didn't connect at all with my children, although by that time my mother's Alzheimer's disease was beginning to take hold of her and he was distracted. But, by all accounts, his relationship with Virginia's step-children was happy and they became very fond of him.

Do you think your views of Ralph have been changed by your writing experience?

Yes. I've allowed myself to look at Ralph more as he was than as I was taught to see him. After he died, I dined out with some of his old intelligence colleagues to see whether I could get closer to the truth about who he was and what he had done. This was good fun because the interviews were entertaining and because the information

I received came to me mainly in the form of hints and pauses, as you would expect from old spies. Making sense of this was hard, but it did explain some things. I sensed that they thought Dad's contribution hadn't entirely justified his reputation, and also that they saw him more as a colleague than friend, but who knows whether that's true. It may just have been old grievance.

He was marked out as a coming man in his twenties and was acknowledged, at the end of his career, as one of the pioneers of Australian diplomacy. He rose to second-in-command of the Department of Foreign Affairs and was highly praised and decorated. He was awarded the Companionship of the Order of Australia and before that, the Order of the British Empire and the Companionship of the British Empire. He was credited with a substantial role in the development of the ANZUS treaty between the US, Australia and New Zealand, which has been the bearing around which Australia's security arrangements have rotated since ANZUS came into force in April 1952.

The fact that he never achieved the top job in his department was always a bitter fact for him, although it's easy to see why this happened. He wasn't a politician or a confidant. He was never seen at the Canberra pubs where the real public service friendships and alliances were formed, and he didn't have mates who would look after his back when the going got rough. He was known for riding his juniors hard, and probably his seniors as well.

When ministers are deciding who they want to run their departments, competence is a given and it's always a question of who will be easy to work with, who will look after their boss's interests and compromise if need be, and who will be a good companion on away trips. My father may not have inspired these feelings. Others' awareness of his training in intelligence, to remember everything and keep secrets until the day when they could be of use, would not have been an advantage. But he seemed to be attentive to and liked by his staff, particularly at conferences and in team situations.

You said a while ago that your family's financial position was modest. Did that worry you, or make you unhappy?

I knew that was the case, but except for a few situations it didn't trouble me. It was the universe we lived in. Of course I would have been pleased if the situation had been different but that was idle speculation. I didn't enjoy the privilege many of my school mates at Melbourne Grammar had but that made me more determined to do well rather than be envious. Public servants in the '50s and '60s weren't paid much. I remember the monthly arrival of the bank statement – purple for credit, red for debit, and the all-important balance, always-in-red overdraft. He always grieved at this, believing that it was unfair for one of his ability to have to be disciplined by his bank manager.

I did see myself as a financial imposition, which didn't improve my self-view much, but again it wasn't something that interfered greatly with my life.

What were Ralph's outside interests – did he have many?

He had some hobbies. By far the most important was a lifelong dedication to Esperanto, a synthetic language invented by the Polish professor Ludwik Lejzer Zamenhof in the 1870s. I'm not sure where or when he developed this interest but it may have been during his time in Oxford. The idea was to create an international lingua franca for improved communication between different peoples, with the aim of benefiting international society.

Dad promoted this to his children and friends relentlessly, to the point where there were some in his life who thought he was beginning to stray onto the fringe. There were parts of the movement that embraced a kind of spirituality and devotion that made it suspect to non-believers.

Nevertheless, my father found much interest and satisfaction in the language as a translator, lexicographer and, ultimately, as a revered father and academician. He also was a regular attendee of the annual Esperanto congress, where he enjoyed the company and respect of his fellow devotees.

Did he manage to develop the reputation and global usage of Esperanto?

Not really. He was a major and respected figure in the movement but it was clear early on that English would become the international language.

His commitment had its greatest day when he was serving as the Australian ambassador to the United Nations in 1977.

NASA, the US space agency, had in that year programmed the launch of two space probes, Voyagers 1 and 2. They were designed to take and send images of the outer planets back to earth, then continue beyond the solar system after leaving the sun's gravitational pull to become the first man-made objects to escape it. NASA and the cosmologist Carl Sagan created identical golden records to attach to each probe that told the story of the solar system and mankind, should one of them ever come into contact with intelligent extraterrestrial life. Engraved on each record was, among other things, a soundtrack containing a compilation of fifty-four peace greetings to the universe recorded in different languages by various UN Representatives. Ralph succeeded in persuading the UN and NASA to accept a message in Esperanto. It's located third-last on track three of the golden records and says, translated:

We strive to live in peace with the peoples of the whole world, of the whole Cosmos.

I wonder what the Department of External Affairs thought of this! Looking back, it's not hard to see how his senior colleagues would have regarded this as an error of judgement. But I am proud to know that the voice of my father will travel through the universe until it ceases to exist.

I rejected my father's invitations to become an Esperantist, but I was still dragged to meetings and functions for years against my will. I didn't want to spend my weekends having to learn what seemed to be an unattractive synthetic language, or to have to associate with his Esperantist friends, all of whom seemed to me to be exceptionally uncool.

Much later, when I began to make my own living, to my father's delight, I made a substantial donation to the Esperanto Association of Australia. I can't say this was because I thought Esperanto would ever be anything but a curiosity, but I wanted to acknowledge Ralph's phenomenal devotion and hard work in the interests of one of the few causes that he loved.

Ralph was also a cryptic crossword fan, and enjoyed stamp collecting and writing his diary and home movie making. He once won a pound for the first correct crossword entry received by the London *Times* and dined out on his victory for a long time.

I guess you could say that Ralph was a challenge for you?

You could. He was not your usual dad. I respected him as clever, knowledgeable and obviously important, as someone who seemed to be winning the Canberra game of thrones and as someone I'd like to have in my corner if the going got rough. All I wanted, though, like every son, was his recognition and praise.

Dorothy – Her Life

I remember you talking about your mother in our early days, and you say you had a closer relationship with her than you did with Ralph, that she was more human, that she seemed to worry about what was good for you rather than what Ralph thought you should do. What was her maiden name?

Elsie Dorothy Sheppard.

And how do you see her now?

She was different; intuitive, observant, sceptical and funny. She made decisions quickly, she was fair-minded and called things what they were. She was curious and delighted in discovery and fresh experiences. She was practical and hard-working, and a lethal card player. But she was far from academic, I suspect having left school early. I loved her curiosity and delight in the mystery of life, her practical, have-a-go intelligence, her need for society, her musicality, her irreverence for egg heads, professors and pomp. And her dislike for symbolic logic. She was someone who looked first at how to get things done, rather than trying to formulate theories. I do the same. But she was not someone who gave love away that often or easily, and for long periods, not at all. And with plenty of prejudices and quite surprising phobias. But she was much loved: she handled official life with ease and amusement and was everyone's favourite at official events.

I saw her as much more of a mate and easier going than Ralph. But even though she was a strong person in many ways, she would never contradict Ralph on the big issues.

The watershed decision for me was to leave me at boarding school at Melbourne Grammar in 1960 when Dad's term as ASIS director ended. She was unhappy with the idea; I caught her in tears more than once. She told me she worried about how an eleven-year-old would cope alone if Ralph was posted overseas again. She knew, and I knew, that this would really be the end of family life for me.

So, tell me more about her history.

Well, my association with her began when I was born – at the Columbia Hospital in Pennsylvania Avenue NW in Washington DC in the great United States of America at 11.37 p.m. on 9 May 1947!

This came about because Ralph was a second secretary in the Australian Embassy to the US. He had met and married mum in Canada in January 1944. Dorothy worked as a senior assistant to the Australian high commissioner to Canada, Sir William Glasgow, where my father was posted before Washington. She was, as we learned many years later, nine years his senior and had been born in Trinidad in the West Indies.

She was a beauty. It took her until her late thirties to marry my father and that lateness is something that has always troubled me. She may have been married previously, and perhaps may even have had other children, but we will never know. Ralph and Dorothy did have a headlong courtship and did love one another. We children once discovered a box of love letters they exchanged. They were the real thing.

Mum was also a talented athlete. She skied and played first-class tennis, and was one of the best badminton players in Canada. She would have made a fine partner for my father in those days when an ability to play tennis was good for your social reputation. She introduced Ralph to ice skating at the Rideau Club in Ottawa, where he did well.

Dad and Mum were regularly invited to play tennis with Eleanor Roosevelt and her friends while Eleanor was involved, with Ralph as a colleague, in helping write some of the core documents in the UN Charter in San Francisco in 1946–47, including the Universal Declaration of

Human Rights. Harry Truman had appointed Eleanor as a US delegate to the UN in 1946, and she was asked to chair the Commission on Human Rights and the Drafting Committee for the Universal Declaration. Dad worked on the drafting committee, although I'm not sure what his eventual contribution to the document was.

Do you owe your sporting ability to your mother, do you think?

Mostly. I'm thankful to her for the gift. Without sport, my life would have been much poorer.

Back in the '60s, there were two kinds of families: the ones that had a decent TV set and the ones that didn't. We didn't have one. My father occasionally relented and hired a TV set during our hot summer holidays in Canberra, but only because of my mother's insistence on watching the test cricket. Being from Trinidad, she was fanatical. One of her great disappointments was my decision to row rather than become a fast bowler. She found the choice incomprehensible, though my love of listening in with her to the telecasts of the tests was some compensation.

Did you ever wonder about her West Indian background and how that might have impacted you?

That was a question mark in my life for decades.

The fact that she had been born in Trinidad created questions, some of which were not solved until after she died, and some have never been resolved. The biggest of these was whether she was ethnically British, which, when pressed, she always claimed. She did nothing to illuminate the mystery. She would invariably deflect any questions about her family or life in Trinidad in general.

As children, we found albums of hers that contained many photos of her in her youth. She and her friends, with her to a lesser extent, looked mixed-race, which meant either that there was Indian or African in her genetics. My mother's discomfort at this discovery was clear and the albums were thereafter lost.

The smoke kept drifting around us as we grew up. My elder sister Virginia and I had notably olive complexions, with dark eyes, jet black, glossy hair and an unusual ability to tan. My younger sister Penny, on the other hand, had blue eyes and a fair complexion with blonde hair. She resembled my father. In my school photographs, the early ones especially, I appeared noticeably darker than my mates. I remember masters sometimes asking discreet questions about my family background.

Did you quiz Dorothy about this?

All the time. I couldn't draw any information from her about the origins or even composition of her family, or why or when she had decided to leave Trinidad for Canada. I was aware that she had several siblings, perhaps five or six, but there were only two who were discussed: Elaine, who was a senior nurse in the US Army, and Tully, who was safely married to an English accountant from Nottingham in the UK.

Elaine visited our family from time to time and my parents visited her when they were on post somewhere within reach. Her visits to Canberra, where my family lived when my parents weren't on post, were looked forward to because she wasn't married (but may previously have been) and always brought expensive gifts, subsidised by Uncle Sam, that we could never have afforded.

Elaine did not seem to raise any ethnic questions, having a fair complexion and reddish hair. I never met Tully and my English cousins, but they were equally uniform in look and accomplishment.

My father wrote a few chanceless pages of notes about my mother and her family background that we found after his death, but they didn't add much. For the work of an intelligence analyst, they were unimpressive.

Did you think that one day you'd be able to shed some light on your mum's origins?

My search for truth was only pursued in bits and pieces because of my laziness and because the reality of my mother was so attractive and warm. Why should I need to look beyond this reality, especially when the discovery of an unexpected provenance would have been awkward? Recall that this was the 1950s and 1960s when the White Australia policy was a given, when Catholics and Protestants were usually not on speaking terms and when members of polite society would never have invited a person of colour to dinner, much less have allowed one to fraternise with their children.

In 2015, I decided that this question should be tackled with modern technology, so I submitted a DNA sample to the National Geographic's Genographic project, which promised to locate my early genetic origin, the migration pathways that my ancient forbears took out of Africa and my racial composition.

I had always been sure that there was some Indian blood in us but when the results appeared, I discovered that around 15% of my DNA came from central Africa, and 5% from Arabia. The remainder was mainly Norse with a bit of Anglo because the Harrys came from Cornwall, which had been overrun by Vikings in the 800s AD.

This meant that one of Dorothy's grandparents was African and had probably been taken to Trinidad as a slave.

To find this out at nearly seventy years of age was bittersweet, but it explained much about me and my make-up. It made me angry that this had been kept from us – who knows what other secrets were buried by Ralph and Dorothy. They were old-fashioned people who found it easy to lie to their children.

Were you happy to discover you were part Black?

I'm proud of it and I've told many people about it, although some of my friends have obviously felt confirmed in their view that I was unusual. I'm spectacularly out-bred rather than inbred, which means I'm unlikely ever to suffer from any recessive disease and I might have a longer than average life span.

What other bits of your mum helped you along?

Her musical talent was powerful and also changed my life. She sang beautifully, and we sometimes managed to draw a piece or two from her in the evenings on our family piano, at which she played by ear with a light touch. I have a warm although wistful memory of her singing me lullabies and rocking me in her arms as I was put to bed at night, burrowed into her perfumed pink cashmere twinset.

From time to time she would decide that the piano should be tuned. She would extract the required budgetary allocation from my father and a day would be set. She had great faith in the ability of the tuners and I recall her insisting that I watch and learn, not just about matters of pitch but also how, with the right talent and training, amazing amounts of money could be earned. Understanding the mechanical complexities of a piano's action was beyond me, much less working out how a tone could be transferred from a tuning fork to three piano strings perfectly. But I have ever since treated tuners of any instrument with respect and a degree of awe.

Did people listen to recorded music much in those days?

Not nearly as much as they do now. The listening process was much more serious and appreciative then.

When my family moved from the United States to Canberra in around 1949, Mum made sure that the latest His Master's Voice radiogram came as well. This I learned to operate early because I discovered, with my usual fiddling and knob twisting, the serials, which for some years I thought was "the cereals" and something edible, that could be made to float magically into the house in the afternoon.

These were thrilling experiences for a small boy and established a lifelong love of series shows on TV. I would do anything not to miss *Superman* or *Dad and Dave* or the *Argonauts Club*, a junior quiz show. *Superman* was a favourite. If he was confronted with kryptonite I despaired; if he rescued a pretty girl I shook with joy. I imagined myself vividly as him, and as every other radio hero I listened to.

Electronic gear of that age was powered by valves. These were small glass tubes that glowed orange and hot after a few minutes' use. A radio took forever to warm up but as it did, the room would be filled with the smell of burning dust and hot resin, and a lovely soft light would appear from behind the rosewood cabinet. It made the listening experience, especially at night, a magical connection with the outside world and gave you the sense that you were somehow in the presence of the person who painstakingly soldered it all together.

My mother also imported a small but well-chosen set of recordings, some of which were shellac 78s, mostly of singers from the USA that she loved, including Marian Anderson, Cole Porter and Louis Armstrong. She also acquired some LPs (long playing) 33 1/3 rpm records that were a mix of stage shows – *My Fair Lady, Oklahoma!, The King and I*; well-known singers of the day – Édith Piaf, Maurice Chevalier, Jean Sablon; and a few keystone recordings from the classical repertoire –Beethoven's *Eroica* symphony, Mozart trios, Strauss's opera *Die Fledermaus*, Tchaikovsky's *Nutcracker Suite* and Mendelssohn's *Midsummer Night's Dream* overture.

I remember Mum telling me that Mendelssohn wrote this as a seventeen-year-old. I went to a concert given by the master Hungarian pianist András Schiff a few years ago, at which he addressed the audience, saying that Mendelssohn's reputation as a composer had been retarded for decades by the antisemitic criticism of Mahler and his contemporaries, whereas he should be regarded as one of the very greats, perhaps on the same level as Haydn, Mozart and Beethoven. Schiff proceeded to play an exquisite, mostly Mendelssohn recital.

I also remember Mum telling me the story of how in 1939 the Daughters of the American Revolution had refused to stage a concert by the Black contralto Marian Anderson at their Constitution Hall on racial grounds, and that Eleanor Roosevelt had helped to re-stage the concert on the steps of the Lincoln Memorial to 75,000 people. Mum always spoke of Marian with pride, perhaps because she saw herself as a fellow traveller in the war against discrimination.

Did you get the chance to go to concerts or live musical performances in those days?

I didn't go to concerts much, mainly I think because I was in Melbourne for most of the year. I know Virginia was taken to ballet and opera performances. She was a talented ballet dancer but as she grew up her height got the better of her and she fell outside the "desirable" height category.

So what did you do for music?

At home it was low-fi AM radio or records, which I played every day. Throughout the rest of her life Dorothy collected recorded music, mostly vinyl LPs. I still have and treasure her collection. Whenever I listen to one of her records, I feel as though she visits me. I was at a lunch a few years ago and was sitting next to an attractive young woman who announced, out of nowhere, that she was a spiritual medium and could see a small figure of my mother perched on my left shoulder. I was sceptical of that pronouncement although I've always felt that she was present in my life in some way.

How did this musical exposure affect you?

From the earliest times, I loved it all. I sang loudly and I could harmonise when songs were being sung in church and on the radiogram. I spent long periods in the laundry with my budgerigars trying, to their annoyance, to develop a vibrato and was awed in the presence of live musicians. I absorbed both classical and popular music as one and found it natural to switch regularly among musical fields. My father wasn't especially interested and had little time to sit and listen, although on long car trips we would sing songs like "Cockles and Mussels" and "Old MacDonald had a Farm" with him to pass the time.

My aunt Elaine helped develop my interest in fine music reproduction. She gave the family a high-quality Japanese Akai reel-to-reel tape recorder one year. I remember the thrill of hearing transparent, rich, detailed sound for the first time. Better still, here was a machine that would record anything I wanted, and before long I learned how to transcribe records borrowed from friends and family, which offered the possibility of an infinite and free expansion of our music library.

Elaine also gave me my own cutting-edge portable transistor radio that made me feel appreciated as an individual and gave me much-needed status at school among my friends. She could not have given me anything more treasured. I still clearly remember its dark brown, glossy leather case and earphones, its rich earthy scent and its shiny silver enclosure. I was a relentlessly curious boy and the explosive development of consumer electronics in the '50s fascinated me.

Tell me something about Elaine.

She was a slim and attractive woman, around ten years younger than Dorothy. She wore neat, light and informal clothing, mostly made of cotton or poplin in the American way. Her sunglasses were the last word in cool, which she wore with flowing scarves. I thought she was the image of Natalie Wood. We envied her access to the US Army post exchange (PX) system. This was a series of army-only stores all around the world where anything was available at a big discount to the normal price. She was a slide photographer and owned a German Contax, a 35mm camera that competed on equal terms to the Leica M series.

Elaine seemed to be interested in what I had to say, and how my life might develop. She went out of her way to guide and encourage me. She died alone in her house in Florida and gave substantial legacies to my children that have made a difference to their lives.

I have felt guilty that such a generous person could have such a desolate end and I blame myself for not having done more to ensure she was looked after. The only thing I asked for from her estate was her Contax, which now sits, pristine, in my camera collection. The camera case still contains the last film she exposed. It will never be developed and I will never part with the camera.

What else was your mother interested in?

Fine art, silver, porcelain, Persian carpets, glass, fabric, clothing design, cooking, cards, sport, film ... everything of quality.

I realised, slowly, that she had faultless taste not just in music, but also in these other things. She wasn't able to buy things of quality all the time, at least in the early years, and even when we children were off her hands she couldn't be too extravagant. But she and Ralph bought original furniture of Charles and Ray Eames and other Herman Miller-sponsored designers, silverwork by Stuart Devlin, a painting by the great Canadian Anne Savage and beautiful silver flatware, china and crystal. She wouldn't be seen dead in clothing or accessories that were ugly or loud; she would prefer to buy one Hermès scarf than a hundred cheap ones.

She was fastidious with her skincare and her perfume was always light and delicious. I would often watch her take her make-up off at night, carefully and thoroughly. The last act in the ritual would always be to moisturise her skin with Elizabeth Arden cream. Later, when the family lived in Switzerland, she substituted Nivea cream. For fifty years I have had a royal blue tin of Nivea at my bathroom sink, and I use it every day. I have, I suppose, been paying tribute to her and her insistence that a good complexion is an essential asset.

She was equally insistent on the value of dental hygiene. Some of my sharpest early memories are of being dragged in terror to the dentist and the horrors of the chair. No child in those days was ever given anaesthetic and the drills were slow, noisy and crude.

She was also a devoted washer of clothes and children. Nothing survived the evening dragnet. We had to be in the bath by such and such a time and to scrub to the point of pain and beyond, or else. This allowed me, however, to explore below the surface of the water and pretend to be an ocean swimmer, a diver or, more appropriately perhaps, a whale, whose purpose was to shift as much of the bathwater onto the floor as possible.

Our laundry was full of detergents and a pastime of mine was to make masses of suds from her Lux white soap flakes in the laundry trough. Like many of my pursuits at the time, this was not appreciated.

There was nothing academic or studied, or socially ambitious, about my mother's pin-sharp sense of style and taste. It was innate and passionate. For her, it was quality or nothing.

Was she an influence on your taste preferences?

Definitely. Her sense of design order led her to be disconcertingly direct with me when, later on, I was going through one of my many perplexing fashion phases. She was a neat seamstress and I would sometimes ask her to peg jeans – meaning convert them from normal leg size to stovepipe. In those days the smaller the circumference of the leg, the more fashionable the trouser. I achieved a respectable fourteen inches at the cuff, in which I could just execute forward movement. There was no such thing as stretch fabric in those days. She would treat me to hoots of derision at all this but I loved her all the more for being a good sport and being on my side.

I know you've always had to battle with your weight. Did that complicate your relationship with your family and especially your mother?

I have had to battle. I was quite round at an early age. Mum's efforts to shame me, and shame my doctors, into some course of action that would result in the appearance of a socially acceptable figure were prodigious but unproductive. She tried every available appetite suppressant, every bribe and every hiding place to keep me from calories. Despite a semblance of control in later life, I have really never escaped the threat of a runaway expansion requiring months of dietary discipline to reverse. It's only now that weight gain has been recognised as a genetic condition, assisted by the impact of processed foods. Being overweight in those days was looked on as reprehensible, a deadly sin. Now that Ozempic is here, the extravagant shaming I and so many others experienced is fading away, and about time.

Was your mum a good cook?

Some of my strongest memories are of Mum in the kitchen.

She cooked more or less in a North American style. My favourites included an aromatic meatloaf, lemon pudding, corned beef, Irish stew, rice pudding with fat raisins, French toast, angel food cake, apple snow, pancakes, summer lemonade and our Sunday lamb or chicken roast. My father was a good vegetable gardener so I was always co-opted with my sisters to shell peas, string beans, peel potatoes and perform other household tasks, though their ability to vanish at the critical moment was impressive.

There would be tea and cake and a good pause from all work every afternoon. This was a ritual she performed all her life even after her mind became unstuck in her old age. We also made sweets the old-fashioned way, by cooking and then pulling long slabs of cooling candy into thin filaments that were then broken up and put in paper bags.

Virginia has now given me Dorothy's *Good Housekeeping Cookbook*, a relic of the early '40s. It's dilapidated but contains the recipes of all the long-forgotten delights that filled my childhood. I've found someone to rebind it so it can be passed on in reasonable condition.

In the end, I like to think that the calorie wars were mainly a game and good fun, although there were times when her fury was genuine. She never gave up believing that if only she could convince me of the ways of moderation, my life would be slim and thus worthy.

My weight always puzzled me because my mother and father were naturally thin. There have been recent studies in epigenetics that might provide an explanation. We now know that hardships experienced by one generation can change the way in which the same genes express themselves in later generations. So, if the first generation, for example, was malnourished, the second can experience difficulty in weight control and suffer from related illnesses like diabetes. My father's family was large and poor and his diet would have been calorie and vitamin deprived during his growing up, much of which was in the Great Depression. We know he was myopic, perhaps for the same reasons. There must be a good chance that this epigenetic transmission has affected me, and maybe also my children.

How did Dorothy see the world – I mean, what kind of personality was she?

She was canny, secretive, richly funny, caring and instinctive to her core. She took instant likes and dislikes to people, but, I have to admit, although she was usually a good judge of character, her reasons for not liking this person or that behaviour were not always pristine. She was, oddly enough considering her background, a believer in the White Australia policy; she didn't like the idea of people of colour living in her neighbourhood; she disliked Catholics, although the family had Jewish friends and she seemed perfectly at home with them. She held her opinions resolutely and often in the teeth of the evidence, but that was her.

When Mary and I visited my parents after our honeymoon, Dorothy was at her worst and best. Because Mary was Catholic my mother assumed she would require fish to be served on Fridays, although as it turned out, Mary hated fish. Our first meal happened to be on a Friday and sure enough, out came a flaccid and inedible fish dish. The sight of Mary in her prim Norma Tullo pleated pale blue dress desperately shunting this food around her plate was very funny, more so because I suspect my mother was well aware of her discomfort.

Dorothy enjoyed the ease with which she could anticipate my behaviour, although preventing it was another matter.

Was she an emotionally demonstrative person?

Well, like many people of her generation, she found it difficult to express emotions. Once we children were beyond toddlerhood, there wasn't much hugging or kissing I can remember. She just came from an era, and I suppose from a family, where it wasn't done. This was one source of her reticence. She never spoke about any pain or illness she suffered, I suppose believing it was impolite and not wanting to reveal anything intimate about herself. Years later in the 1970s she developed breast cancer when she was living in New York with my father. She was put on a brutal course of chemotherapy when the treatments were new and unrefined. I never heard a single complaint. She came to every meal when I visited; apart from the occasional lie down, you would have had no idea she was in the midst of a miserable chemical assault. It may have been polite, but having to suffer in such silence and solitude surely must have been costly.

This physical and emotional restraint became ingrained in me as well, and would not have helped my social and emotional adjustment.

You know that Ralph, from earliest days, travelled overseas regularly to this conference or that international gathering. Often these were United Nations affairs in Geneva or New York where he was a delegate for the whole of the two- to three-month conference sessions. My mother would take responsibility for the family while he was away. She would tackle these periods grimly, but there were many times when I would surprise her in her room in tears. Despite the strain this placed on the family and her relationship with my father, she never stopped praising him and impressing on us our good fortune to be the children of such a great and respected man.

Was Ralph completely straight, or did he have secrets? Did he have many female friendships, or loves?

I have no idea. I've been told that he was attractive to women although, being as socially backward as I was, this was never obvious to me. He was tall, with strong and regular features and dark, severely combed-back and Brylcreemed hair. Brylcreem, you might remember, Jimmy, was an oily, white hair-styling cream in a tube that, when applied and combed, would set hair in a gleaming and perfect shape that dried like rock. It was like a hat, or shiny black shoes – it informed one's superiors that one was committed to workplace conformity and that one rejected anything avant-garde or fashionable.

I have a strong feeling, corroborated by oblique signals emitted by his old colleagues, that from time to time, especially when on long trips, he had had friendships with other women, though how close we will never know. He was an intelligence craftsman and any trail would be ice cold.

Sport

Can we take another one of our side trips to discuss other pieces of you? How about sport? I know it was a big part of your early life, but did that continue?

It did. Sport for me, as a player and also as a fan, has been a massive interest, and overall has been good for my health, my self-opinion and my mateships.

Ralph tried to convince me that spending time on sport and sports people was a dalliance, essentially a waste of time, just as he did with film, music, acting, photography, cooking and most of my other passions.

Sport is battle, which man has evolved to be very good at because it was a primary survival attribute. It's an essential part of human expression. How could anyone think that it's unimportant?

Did the fact that you were overweight become an issue with sport?

Despite my circumference, people began to notice that I was strong as a boy of seven or eight. I also was starting to show endurance with long-distance bike rides and walks and could hit a golf ball further than my father from the age of ten or so.

My mother was always on the lookout for ways to curb my weight, so she signed me up to do a course of weights and calisthenics at a Findlay's Gym in Bridge Road in Richmond at around that time. I hated it because I had to find my way up there after school on the tram then find my way back to our house in Malvern, which meant my entire afternoon barnstorming around the neighbourhood got scrapped. The one part of this smelly and boring experience that I enjoyed was that you could change weights on a bar and test your strength properly. I remember the day on which I lifted 100 pounds overhead. Not many ten-year-olds could do that. I always hated gym training from then on – no wonder.

Was there any sport at that stage where you stood out?

Swimming was good for me. I spent my life in a pool when the family lived in Singapore, and raced well. When we moved back to Melbourne, I usually won at school and interschool meets. I could also sprint and jump. I didn't make it to the A football teams because while I had speed and strength, running long distances was not my thing, and maybe because round boys didn't attract interest from the selectors.

Two developments put me into a more serious sporting environment. The first was when I was fooling around in the school high jump pit one Sunday morning when I was fourteen or so and I saw David Baillieu, then the school senior shot-put champion, training nearby. I remember being attracted to the idea of throwing a shot: it was quick performance, quick reward, which suited my impatient temperament; it favoured boys with speed and strength; and it didn't require great aerobic fitness and hence I wouldn't need hours of training.

The second was that a friend of my parents sent me to see a man called John Thomas at Mercantile Rowing Club one day to see whether rowing was of interest and if it might help diminish my circumference. I recall my first row, in a dilapidated clinker four, with absolute clarity: I was hooked and dying to do more, although it would be another three or four years till I took it up regularly.

My shot-putting career was limited to school with a smattering at university, but it put me on the map as a leading athlete in the Associated Public Schools and the best-performed shot-putter on record from Melbourne Grammar.

I remember you at school being a kind of sporting celebrity. We all had to turn out at the interschools athletics sports. You were expected to break the senior all-schools record in 1964; when your win was announced and there was no record, I remember the whole school groaning loudly, as though they'd been let down. It must have been disappointing.

It really was. It wasn't as though I'd failed! I broke the under-16 school record by ten feet, and the senior school record by five feet; and I won the all-schools championship in 1964 and again in 1965. My school senior record was two feet longer than the all-schools record. But I had no coach, and set my own training program; I had almost no preparation such as weight, endurance and sprint training, which would be routine now. How the school allowed this to happen I don't know, but there it is.

Anyway, my successes earned respect around the schools community, which was helpful. I was invited to train with the then well-known field events coach Franz Stampfl in 1965, but he told me that even though I had Olympic potential, I would need to move from around 100 kg in weight to 150 kg to be competitive. Franz, who was a migrant to Australia from Austria, had coached the famous Roger Bannister and was later implicated in steroid use; it's obvious now that this weight gain could only have been achieved with a steroid program. I told him that I wasn't interested and there my field events career ended.

I know you were mostly known as a competitive oarsman, but I don't know any of the detail?

Rowing was my great love and where I had most success. My first crew was the boarding house eight in late 1962 in the interhouse rowing competition. I'd never raced a stroke in my life and I was in the 4 (stroke side) seat. The Perry boarding house crew lost its heat but I managed to keep up and I decided, with some persuasion from Gordon Sargood, a master and keen promoter of rowing at the school, to take it up. He told me that I was unlikely to become a test cricketer and urged me to try out for a

Melbourne Grammar School crew in 1963. After early season trials, I was selected into the MGS third crew, coached by Noel "Dogger" Banks, which came second to Geelong College at the Schools Head of the River Regatta.

I remember Dogger as a good bloke, and I remember you in his Greek history class, which I was in too.

He was a big supporter. He told me after our race at the Barwon in 1963 that I'd probably be in the school first eight in 1964, which was great to hear.

The winter of 1963–64 was full of discussion and planning around the campaign for the following year. Christopher Dane was convinced that we had the horsepower to win the Head of the River, although it seemed like Mount Everest to me. Chris in the stroke seat of the MGS eight had been soundly beaten in 1963 so there was no reason for me to be optimistic. Chris wasn't much of an oarsman, but he was cocky and funny and probably suited to stroke a crew of mainly sixteen-year-olds.

I was then told semi-officially that I had been chosen to row in the 5 seat of the 1964 eight, which was astonishing but scary. I couldn't understand how all this could have happened in the two years since I started. You probably remember that rowing then was high prestige, not just at school level but at a public level as well, and it was usual to have 50,000 spectators at the Head of the River regatta on the Barwon as well as regular press coverage.

Who finished up coaching you in 1964?

Gordon Sargood. I liked him. He was a slender, reserved and scholarly man who had coxed at Cambridge and taught history. He told me to lose ten kilos of my shot-putting weight over the 1963–64 summer, which I did. I remember going down to the boatsheds on the first day of training and getting on the scales. I was a bit less than ninety-two kilos. On the money. The rest of the crew was happy too.

Gordon coached the crew patiently and we developed into a stable, smart and fast combination. Suddenly life had flavour, excitement and promise, and I was surrounded with eight other great mates who had my back. It was a period when I felt as though if one miracle could occur, maybe others would and my life might make sense after all.

Gordon watched out for me, including persuading the matron of Perry Boarding House to make me special salad meals in the evenings, which I ate alone and in great splendour in the empty Perry dining room. I found being respected and talked about much to my liking. Masters from my prep school, Wadhurst, who had written me off as a potential sportsman, began to stop me to chat about the crew with obvious surprise at my development.

We won the 1964 Head of the River one sunny, sparkling March afternoon on the Barwon River. I remember every detail of that day; the precise feel of the heavy, salty water on my oar, the easy precision of our bladework, the glue dripped on my seat to keep me anchored during the race, the lamb fat on the oar swivels, the agonising pre-race nerves, the blast of the starter's shotgun and the roar of the massive crowd as we rowed to the finish line. I don't think I was ever as spent in any other race; it was pure joy and relief. Boat race night was a happy blur of dinner, dance, afterparties and disbelief that we – we! – were the heroes. I was now a winner, respected and noticed, but, for a long time, still disbelieving. That one day was precious, always to be remembered.

Do you see much of the 1964 guys these days?

I do, though maybe not quite as much as I'd like. My stroke Chris Dane in particular became more and more a recluse as he aged. He died of pancreatic cancer in 2022 and we miss him. The other members of that crew are still my beloved friends; we are, other than Chris, all alive and together after more than fifty years and see one another regularly, except for Simon Holland, who was diagnosed with schizophrenia at university and was committed.

I know you went back to school for a second Year 12 in 1965 as a kind of gap experience, which just doesn't happen now. Did you row again?

I did, but we were poorly coached by Tony Smith, who had a filthy temper and not much emotional discipline and was unsuitable as a coach of young men. Despite talent, we lost our heat to the eventual winners, Wesley College, by a few feet after being headed by over a length at the halfway mark. It was a poor effort by a crew with no confidence. We won the intermediate final by several lengths, and if memory serves me, in a faster time than Wesley in the winner's final.

I also was a core member of the Melbourne Grammar Rugby First XV, and so emerged with triple sports first colours. This entitled me to wear a first colour blazer – a magnificent traditional jacket on which the school's crest was embossed in navy, red, white and gold.

I emerged from school with a reputation as a successful sportsman, which has followed me all my life and into some unexpected places.

OK, so now you're at uni. It was a vibrant time, being at the beginning of the '60s revolution, so there must have been a lot of distractions?

There were. Just being at university with no parents, no rules really, I was making up my life as I went along. I wasn't interested at all in organised university sport. I thought success at school was going to be the end of rowing for me.

But I was persuaded to row in the intercollegiate boat race for Trinity in the first term of 1966. It was a super-short season of three weeks, so no great commitment. We lost dismally in the heat to Ormond College because two members of the crew turned up drunk most days and ruined our sessions. I was then selected into the intervarsity crew to race in Mannum in South Australia, under Harvey Nicholson as coach, and came second to the University of Tasmania after our 6 man collapsed fifty metres from the finish. The race was contested over three miles, which took an endless thirty minutes to row. It was the second last of these marathons to be contested.

Sorrow fell over the trip when we learned that two members of the Adelaide University crew had been killed in a car accident on their way back to Adelaide. We joined the Adelaide guys at their sheds the next day to drink to the passing of their mates. It was a day that few of us can remember but that we'll always recall.

The following year I rowed in the 7 seat of the Melbourne University Junior VIII with the famous cartoonist Peter Nicholson, Harvey's son, in the stroke seat. Peter was a huge fan of the famous German coach Karl Adam from the Ratzeburg Rowing Club, who had revolutionised rowing technique and training methods in the late '50s and '60s. He advocated a style of rowing that required an upright and calm finish, an acceleration into the beginning of the stroke and high race ratings of 40+. We adopted this method wholesale and were very fast for 1,500 metres, followed by an inevitable blow-up, although we came second in our state championship race on Lake Wendouree.

The season began with the traditional Christmas Regatta season in Rutherglen and Yarrawonga, which was hot, tiring and alcoholic but successful for my crew. Australian radio was full of the Supremes, Gladys Knight & the Pips, the Temptations and Marvin Gaye, and we would always carry a big transistor radio blaring those songs on our many winery visits. The hottest song that summer was The Toys' "A Lover's Concerto". You can find it on YouTube.

I mostly wore a navy shearer's singlet, which I hoped would attract a retinue of female admirers, especially with a baby oil gloss on my buffed arms, but no real luck. I had no idea how to turn interested glances into productive communication.

I was then selected into the 1967 Victorian King's Cup crew from that Junior VIII, the first time that a Victorian oarsman had not come from a Senior VIII.

Can you explain what the King's Cup was about?

OK. The King's Cup is a competition for the eight-oared rowing championship of Australia. The cup itself was first competed for in the Peace Regatta held at Henley-on-Thames in 1919, in a race between crews representing the Allied armies that had fought during the Great War. Australia, stroked by Clive Disher of Melbourne University, won the event, so the cup was donated by the royal family to Australia for perpetual interstate eight-oared competition.

The Victorian King's Cup crew in 1967 was no good – there were several older crew members who, as it turned out, were past it and we finished lengths behind New South Wales, but the trip was magical for a twenty-year-old novice. My roommate in Murray Bridge was Bob Lachal, who had just returned from a twelve-month stay in Antarctica as a cook with the Australian expedition to Mawson. His stories of the goings on at Mawson left me helpless with laughter night after night, so our loss wasn't such a disappointment. Bob also arranged for the mayor of Murray Bridge to come and christen our boat, which Bob had named Snoopy after the then popular song "Snoopy vs. the Red Baron". Bob had commissioned a signwriter to paint Snoopy on the bow and also a PA system to play the song during the ceremony. The whole thing was a send-up and the flustered mayor, who by now was well aware of the piss-take, broke the bottle of champagne over the boat and fled amid the helpless laughter of the crew.

I know that you were part of a crew around this time that had great success overseas and led to you being inducted into the Victorian Rowing Hall of Fame.

I was, and the experience will always be treasured. Hubert Frederico, or Freddy to us, decided that the younger members of the 1967 Murray Bridge King's Cup VIII should form a coxed four to race in trials to be held on the Nepean River north of Sydney for the right to represent Australia at a regatta to be held in St Catherines in Ontario, Canada, at the inaugural North American Rowing Championships. The regatta was convened by FISA – Fédération Internationale des Sociétés d'Aviron – the world rowing body. This also coincided with the staging in Montreal of Expo 67, an international exposition timed to coincide with the 1967 centenary of the Canadian Confederation.

The crew consisted of Tom Daffy as cox, Graeme Boykett as stroke, me as 3, David Douglas as 2 and Steve Gillon as bow. We had three weeks of training before fronting up on the Nepean for the trials but realised that we were quick. The coxed fours competition would be fierce: the winning New South Wales King's Cup VIII would divide into two fours, one of which had competed successfully in Europe the previous year and contained Peter Dickson, John Ranch, Alf Duval and Chris Stevens, the best of the New South Wales VIII: huge and experienced competitors who outweighed us by at least ten kilograms per man and had trained thousands of kilometres together. And there were around ten other boats to contend with.

So you were seen as also-rans?

Definitely. But we sailed through the heats. The final was going to be a two-boat affair – us and the big New South Wales four. To everyone's surprise, we led the whole way, only to be beaten by a foot on the line. It was a victory for efficient technique and youthful exuberance, but our imperfect conditioning let us down. Freddy wasn't a skilled trainer – he didn't like gyms, running and testing – and so all of the Freddy crews I rowed in lacked toughness. He was also quirky about selections. He didn't like anyone asking questions and he dropped some spectacularly talented oarsmen.

In the end, the selectors chose our four to compete in St Catherines and also at the USA Championships in Philadelphia and European Championships in Vichy, France. They thought it would be good experience for a group of younger athletes who would be in the running for Olympic selection for Mexico City the following year.

I'll say a bit more about 1967, but as for the rest of my competitive résumé, readers can consult Andrew Guerin's splendid archival website at rowinghistory-aus.info.

How did you feel to be in an Australian crew having been in a Junior VIII less than six months before?

Beyond excited.

Naturally there were problems. The trip was to be three months, so I needed a leave of absence from the law school. This was quickly granted by the dean, Julian Phillips. In those days there was no term-by-term review process, just year-end exams. So it would be up to me to cram in as much as I could in the six weeks after my return and hope for the best.

The second was money. Ralph offered me a small subsidy but I would need to raise the bulk of my expenses myself, which I did with night jobs and crew fundraisers.

The third was training. Because it was winter in Australia, we had to work entirely in the dark except for weekends. I was waiting for weight training and other out-of-the-boat conditioning to start but Freddy stuck to rowing.

We broke our trip on the way over in San Francisco in mid-July. This was the famous summer of love when the hippy movement was at its peak. It evolved from the 1950s Beat culture of Jack Kerouac and Allen Ginsberg. Hippies preached free love, anti-establishment music, opposition to the Vietnam War, communal living, peaceful cooperation, giving, cannabis and flower power. The musical bards of the time were the Charlatans, Jefferson Airplane, the Grateful Dead, Quicksilver Messenger Service, Big Brother and the Holding Company, and Country Joe and the Fish. The Beatles had just released *Sgt. Pepper's Lonely Hearts Club Band* and it hit us like a truck when we heard it on our arrival.

The '60s weren't just hippie culture and music. In fact they were groundbreaking years in politics, science, literature, music and art, that deserve more discussion.

Our first stop was the legendary Haight–Ashbury intersection, the acknowledged centre of the movement, which had always been a cheap residential area for students. There were bells, kaftans, incense burners, leaflets, psychedelic artworks, trinket vendors, hustlers, topless women, preachers, drug dealers, seedy bars, loud music, anti-war badges. We were like the country cousins, dazzled, hopelessly at sea but realising that we had been a small part of a history-making time.

So where was the competition site?

St Catherines in Ontario, a small town located on the now disused third Welland Canal, near Port Dalhousie. The canal was part of the St Lawrence Seaway, joining Lake Erie and Lake Ontario. The course itself was located alongside Henley Island, and was the traditional site of the Royal Canadian Henley Regatta.

Our first accommodation was at Ridley College, an old and prestigious boarding school located in the town. Between rows, I haunted the Ridley sound lab, with its collection of jazz, blues and popular LPs. It was where I first heard Aretha Franklin and *Sgt. Pepper*. Mesmerising.

After a couple of weeks we were relocated to the Welland Hotel and then to the house of a Canadian called Jim Burrows, who adopted us. He introduced us to the latest music, the cheapest bars, the best restaurants, and drove an MG. His house walls were covered in Playboy centrefolds and he knew the counterculture from the ground up. How cool could you get.

Compared to the way modern Australian crews are prepared and managed, we were underdone. We were having a brilliant time, but we had to accept constant accommodation changes, borrowed equipment, uncontrolled nutrition, no health monitoring and a seat-of-the-pants training program. Other Australian crews at the time were much the same and usually did poorly in international competition.

We trained at the course twice a day and improved with every row. We had brought our own English Ayling oars but these were wooden and becoming stretchy, not ideal for racing.

We were given an American Pocock boat of 1950s design, which was quite new, although it was heavy. Pocock fours were in the 200-pound (90-kilogram) range and a modern Empacher would be in the 120-pound (55-kilogram) range. Even so, we were generating excellent pace but the question was whether we could sustain this over the full 2,000 metre race distance. The physics are clear – as the mass of an object increases, assuming constant force, acceleration and thus terminal velocity will decrease. So even a 10% boat weight surplus would mean time added across 2,000 metres. If force decreased, as it would in the final quarter of a hard race, the impact would be greater still.

Our speed became known to the Canadians, who planned to boat their national four at the Canadian Henley Regatta as a warm-up race, and there was pressure brought to bear to take away our boat and substitute an older and slower boat.

At Canadian Henley we won easily, against mostly Canadian and US crews. Thereafter we found it hard to find any help from the Canadian hierarchy.

After Henley, our training was relocated to Buffalo in New York State, where we were accommodated at and boated from the Buffalo Rowing Club. Here we were given another Pocock built for the 1956 Olympics. We stepped up to training three times per day and were feeling sharp and connected.

The great championship regatta was soon upon us.

We won our heat easily on a sunny but blustery headwind day. Our final consisted of Australia, the USA, Denmark, England, Canada and Switzerland.

I was, as usual, overcome by nerves and the trip down to the start was a nightmare for me. People who have never rowed can't imagine the pain involved in racing. In those days of slow boats, a coxed four race would last for around six and a half to seven minutes. Now, coxless fours – the standard – take well under six minutes. It meant that the last 500 metres of any race might be a problem, especially with our lack of deep conditioning.

The day was bright but muggy, with a light holding head breeze. International racing then, as now, was conducted under the racing riles of FISA. After we had backed our boats into our starting positions, the starter lifted his starting flag, asked each crew in turn whether it was ready, then simultaneously shouted "Partez!" (the French for "Go!") and dropped the flag.

Our raw boat speed was phenomenal and we shot into a quick lead. We were rowing beautifully-the boat sang and as each mark passed we gained on our opponents, and after a major effort at half-way we were four lengths clear-an unheard-of margin in an international event. But we were exhausted by the three-quarter mark, when we ran out of gas and struggled home to win by a length and a half. I remember little about the second half of the race.

We had been the first Australian sweep-oared crew ever to win gold at an open FISA Championship Regatta, an historic achievement.

The post-race celebrations were long and delirious. It was impossible to comprehend how a young and raw group of boys had been able to beat the world's best. A fairy tale! We were swamped in calls, telegrams and well-wishers for days.

Now, Australia has a world-class rowing program and Aussie crews routinely win medals at Olympics and world championships. Then, the idea of Australia winning anything in international competition was seen as hopeful at best.

We moved to Philadelphia for the USA Championships where the conditions were hot and humid. Again, we were three lengths in front in the final with 500 metres to row. This time, the fade was fatal and we were rowed down on the line by two feet by New Zealand.

Our last stop on this crazy odyssey was Vichy in France for the European Championships, where much the same thing happened as in the USA: we were in a position in our semi-final to go through to the final and were rowed down by the USA crew we had beaten easily in St Catherines.

The crew was exhausted and homesick.

Of the six finalists, four were crews from Eastern bloc countries who ran drug programs and whom the Western crews had no chance of beating. We didn't know that performance-enhancing drugs existed, much less the dramatic results they produced. But we were thrilled with our success and the wild and carefree experience of three months on the road with our closest mates.

Why did all these fades happen?

We were a young and unseasoned crew that had spent far less time as a together than our other competitors, and almost no time in international competition. We were not well-prepared for strength and endurance. Our race plans were inflexible: we programmed efforts where there was no need for them and spent unnecessary energy early in races. Now we know that maximal efforts lift blood lactates dramatically and permanently, meaning that deliverable power in the later race stages is compromised. We were given too much high intensity training between regattas, meaning we had insufficient opportunity to recover. And our equipment was substandard compared to other crews.

In short, our campaign wasn't the best it could have been and St Catherines resulted mainly from raw athletic ability.

After 1967, I won two Kings Cups (1969 and 1970) out of the seven I rowed in, and won the Mexico 1968 Olympic four-oared test race but was that crew was excluded from the team owing to an Australian Olympic Committee decision to reduce the size of the rowing team for financial reasons, in what was probably the most disappointing experience of my life.

So, Johnnie, what did rowing do for you and are you happy with the way your career turned out?

Most of my best friends are from that time and they've been kind and loyal, a gift that many blokes don't have. I still see them regularly and I'd be unhappy without them. They're dying off one by one and some of them are losing their way mentally, but we'll keep celebrating till the last man's down.

I represented my school, my state and my country successfully so I was one of the lucky ones.

I retired at twenty-six to look after my family; I sometimes regret the early exit but who knows what would have happened if I'd gone on. I think my trajectory might have been different had I been rowing in modern times, because I would have been better managed and conditioned, but again, who knows. I was a big man who ate and drank unwisely off-season and it was always hard for me to regather my fitness the following year.

I've certainly always had a sense of pride and accomplishment looking back, which was a comfort to me in bad times.

Are there any other sports you should mention?

Several, but by this stage the reader will be bored solid. I was a keen sailor for many years in many classes, including Port Phillip Couta Boats, J24s and one-tonners. I played squash indifferently with some rowing mates; I was an avid walker and completed the 800-kilometre Spanish Camino de Santiago, as well as a two-month high-altitude trek in Nepal in the Annapurna area.

For years I was part of a cycling group made up of old oarsmen that rode from Princes Bridge to St Kilda twice a week. The group competed in four "Round the Bay" rides: Melbourne to Portsea and return, around 230 kilometres. I wasn't the right shape or weight really so my long-distance cycling career then came to a permanent and welcome end.

That's enough, I reckon.

I look at my watch and it's getting dark outside.

"Jim, you're probably drifting away a bit because none of this is all that riveting. Let's go outside and watch the sunset and open up another bottle. I'll cook you dinner and show you your room and maybe we can start back a bit later?"

"Great idea, J," Jim says, "I just need you to tell me what we're having because I'm on a low-fat diet these days."

"I thought we might try a pasta of some sort, probably verde?"

"Sounds fine," Jim says.

I know that the low-fat diet's because Jim's liver is stuffed but I don't say anything. He knows I know. I just wonder how long it's going to last because Jimmy never could resist temptation for long.

We stroll out the back door to the big American white oak table on our west-facing terrace, loomed over by Mount Victoria. After years here I know which notch in the forest line the sun sets into at different times of the year. We're close to the September equinox, which I can now predict within a few days from the sun's setting point.

The air is fresh and clean here, and in the half hour before the sun sets, dew falls and releases the musky perfumes of grass, trees and blossom from our spring flowers and from the wattles and barks in the nearby bush.

We're surrounded by forest, making this one of the most bushfire-prone zones in Australia, but we are one of the first families to leave on Code Red days – I'm too old to stay and defend the house, plus we have a solid over-house sprinkler system fed from a high dam, meaning we don't rely on pumps or electrical connections.

I go back into the house to find some more wine and a couple of fresh glasses, plus a Cuban cigar from the stash given to me by my mate Nicola Pero, which I raid once in a while when I'm feeling like a celebration.

"Seems a pity to mess that lovely air up, but I reckon we've got off to a good start so I hope you won't mind if I have one of these?"

"Not a problem," says Jim. He used to smoke as you would on long sailing journeys but that's hit the dust now too.

"So, Jim, here's another wine for you to try – it's our 2019 cabernet sauvignon made from fruit from the famous Funder & Diamond vineyard down the road. It's starting to hit its straps now. I reckon Valley cabernet is well underrated. It's rich and layered with great sweet fruit and fine tannins."

Jim hands me his glass pronto and I gurgle in a reasonable share of the bottle.

I start making Jim the pasta verde with stock, spinach, edamame beans and celery, and we sip our way along. There's lots of nostalgia in the air – stories from school and university days, women we both loved and lost, dishonest men we'd swept from our lives at one time or another, fears of the grim reaper, tall tales of surf and mountains, of yachts and the sea, of wealth and happiness.

Soon dinner is on the table and we chat back and forth. The best part of having a kitchen garden, I find, is herbs. So lovely to run up the hill for a handful of fresh parsley or tarragon or thyme. I cook OK but I know that if you want to be excellent, which I'm not, you need to be imaginative, precise, have a great nose and tastebuds, and most of all, be at it constantly. My next project is to learn Japanese cuisine. The most exacting and time-consuming of all. One of the difficulties here is that an average day on the farm is tiring – there are always dozens of jobs to be done. By six p.m. and after a whisky, I'm spent and find it hard to work in the kitchen. But we get by.

"Should we get moving again?" I say, without much conviction.

"Aaaaah, if we have to!" Jim sighs. I know what he'd prefer to be doing now – popping another cork or three and going gently into his dreamtime. But I haven't got him for long, so I'm being hard. I know how much work we've got to do. Maybe too much, but getting stuff done is something of a compulsion for me, unfortunately.

We settle back down in the couches in the main living room, which is high-ceilinged and airy. It was built as part of a house extension we did a few years ago now. I designed the layout, paying attention to the dimensions of this room, which has a rectangular concert hall form to provide a clear and balanced acoustic result for both recorded and live music. I hoped we might stage small-scale concerts here but the Covid pandemic brought that plan undone.

Jim sits up, summoning all his stamina and patience for the next stanza of our journey.

My grandparents, Arthur and Ethel Harry.

The Ralph–Harry family at 8 Tennyson Crecent, Canberra, 1954.

My father Ralph Harry with the Hon. Herbert Vere 'Bert' Evatt
at the United Nations, New York, 1947.

Portrait of my great-grandfather Sir Frederick Holder
KCMG, first speaker of the first Australian federal
House of Representatives, by his daughter
Rhoda Holder.

Ralph Harry addressing the United Nations General Assembly
in 1976 as Australian Ambassador.

In a commemorative 100-year anniversary photo of the students of Wadhurst, Melbourne Grammar, 1958.

As a member of the winning Melbourne Grammar first VIII at the public schools Head-of-the River championships, 1964.

At the wedding of Virginia Harry to Martin Braden, 1965.

Training in the shot-putting ring, Melbourne Grammar School,
Domain Road South Yarra, 1964.

Australian Rowing Team departing for North America and Europe, August 1967.

Ralph Harry escorting Queen Elizabeth II on her visit to Tyne Cot Cemetery, Belgium, 1968.

Training for the first FISA North-American rowing championships, Buffalo NY, 1967.

Victorian Kings Cup crew training, Lower Yarra, 1969; I'm seated at five.

In Bundaberg, Queensland, during training for the Kings Cup interstate eight-oared rowing championship, 1969.

With my mother Dorothy on my wedding day, 14 December 1970.

Sarah Harry, 1976.

Pip Harry, 2010.

Some Philosophy

Can I ask some deeper questions to see where you've arrived at now that you're, what do they call it, a septuagenarian? That seems right to do in the evening.

Of course.

We chatted earlier about why you were interested in doing this and one of the things you said was that if you looked too far into issues like the nature of reality and knowability, and of purpose and meaning, you might not just wonder whether a memoir made sense but whether living made sense. I think your answer was to say that we needed to make assumptions like: if a glass of wine was on your table and it looked and tasted like wine, it was wine. Or, if you were in a boat, you should allow yourself to believe that it would continue to float. Can you describe some of the questions that have bothered you?

I'll try, but you know I'm not a philosopher, Jimmy. I don't think my mind is well enough trained, or as capable as it would need to be to grasp that landscape fully. I have some idea about some of the concepts, but I also know that, as in many other disciplines, there are many schools, much disputation and no predominant views. So I'm in good company when I say I feel inadequate in this arena.

Just have a go?

OK.

The prevalence of evil and injustice in our world has been most troubling to me. A cliché to say, I know, but it's been one of my life's puzzles and disappointments. A lot of my mates seem to be able to ignore it and maybe that's healthy or at least a survival skill, but it drags me down.

I once sold a second-hand car to an acquaintance of a friend at a fair price. He came back to me a couple of months later to tell me that he'd found some mechanical problems and that it was going to be expensive to fix and would I foot the bill. I said I'd make a contribution but since he was aware that I hadn't given him any guarantee about the car he'd have to pay the majority. He seemed unable to accept this and went away looking thunderous. A month or so later my friend told me that he'd committed suicide. I found out that he'd been clinically depressed for years but I always blamed myself for not seeing this and felt guilty that I might have been partly responsible for his decision to end his life. He must have suffered terribly, and for a long time, to arrive at that point.

Donna and I have had some tough experiences recently with people we trusted and to whom we had been kind. One was a former friend we employed in a business who essentially threw that business under a bus. The other was a builder we'd known forever who walked out halfway through a renovation contract without a qualm, stranding us mid-project and costing us a great deal. So we've had close and recent experience of disappointment.

Who can understand why we injure one another without remorse, whether in war, in social media, in the courts, in parliament, in the streets, in the school yard, in the press, on the stock market?

Violence, theft, tribalism, brutality and abuse are an inherent aspect of human nature. You might say that it's just the way the world works and that we have to learn to live with it; but as we see in, for example, the MAGA experience in the US, it takes no time for those characteristics to multiply when a state's institutions and leaders become confused and unprincipled. One of the core purposes of civilisation is to repress that multiplication, so what we see today, in fact, is civilisation breaking down.

We don't often think about how much ordered daily life depends on efficient institutions like banks, insurance companies, supermarkets, schools, railways, councils and police forces. As beneficiaries we don't pause to think about how important it is that they work well, how much we take the seamless delivery of their services for granted. Each of them is a complex and vulnerable organisation that needs maintenance, support and especially our confidence. What developed over time was a pattern of dealing, or a social contract if you like, that required trust and ethical dealing on both sides, without which the delivery and acceptance of the service is at risk. You don't have to be too smart to see how much that contract has become challenged by greed and incompetence, and outright unlawful behaviour, on the part of modern institutions.

Look at the US Supreme Court, which we looked up to for decades as the exemplar of calm and wise justice. Now it's just a political bull pit. Cardozo and Frankfurter wouldn't have believed it.

You don't have to look too far down that track before you start to see irrationality, absurdity, senselessness and chaos.

I saw this in my law firm. As time went by and as the firm became larger and the market more competitive, partners started to take a looser approach to ethical decisions that used to be obvious.

Today I ask what I can do to turn this tide back. Now, when some business tries to cheat me or take advantage of me, I push back. This has produced some satisfying wins. If everyone wronged did that, the world could be a different place.

I recently floated, with an ex-federal parliamentarian friend, the idea of creating a bipartisan political incubator to identify and train young Australians interested in a political life. It would be a long and exhausting project to accomplish but I mean to pursue it because it might succeed in raising the general competence and ethical sensitivity of members of parliament. That might be one contribution I can make.

What do you think of modern media departments and premiers' offices whose job seems to be anything but telling the truth?

I have no patience with language as deception or avoidance. The greatest sinners, as you say, are the holders of our highest offices – in politics, in business, in the media. I'm annoyed every day to have to listen to the stream of fudges, distortions and ambiguities that emanate from Canberra, from current affairs shows, from pundits, from boardrooms. Go back to the PR campaign Qantas subjected us to over the past year, trying to excuse itself from simple theft; did we hear a single genuine apology? All a minute too late and a dollar short.

My old school housemaster Reynard Jukes may have had his faults, one being a taste for administering corporal punishment to young men, but on the wickedness of evasive and misleading words he had no doubts. It was the mark of the charlatan and scoundrel who were to be cancelled, in modern language, forthwith. The thought that the first port of call for any politician in strife today is the spin department is genuinely sickening: you and I allow our taxes to be used daily for propagandising and deception. How do you feel about that, Jimmy?

The same.

I do sometimes see too many problems with the kind of world we live in and the kinds of beings we are, and I do accuse myself on the one hand of naivete in being too trusting, and on the other of not doing enough to help roll back the tide. If you have any ideas, I'd love to hear them.

We seem to be so isolated in our self-selected media bubbles and identity boxes that we've lost the ability to see the world as a whole. If you look around with open eyes you can see that there are big, broadly based problems everywhere.

Yes, there are. The world is a much more cruel place than we think, we are much more flawed than we think and we suffer more than we admit. It's easy to see why many of the world's most visionary and aware humans decided that faith in a god was the only rational choice to make: otherwise, we would be forced to hate ourselves and live desperate lives knowing there was no answer and no redemption.

And yet, I love the world and humanity. Have you seen the photographs from the James Webb telescope of the edges of the universe? Light emitted billions of years ago now opening the window to knowledge that we could never have foreseen, making our universe more and more complex and mysterious? Last night here was a good night for star visibility, which there aren't very many of these days, and even though our galaxy is magnificent, how much more so are the visions that this instrument brings?

Can I ask about whether there's been a spiritual dimension in your life?

There has been, but a quiet and uncertain one. My mother was a churchgoer, not just for social reasons. She imposed Sunday observance on the family from early on and got to know all the reverends and Sunday school teachers, and produced piled plates of cakes on days of celebration. When we travelled she made sure the family visited the local cathedrals and went to liturgical music performances like the *Messiah* and Bach's Mass in B minor.

When I was at school, the boarders had to attend chapel twice on Sundays: once at Matins and once at Evensong or, if it was a special Sunday, at Compline. I became an altar server, which meant assisting at the eight a.m. Sunday communion service. I was then not required to go to Matins. There were never more than a handful at communion so there was plenty of time to think and wonder about what religion meant.

It always seemed to me hard to believe that Christ's fundamental message of love and redemption could be properly conveyed by priests. I saw them as just a part of a desiccated establishment that cared too little for me and too much about itself.

The moments in which I thought I could see a glimmering of the other were often musical. Our chapel choir was well-trained and the choice of repertoire was wise and beautiful. The school's music master, Donald Britten, was a fastidious and scholarly Englishman who trained the boarders, most of whom were Western District farm boys, to sing antiphonally. One Evensong we received a visiting priest to deliver the sermon. After an antiphonal psalm, this man burst into tears as he ascended the pulpit steps and took some time to regain his composure. He told us that this was one of the most sincere and beautiful experiences he had ever had. I saw commitment and belief in him and wondered whether I should listen more carefully to God.

I regularly come to tears when I listen to music, whether it be a Haydn concerto, a Bach cantata, Maria Callas or Tina Arena. Creation of any kind must spring from somewhere, and the more profound my musical experience is, the more I consider the divine.

How can the universe have come from a singularity? The more we look at it, the more absurd the idea seems, and yet the mathematics tell us it's true. Is that mathematics the revelation in some form? Or have we simply taken a huge wrong turn, or are we incapable of seeing and understanding reality?

So yes, I feel other dimensions and sense the empathy of something beyond me, like that kindly spirit of fire.

I know, though, that one day, when the sun goes out, the last human will die, ending human history and knowledge. The bleakness of that thought is unfathomable. What then of the divine? I also wonder how much of my life I made, and how much just happened: was the thought that I had genuine agency a fallacy? I suppose this volume is shouting *Yes, I do have agency, and here is the evidence.* It will just be ink on paper, not me, but I tried.

I also know that no one's life has been or will be like mine, and in that sense I'm alone, that when I die I'll be extinguished forever.

How do you feel about yourself?

I try not to assess myself, although as I said earlier, I don't dislike myself as much as I used to. My view of me is like dry leaves in a stout breeze: never in one place. The trauma I experienced as a child, which implanted doubt, anxiety and lack of confidence, did so for all time. It will never leave me; but I now recognise it as a bad memory that I'm not responsible for, confined to a remote box, and not a living thing trying to strangle me. Because I am, and we all are, creatures of our DNA and so to a great extent predestined, how much does the question of self-love make sense? I suppose the answer is that, regardless of pre-destination, it's better to feel comfortable about one's self than not.

One thing I can say is that nowadays, people treat me with kindness and respect, and they listen to what I say. They also seem to like me. I know that part of the reason is that I now reveal myself more often, and I am happy to engage in a relationship for as long as it takes, rather than trying to exit from contact as quickly as I can, thinking that whoever I'm talking to believes I'm an idiot and can't wait for me to go away. I wish I'd learned this a long time ago.

One thing I'm convinced of is that I know what love is and that it exists and sustains us. When I doubt that, I think of the Melbourne Football Club and how despite every setback it has experienced, I adore it beyond expression. Even though loving myself is a difficult discussion, I believe profoundly in the idea of duty, of helping others, of the importance of loyalty, respect, kindness and generosity. In one way or another I try to better my fellow man most of the time.

And the churches?

A calamity.

Well, that wasn't your usual set of life reflections! Probably enough?

Yes. Enough.

Harry Family History

Let's take a look at your broader family story. You were born in the USA. When did your family come back here?

We moved from Washington DC to Canberra in June 1949. We travelled by sea on the passenger liner *Aorangi*, an old New Zealand/British ship that had been in service since the 1920s. Our point of embarkation was Vancouver in Canada, according to Dad's passport. I can't remember anything about the trip.

Canberra was chosen as the site of the future national capital at around the time of Federation in 1901, and a new parliament house was opened there in 1927. When my parents arrived it was still a small and isolated settlement.

So what was your family's first house?

Our first lodgings in Canberra were at the Barklay Avenue house of Alan Watt, a colleague of Ralph's. We moved from there into a tiny government-built red brick bungalow purchased by my father, at number eight Tennyson Crescent in the inner suburb of Forrest. The house was on a block of one acre. Forrest in time became one of the fashionable locations in Canberra, so this proved to be a valuable asset. The first version of the house would have been not much more than 100 square metres in area. There was an internal toilet with blue streaky linoleum on the floor and an open slatted chicken wire glass window that poured the bitter Canberra winter winds straight down your back. There was a small living room that did no justice to our Eames modernist furniture, an equally small kitchen and a laundry with concrete troughs, a wood-fired copper boiler and a hand wringer.

There was no heating, just one fire. In those days, heated bedrooms were regarded as decadent. We had a thick pile of Laconia wool blankets instead.

The house purchase was financed under the War Service Homes Scheme established by the federal government to benefit ex-servicemen of World War Two. My father was always proud of this.

Tennyson Crescent was a paddock when we moved in. Every tree, path, driveway, tap, lawn and shrub had to be installed by my parents and it was years before the windswept and empty look was softened. One of my earliest memories is watching a horse and plough turning over the soil in the back garden, and the endless raking of the new lawn beds before seed was cast and watered. Dad planted a strictly European garden, with elms, oaks, maples and silver birches, azaleas and rhododendrons, hydrangeas and daphne.

A major task in the civilisation of the property was the building of a long concrete semicircular driveway. Dad did most of the work. I remember the constant chugging of the cement mixer, the levelling and smoothing of the concrete and the hessian bags that he spread on the newly poured sections and moistened regularly with the hose. Of course, I created havoc in the piles of sand and gravel and was always up to my armpits in the water that he used to leave in the cement mixer overnight, which had a rainbow-coloured slick on it.

Do you remember the local area well?

Of course. In those days, kids were free to roam far and wide and I knew southern Canberra end-to-end. I remember Red Hill, to the south of our house, that we used to play on and look at from the back steps, which burned out in a bushfire one early year. I remember watching the flames slowly cross the crest of the hill and move toward us, the sour smoke swirling down to the house and the angry red embers glowing for days after the main burn had passed.

I remember the panic that swept the street when the fire appeared, with many households moving furniture and household goods onto the nature strip, and a recurring nightmare about being caught in the fire and having no home. My aunt Marjorie drove me up the hill to see the damage the fire had done a few days later and I was frightened by the devastation.

Was Canberra a happy landing for your parents?

Well, Dad was pleased to have the house, and proud that his work was moving the property in the right direction.

For Mum, coming from North America where even in the 1940s every house was centrally heated and appliance-laden, there was the shock of the freeze in winter, no cooling in summer, a wood-fired kitchen stove, an ice-box fridge, few electrical plugs, no insulation, a tiny reserve of hot water and no equipment to speak of. You can imagine her dismay at having to endure deep, crunchy white frosts every winter morning, ice in the laundry trough, the uncarpeted floors and having to hump firewood fifty yards up a steep hill to get the stove lit and start cooking breakfast. There was no such thing as processed cereal then. In winter, the oatmeal was put in a large saucepan to be salted and soaked the night before it was cooked, otherwise it wouldn't make porridge tender enough for the kids to eat in the mornings.

Milk, bread and ice for the fridge were delivered by horse-drawn cart to the front door. The milkman would ladle fresh, full-cream milk into my mother's jugs from a large milk pail with a one-pint scoop, producing an unforgettable frothy suck and gurgle. The bread would arrive fresh, crackly and hot in a box insulated with straw, in the form of a huge high-top loaf that would soon have its centre scooped out by marauding fingers. I'm not sure how we shopped for fruit and vegetables, but I think we also had visits from a greengrocer's cart, although my mother would have shopped for meat.

There was a retail centre in Manuka, a twenty-minute walk from our house. There was a movie theatre there, which we kids were allowed to visit only on rare occasions as Ralph was against commercial entertainment.

When we were allowed to go, we would be given the ticket price of threepence, often in the form of large copper pennies, and another one or two pennies for sweets. You can still find utility shops called milk bars today, but then a milk bar was just that – a stainless-steel bar in a small shop-front supervised by a kindly old lady where you could order milkshakes and spiders, with an ice cream freezer and a lolly cabinet that offered a mouth-watering choice of confectionery. This would be presented in shoebox-sized cardboard containers full of every colour and design, over which we agonised and chopped, changed and chopped again until the choice was made. Our favourite milk bar was Gumley's in Manuka. When we shopped with Mum and we were good, she would buy us all a bakery cream bun.

You could buy items up to ten-a-penny, so twopence brought a full, fist-sized white paper bag. My favourites were liquorice bullets, chocolate-coated caramels called buddies, violent pink musk sticks and Caramac, a kind of caramel chocolate. An ice cream would cost threepence and would consist of two huge scoops of rich, real ice cream in a big crunchy yellow cone.

On days when I'd successfully lightened mum's purse of a copper or two, it was a feast. I felt guilty about my domestic larceny all my life until my kids discovered and emptied my change box daily, no matter where it was hidden. They were so persistent and successful as burglars that it became a family joke, as it should have.

What about you? What was life like for you in the early Canberra days?

I was an adventurer from the first. I was always investigating something, someone or somewhere, and had no sense of risk or awareness of the need to stay near home or maintain contact with my mother. I was always falling into something, scraping this or breaking that, getting lost, being late, conducting experiments with household chemicals, chewing unidentified pills and other substances, being hospitalised for poisoning, burns or abrasions, chasing animals, poking away behind radiograms and spending what was left of my time asking a million questions about everything.

Once, I was chasing Penny into the living room because of some insult, when she slammed the glass entry door onto my outstretched arm, causing a laceration from my wrist to my elbow. My mother managed to wrap the arm in a sheet and get me to hospital where a clumsy intern sutured the wound, leaving a long and ugly scar. I was lucky to escape major damage.

So, I attracted much more than my share of discipline, but this failed to affect my behaviour much. There's a photo – the one on the front cover of this volume – taken at about this time of me seated on a fence with my father. In it I look solemn, determined and burning to be independent. That is exactly who I was at the time and much like who I still am.

I guess you had your first schooling in Canberra?

That's right. I was enrolled at the kindergarten at the Canberra Girl's Grammar School, located up the Tennyson Crescent hill at the corner of Melbourne Avenue. I remember our classes and particularly hand painting, cutting out, plasticine modelling and playing with blocks. There was a large playground with old tyres hung on ropes from a tree from which my teacher found it very hard to detach me.

Because Canberra was small and it would have been hard for me to be lost for long, I was soon spending more and more unsupervised time away from the house and creating my own adventures and projects. I still can smell the eucalyptus, the wild fennel, the dust, the rain on dirt, the freshly scraped fire ash, the steam from the stove, the clank of the double boiler cooking yet another lump of corned beef, the summer heat and the winter mildew, the burn cream, the Dettol, the bandages for my injuries and the magnificent aromas of a vanilla malted milkshake.

I can still feel the pain of green gum branches cracking me on the back during the many gang battles that I fought in, the burns that I received as I constantly tried to steal previews of our dinners while they were on the stove, the chilblains in winter, the exhilaration of reaching the tops of big trees and the exhaustion of climbing Red Hill. I remember falling in love with a young and ethereal Queen Elizabeth when she floated onto the screen of the local cinema in her buttercup-yellow gown, soft, beautiful and utterly beyond reach, during the playing of the national anthem, which was required by law prior to any public performance.

Did you spend much time in the Australian War Memorial?

I did. It was a long bike ride from Forrest but I would have visited every two or three weeks. It was cool, silent and sad, but of course, magnetic for me. Especially I remember the Pool of Remembrance, which we all walked past on the way in, and which was full of glittering coins that visitors had thrown in to help with upkeep, and also for luck. I couldn't believe that anyone had enough money to be able to afford to throw it away. The building was completed in 1941, just over ten years before we arrived in Canberra, but it always seemed monolithic, severe and old, as though it had been there forever. The great war diarist C.W. Bean was a major contributor to the War memorial project. One of my most cherished possessions is a set of every volume of his history of World War 1.

In around 1951, my mother became pregnant for the fourth time. One day late in her pregnancy she was taken to hospital for what we assumed would be the birth of another brother or sister. I remember her being brought back to the house looking pale and broken. There had been a still birth. A grey spirit fell over the household for many months, it seemed, before life got back to normal. I don't know whether there was a grave and burial and I feel tears rising when I think about it. I feel remorse that I did nothing to investigate or recognise my lost sibling.

I'm not sure how much time I spent at the kindergarten but soon enough I was sent to the prep school of Canberra Boys Grammar School.

Canberra was still a small town so everybody walked to whatever they were doing in the mornings. It was a joyful experience to join the swelling crocodile of small and noisy boys trailing through the paddocks with their satchels and treasures in tow.

In winter, the puddles froze and we would break all of them open. The ice would have dirt and grass frozen into it in lovely patterns. By the time we arrived, our hands and feet were red and numb and it would be an hour until we could write properly. In summer, we hunted tadpoles and frogs in the streams and rode our bikes miles every day in search of adventure.

What do you remember of the guidance you received from Ralph as a boy?

He taught me to put on a tie and I remember his solemn advice that I should never wear a Windsor double knot, as this was for bookmakers. I would often sneak into his room to rummage through his boxes of cuff links and other treasures and look at his shoes and clothes, which always smelled tweedy and sour. He dressed neatly and modestly and always wore a smart grey felt hat to and from his office in the East Block administration building.

Ralph once took me to the annual fete of Canberra Boys Grammar. It was an unusual event because even with the most sustained badgering, he would never willingly waste time on things he considered unproductive, which entertainment like fetes, concerts, movies and theatre he believed most assuredly was. I remember feeling that I should be grateful for the privilege of being in his company. I would have been hard to manage and would have tested his patience with the usual barrage of questions and negotiating for yet another ride or toy. But he gave me two experiences that still are important to me. The first was paying sixpence for me to look through a telescope at the daytime moon. It seemed a miracle to be able to see all of the craters and mountains in their remote pale blue and white beauty. I was captured by astronomy on the spot, and I've never lost my sense of excitement and wonder at the night sky, satellites, space travel and cosmology. The second was being provided with a stick of pink fairy floss. This was a rare indulgence. The shiny aluminium sugar-spinning machine seemed a far greater display of ingenuity than the telescope. My father clearly didn't think so but I knew I was right.

On the night of the 1961 Federal Election in which Bob Menzies was challenged by Arthur Calwell, I remember Dad taking me down to the Canberra tally room where all the votes were displayed with tin numbers on a large scoreboard. Menzies looked to be in dire straits because he had recently imposed a credit squeeze to get inflation down. He was saved at the death-knell by Jim Killen, who won the seat of Moreton in Queensland by 131 votes to return Menzies with a two-seat majority, and one seat after election of the speaker. It wasn't especially engaging for a small boy but I've always been grateful for the memory of having been on the spot to witness a great moment in Australian history.

You mentioned that you had some family relatives in Canberra at the time?

There were some, but they seemed few and far between. My father's elder brother Egbert had also found his way to Canberra. He worked in the office of the Commonwealth Statistician and was married to a dark and unhappy woman called Thora. There were four children: Brian, Ann, Michael and Paul. The family was, like ours, respectable, though less so than ours, my mother thought.

We would be taken around to see them from time to time but there weren't too many sparks. My mother made it clear that she didn't enjoy their company, and it was true that they weren't much fun. I remember conversations in which there was starchy speculation about the real reasons for a hasty engagement, a pregnancy or a bad job choice. Looking back I'm sure my mother also wanted to discourage closer relationships, having concluded, in her iron way, that this would be of no help to us.

I mentioned earlier that Ralph's younger sister Marjorie had also ended up in Canberra. She was a librarian and academically accomplished.

She wasn't blessed with good looks, nor was her manner especially easy, although I think she had a good heart. I found her lectures on the Dewey decimal system of book classification obscure and frightening, and, like Esperanto, to be avoided at all costs.

Most people had long given up the idea that she might marry but she surprised her world by announcing her engagement to my Slivovitz hero Jan Dabrowski, the elderly Pole who had been a lawyer in Warsaw before the Second World War.

Marjorie and Jan had one child, a son, named Robert. He seemed to prefer Dad's company to mine, maybe because he was on the bookish side. I haven't seen or spoken to him for many years.

Switzerland

I remember that in our French classes at school, our teacher Albie Twigg would forever be calling on you to read pieces from French books because you had a good accent, and I know your family lived in several places overseas because Ralph was on post; when was the first move?

Dad's first diplomatic posting as head of mission was to Geneva in 1953. He announced to the family that we would soon be moving to Switzerland because he had been promoted to the position of Consul General for Australia, including responsibility for Australia's Geneva United Nations presence. Geneva was the location of the European UN headquarters and it hosted the offices dealing with health, human rights, refugees and migration, and disarmament. Dad had been involved in many of these areas when he worked in the UN in New York in the late '40s.

Ralph became involved in the resettlement of war refugees in Australia from their camps all over Europe, and the process of removing the Soviet Union occupation from Austria and other countries, which Stalin had agreed to with Churchill and Roosevelt at Yalta to leave postwar.

I had difficulty understanding the concept of foreign countries, much less where Switzerland was or what it might be like, but this was the first time my father would be in charge, and we all understood how important this was to his career and that our lives were about to become different.

The next weeks were unbearably exciting. It had been decided that we would go by ship even though flights to Europe from Australia were available. Maybe flying was still thought to be on the risky side for diplomats.

The great day came and we flew to Sydney on a Qantas DC3 – a crude, slow and noisy wartime plane – to board ship the following day. We embarked on the *Neptunia* at Circular Quay, only after I had finished a last vanilla milkshake on the wharf, on a sunny June afternoon in 1953.

In those days the embarkation process for a long sea journey was a festival. You invited all your friends to come aboard to look at your staterooms, to have tea or a drink and to say goodbye. All non-passengers were then herded off the boat, and you pushed slowly off the wharf as everyone on and offshore threw out coloured paper streamers, to maintain a slender contact with their loved ones till the last possible moment, when the streamers would break and the journey would really begin.

Diplomats in those days were Brahmins who got VIP treatment. So, we travelled first class. It was my first experience of being visibly privileged and literally looking down on the lower decks. I found this strange at first but I was happy to accept our circumstances as it meant better and more food, the best swimming pool, a live band in the dining room at night and the smartest and kindest attendants.

The trip must have made a big impression on you.

It did, and it seemed to go on forever. We steamed north and west, stopping in Jakarta, Colombo, Bombay and Aden, finally disembarking in Naples. I recall the ship in all its detail – the salt-stained brass with green edges, the white scrubbed teak decks, the smart white uniforms of the staff, the emerald water in the swimming pool, the flying fish, the seasickness, the social competition among the passengers, the guitarist who played every afternoon for the tea drinkers, the wonderful white chicken sandwiches, the damson and azure-coloured petit fours, the terrifying captain's table.

When we crossed the equator, there was a big party. The adults all dressed in costumes and drank whilst we kids ate ourselves sick, burst all the balloons and ran away with King Neptune's trident. We threw sparkling coins into the cobalt water in Aden for small Arab guli-guli boys to dive for and ate pasta on the docks in Naples. Going through the Suez

Canal, we saw the UK, French and Israeli warships that had been sent to the canal to take it back from Gamal Nasser after he had nationalised it. Eventually, these countries were forced by superpower opposition to retreat, leaving the canal and its operations firmly in Nasser's hands. We kids of course understood none of this. We just continued to go black from the sun and make friends with everyone we met, feeling that if a paradise existed, we must have been in it.

These months were the only time I can remember Ralph being tied to the family full-time. No cables, no cipher machine, no phone, no meetings. I can see him tanned, smiling and relaxed. A different man, though not for long.

And how was the arrival in Geneva? It was the first time you'd arrived in a new country to live?

Yes, it was. After a couple of hot and sunny days in Naples looking at shops and monuments and eating spaghetti carbonara, the family boarded an overnight Swiss train bound for Geneva. I had never seen a train like it. Modern, quiet, gleaming and fast. This Europe was an interesting place.

On the morning of 27 August 1953 we were installed in a suite in the traditional and starchy Hotel La Residence, in the Route de Florissant, while our parents looked for an apartment. It wasn't long before I swung a curtain rod through a large old painting hung near the stairs to our suite while playing soldiers. Ralph received a tight-lipped delegation from management while I cowered in a cupboard nearby. I was found and beaten with a large and heavy ruler. This seemed a disproportionate penalty for a minor accident but no one seemed to agree with me.

Were you taught any French before you left?

No. But I was worried about how I'd communicate and what sort of school I'd be put in. My parents' solution, after I spent a short time in the UN International School, was to enrol me and my sister Penny in a nearby traditional French-speaking Swiss school called the Ecole Privat. Virginia stayed in the UN school, which was populated by children and teachers from all over the world and seemed to be more generous and cosmopolitan. The decision was, I think, that she was older, and thus needed to remain in a system that was more familiar, and maybe also that she might have more issues than Penny and me with learning French.

Switzerland was federated in the thirteenth century. It has always been resolutely republican and democratic and has always existed in a state of armed neutrality. So, all men up to a late age are required to be in a military reserve and to attend annual military training. The Ecole Privat took these traditions seriously. Our uniform was a red and black paramilitary smock. On arrival we were taken to a large gun hall where we were allocated a locker, an old muzzle-loading rifle and an ammunition pouch containing one bright pink copper percussion cap. We were required to do military drills with weapons in the school courtyard and attend Saturday excursions and weekend bivouacs that always had a military flavour. I was six and a bit years old.

One hall of the school was set up as the site for what was called Le Jeu de la République, or the Game of the Republic. The whole school would play the game on Thursday afternoons. New students would role-play from a range of occupations: doctor, lawyer, shopkeeper, politician, manufacturer; they would receive a stall, some raw materials and a supply of play money and then be left to their own devices to become what they wanted. To be cast into this with no French was uncomfortable. Penny and I were, at least at the start, alien to our fellow students, because we looked, acted and spoke so differently. Conformity is something children insist on and we were a succulent target for gossip, teasing and sometimes abuse. European culture then was not much different to the way it had been in the nineteenth century – meticulously hierarchical, stiff, conformist, academic and intolerant.

So did you get through the transition process OK?

I survived, and soon enough – almost without knowing it – I was fluent in French and the school environment. I was often bullied but overall I found my time there absorbing and a fast learning experience. I remember my teachers as strict but fair. On the odd occasion, when I received the dreaded black square in my weekly report, denoting faible or fail, rather than the pink square for excellence, I would be depressed, but I accepted the discipline.

Penny and I became so used to French that it was our play language around the house and was convenient for concealing our more questionable activities from our parents.

Did you make friends with other students?

Yes, but I had more social contact with boys from the apartments nearby. There was a big park just up the road from us with play equipment where I ran into other kids and soon I was a made member of a local gang. Our gang had a meeting place in a nearby building site where we conducted secret rituals. Most nights I would leave the apartment soon after coming home from school and not be seen again till dinnertime.

What were the things about Geneva that you have good memories about?

The food was enticing. Breakfast would always include fruit, perfect Swiss yoghurt in rainbow colours that would be delivered to our apartment fresh every day, along with cheese, breads and chocolate. A regular part of my school lunch was pain au chocolat, meaning a superb fresh white roll stuffed with bars of Nestlé milk chocolate. Much better than Vegemite. Dinners would include stroganoffs, roasted meats and pastas that had been too exotic for us in Canberra.

Especially in winter, Geneva was a dazzling feast for a child's senses. There was a chocolate shop on every corner, stuffed with barrels of toffees, marzipan, chocolate bars, pale pink, green and blue candied almonds, large chocolate statues and candy canes. I would stand outside the door of the local shop and just inhale the gusts of hot, sweet, toasted almond air that would emerge as people walked in and out. I remember my first triangular Toblerone bar to the final crumb. If I didn't love the Swiss before, I loved them then.

In mid-December each year there would be a great event called the Fête de L'Escalade, or festival of the ladder, to commemorate the defeat of an invasion of Geneva by the Duke of Savoy in 1602, when his troops tried to climb the walls of the city and were fought back by the women pouring cauldrons, or marmites, of boiling soup on the wicked French.

Part of the celebrations would involve families, including ours, buying chocolate soup cauldrons filled with marzipan which had been wrapped in the yellow and red colours of the city, and smashing them for the children after the celebration dinner. What joy. Hot chestnut vending carts were all around the city and I would die for a cornet of these hot, sweet, smoky snacks. Patisseries were everywhere, and the heaped displays of cakes, pastries and sweets were delicate, ornate and miraculous.

Did sport become a thing for you in Geneva?

Yes. I loved winter sports. I pestered my mother for weeks till she bought me ice hockey skates, an ice hockey stick and puck and drove me out to Lac Leman where the winter winds had swept water over the stone lake wall onto the paths around the foreshore. There it had frozen into a long, deep blue sheet where boys would go to practice. The white ice wave on the lake wall, like frozen surf, would get thicker and more twisted as the winter went on.

We would also visit the local outdoor skating park where Virginia went to figure skating classes and I would race around being a nuisance to everyone. We would long for the cold weather and the annual freeze to arrive. Our apartment windows looked out to the Jura mountains to the east. When the first snowfalls appeared we knew that the ice wasn't far away, and we would gaze out every evening as the last shafts of the deep rose winter sun would strike the white peaks.

You told me years ago that one of your happiest memories was skiing.

It is. I've skied all my life, and a fair bit of it with you, and it has brought me to out-of-the-way places, introduced me to lifelong friends and given me peace and happiness. My parents were skiers in Canada before they came back to Australia, so they decided to introduce we kids to skiing at a small village in the Bernese Oberland called Schonriedt. This is just up the hill from the old and ritzy resort of Gstaad.

Somehow Ralph found a chalet to rent from a farming family called Frautschi, which was the top floor of an outbuilding where the cows lived under our floorboards.

The first year we were driven up by Ralph's chauffeur, Gerard, in the consulate's official car, which was a highly polished black Humber Snipe. I had never been above a snowline before, and I will never forget the thrill of seeing thick white snow cover for the first time. In those days, the road clearing was limited and because global warming hadn't begun, the height of the snow bank beside the road was often three or four metres.

Our chalet was warm and comfortable, with the rich smell of hay and the wintering cows drifting in and out. I couldn't sleep on our first night, and spent hours looking out of the hoarfrosted windows waiting for dawn, which eventually appeared, at first midnight blue, then grey, then dazzling white.

We were put in a morning ski school, with free skiing in the afternoons. The school was, as you would expect in Switzerland, formal and serious, with exams that had to be taken to achieve at first bronze, then silver and finally gold accreditations. I took these over the three seasons we spent in Schonried and became a fast and safe skier. In those days, slope grooming was unknown, so you skied all day on rough terrain, which meant that basic skills and safety routines were much more important than now.

Our equipment was primitive. We used long wood skis with red melted-on Kofix bases that needed waxing every day and replacing once a week. The bindings were non-safety and if you crashed, your skis stayed on and you just hoped for the best. Your boots were floppy and laced up. No quick exit for lunch or afternoon tea. Edges were screwed to the skis in sections and often broke off. Being adventurous, I broke skis but no bones.

I fell in love then, and stayed in love for the rest of my life, with quietly falling snow and the alpine life. There was something creative and satisfying about leaving neat tracks in new, icing sugar snow. I loved being able to ski better and faster than Ralph, and I roamed all over every mountain I could find, and often well away from recognised runs, trying to improve my craft and proud of my independence.

Penny and Virginia were good skiers, but were more prudent than I was. We would often visit Gstaad to use the ice rink near the Palace Hotel, and then have afternoon tea there, a great treat because the cafe was usually full of royals, spies, poseurs and millionaires. Princess Caroline of Monaco, who was about our age, was usually there, and we were part of the same kids skating group.

I remember the good times you and I had at Mount Buller. Like you, skiing was always something I loved. Even if you weren't fit you could still go and ski OK in winter somewhere nearby, and it was great for the family as well.

We taught our kids to ski early on, like you, and we had many happy winters at Omski. They learned to ski well. Pip has probably done the most skiing as an adult, mainly because her husband Dale is a committed snowboarder, and because at one time Pip's job involved travel to Europe and North America, where she would usually find a way to get to the slopes for a few days. She turned into a graceful and courageous skier. Watching her on the slopes made me so proud.

When the kids left home I went away regularly on ski holidays with friends. Even though I'm slow and stiff these days, I'm still involved. I'm grateful to have had the chance to see many of the world's great resorts in the USA, Canada, Japan, New Zealand, Finland, Switzerland, Austria, Italy and France.

What about your memories of Geneva itself?

Too many. Geneva is one of the world's most lovely cities even if it's a bit chocolate-boxy. It surrounds the south-western end of Lac Leman, known to us as Lake Geneva. Many of my memories involve the lake somehow. Also, some of the greatest ski terrain in the world lies in the alps to the south and west of Geneva, including Chamonix, Megève and Crans-Montana.

Ralph and Dorothy were introduced to a bathing club on the lake shore, which they joined as members so the family could spend time there on sunny summer days. There was no beach but there was a long lawn approach to the water's edge where we would all picnic and sunbathe. There was a deck you dived off into the water, inhabited most of the time by white swans. Quite a bit of the lake froze in winter, and on even the warmest of summer days the water was still cold and full of fluoro green slime. Still, we got used to it fast and we would swim out to pontoons offshore to annoy the older bathers. There was a strict rule that no children could enter the water until one hour after lunch because of the risk of cramp, which was real.

This would have been my first encounter with the almost-fully-revealed female form. I embarrassed my parents with my constant questions about anatomy and sexual difference. I remember one day finding a sex-ed book in my sister Virginia's room, into which I had launched an unlawful raid, and pestering both her and my parents for days about the meaning of what was in it. It was clear that I was at the threshold of a mystery of importance – although it took a long time for me to make sense of anything. This was a time in which parents believed that the last thing they should do was give their children information about reproduction. I suspect Virginia's book had been obtained by her from somewhere outside the family, as it was never offered to me.

The bathing club was a Swiss institution where only respectable foreigners like diplomats were admitted, and even then, grudgingly. Social conformity was required, especially for the insular and conservative Swiss, so children were harshly disciplined. This didn't suit me at all. The worst insult that could be levelled against parents was that their children were badly brought up; Ralph and Dorothy were on the receiving end of many observations about my noisy and undisciplined habits.

I would also find my way down to the quay around the lake to watch the old fishermen trying to coax up freshwater perch. They used long, thin bamboo rods and old iron buckets for their catch. I hadn't been fishing much before and the experience of seeing a writhing fish flicked out of the water and dashed to its bloody death on the flagstones was new and uncomfortable.

We would sometimes be taken out on the long, slender, elegant white paddle steamers that took traffic around the lakeshore. These were built between 1900 and 1925, during the Belle Époque, the golden age between 1870 and the outbreak of the First World War, and are regarded as the most important paddle steamer fleet anywhere. I remember the splash and thunk of the fluoro slime paddles through the blue lake water, the grimy and choking engine smoke, the bright summer sun on the wake and the smart navy blue uniforms of the crew.

Geneva being in middle Europe, you must have had some exposure to musical performance?

Yes. In those days, there were FM broadcasts of classical concerts. FM radio didn't arrive in Australia for another thirty years. My mother would tune in regularly on FM radio to the Amsterdam Royal Concertgebouw Orchestra or the Berliner Philharmoniker. You would also find classical duos and trios playing in the smarter hotels, gypsy accordionists and guitarists playing Django Reinhardt tunes in the squares and coffee shops, and also free concerts in the parks featuring more popular singers.

We went to afternoon concerts at the Geneva Conservatorium to hear the Orchestre de La Suisse Romande that had been founded by Ernest Ansermet just after the First World War. Ansermet was still with the orchestra in the mid-'50s, and still completing the now-legendary recording series with Decca Records, including some of the earliest stereophonic LPs ever made.

My mother decided that the time was right for me to begin my musical education seriously. I was to become a concert pianist. In Switzerland at this time, no music teacher would accept a student unless he or she had passed a course in musical theory, pitch recognition and sight reading known as solfege that relied on allocating simple syllables to notes like do, re, mi.

So, at the age of seven, I was enrolled at the conservatorium for my year-long course. This was taught by old and impatient instructors who were not fond of young people, especially foreigners. You can imagine the stress of the final examination, which was oral. I remember staring upward for what seemed like miles to the dark wood bench at which my examiners sat in front of their inquisitorial blackboard, their eyes piercing me.

Anyway, I seem to have passed, and the joyous day arrived when I went to my first piano lesson. I had a good ear and made rapid progress, but I was never a good sight reader because I would memorise all the notes – it seemed easier but it meant that when music became complex I struggled to decode it. However, I formed a lifelong love of the keyboard and other instruments, which has brought me thousands of hours of happy play.

For the first time in her life, my mother was able to afford some domestic assistance in the house. When we first arrived she hired an older woman to help with the chores and act as a babysitter/governess for the children. I can't recall her name, but while she was strict, she was fond of long walks and we explored Geneva together. I think I asked too many questions and told too many tall stories about my imaginary adventures in Africa and Arabia, but we seemed to be good mates.

Then along came a pretty young German girl who was much more fun. She had been in Hamburg during the Second World War – bear in mind that this had finished only ten years before – and she once showed us the shocking scars she had from injuries received during Allied bombing raids. I would pester her constantly for wartime stories and she was usually happy to oblige. It was the first time I had seen evidence of the results of war. My main memory is anger and bewilderment that this lovely girl should have been ripped apart by bombs for no reason.

Did you get around Europe much for holidays?

We did. Ralph was an explorer. He would always arrange holiday car trips to interesting places in France, Austria, Germany and Italy.

One year he decided on the Ticino – the lake area of northern Italy closest to the Swiss border. We stayed at a guest house in Ascona on Lake Maggiore, and the next year at Sirmione on Lake Garda. Getting there involved a car trip across the Furka and St Gothard mountain passes, both frightening switchback climbs along narrow, ice-bound and unprotected roads. I remember being car sick, although this would have been caused as much by Ralph still smoking as it was by the twisting and turning. These were lovely interludes. The lakes were very beautiful, although, like Lac Leman, intensely blue and freezing.

Geneva is quite close to the French border, isn't it?

Yes it is, and we often would take day trips into nearby French towns like Annecy and Aix-les-Bains. Dorothy would buy cheap wine and other luxuries that the French taxed less. There was a limit of a couple of litres of alcohol, after which a declaration had to be made. Invariably Dorothy would load the boot with far more than the permitted amount, hoping that our diplomatic number plates would persuade the grim Swiss border guards to wave us through. She went undetected for some time, until her car was searched one afternoon to her loud protests, revealing a large stash of contraband. We were helpless with laughter as she fumed and, in her imperfect but perfectly understandable French, protested loudly and long to the guards, hoping to the last for a back down. It was an expensive afternoon and led to a communication black-out with Ralph for some days.

What about other extracurricular activities?

Cubs was one. My mother felt I should join a pack despite the fact that with school, the conservatorium, my gang and sport I was too busy for someone my age. This was fun for the most part. We went on many weekend bivouacs but I was to experience the hard edge of sledging from the local boys about my weight, my nationality and all the other things that cause small boys to single out others for attention.

At one camp, I was wrongly accused of having concealed a prohibited knife in my gear. This led to an uncomfortable search through my bags and my clothing, although, happily, to acquittal. It was an early introduction to the sour taste of prejudice and the pile on.

Occasionally Ralph would decide that I needed a taste of the life I might have when I grew up, and would take me with him on an official engagement. We listened in to a few debates at the United Nations; went to his office while he was working; and on one famous occasion to a nuclear research reactor, which in the mid-1950s was new and rare. The reactor was built in a water pool and glowed neon-blue deep below the surface as the controlled chain reaction got under way. I couldn't work out whether the surface of the pool was glass or water and it seemed logical for me to test this by dipping my foot in. It was water, but this act unleashed a storm of activity from attendants and security guards, including me being herded into a decontamination room and having a Geiger counter applied to my foot. I thought it was a wonderful trick and although it blew over quickly, Ralph was far from amused.

Where else did you go?

Well, we travelled to other parts of Europe, which one could do easily because everything was within reach. We spent time one summer on the Dutch coast at a town called Scheveningen, close to The Hague. It was grey and cold and there was to be no swimming or sunbaking. It was also difficult to get to the beach because large areas of the foreshore had been mined during the war and were still not cleared. I remember the big red skull and crossbones signs and the barbed wire fences up and down the minefields. It was lucky that I didn't go wandering around in the danger zone. It was the kind of thing I would have done then.

On the same trip we went to Hamburg for a couple of nights. The city was still in much the same derelict condition it had been in at the end of the war, with ruined and charred brick buildings everywhere from the Allied bombing campaign. This made a deep impression on me. I connected the grim landscape to the scars and war stories of our young maid and started to form a concrete impression of what the war must have been like for the Germans in those big cities. It also explained the abuse that the Swiss and French still directed at the few German children I knew in Geneva. They were les sales Bosches – the filthy ignorant Germans.

So how long did your Swiss experience last?

Ralph's posting to Geneva was for three years. There was still much war-related work being done. I mentioned that one of his responsibilities was the coordination, with the UN agencies, of Australia's assisted migration program for refugees coming to Australia from central Europe. Ralph often visited the Russian-controlled refugee camps there to help with selecting and processing migrants. It was during our stay in Switzerland that arrangements for the departure of Russian forces from Austria was negotiated. Austria had been occupied by the US, France, the UK and Russia after the war but instead of being partitioned like Germany, it was given its independence and freedom from occupation in 1955.

Switzerland was an important time for me. I became fluent in French, began to understand and play music, started to show some academic ability, was exposed to a complex, dense and sophisticated culture, learned about prejudice and human weakness and began to pick up the distant signals of the hormonal deluge that would soon drown me. I began to understand that my life was privileged and that this would in some way improve my odds of a good future. But any concept of discretion, social adaptability, softness or judgement was, unfortunately, far away. I was loud, inquisitive, rough and not a little boastful. The lessons I needed to learn to navigate my relationship with the world well were nowhere in sight.

Singapore

What was the next staging point for the family, then?

My parents sat us down one evening in 1955 and told us that we would be going to Singapore. This meant as little as Geneva had meant before we left Australia, although I do remember helpful adults explaining the concept of an isthmus, which Singapore wasn't. I gathered that as Singapore was Asian it would be more exotic and complicated than anywhere else I'd been, and that I'd need to go into a new school.

We were all proud because Ralph's new role was to be Commissioner for Australia (one step below High Commissioner) early in his career. I suspect that he was promoted because Singapore was likely to be given its independence before long, and Australia needed a hard representative to assess the contenders for leadership and, if possible, influence the outcome. There was a concern that Lee Kuan Yew was unstable and possibly communist-oriented. Ralph had always been keen to have a post in the Asian region and his agreement to go to Switzerland may have been on the basis that Asia would follow.

My parents decided that Virginia would not come to Singapore, but would board at Canberra Girls Grammar School instead. The decision seems wrong now, but they may have felt that it was time for her to settle down academically.

And did you go by sea again?

No. It seems the policy had changed. The family took a plane. This was my first experience of the Qantas Lockheed Super Constellation. The Connie was a transport aircraft designed during the war, powered by four Pratt & Whitney R-2800 supercharged 18-cylinder engines. It was noisy, slow (less than half the speed of modern passenger planes) with a comparatively small cabin four seats wide, with a short range. I remember our late afternoon take-off and ascent above a beautiful patchwork of small Swiss farms, lakes and mountains. Night fell quickly, and a rich dinner was served from slender service carts manned by stewards in black trousers and white coats with polished brass buttons. As soon as the service was over, smoke filled the cabin as travellers lit up with their coffee and liqueurs. Cigarette tips glowed throughout the cabin all night. The engine exhausts turned pale pink from the heat of the avgas burning. We landed in Milan, then Calcutta and Bangkok for more overnight stops before arriving in Singapore.

I have no memories of Milan, but Calcutta made a deep impression. We travelled to and from the airport in large official cars, but in those days there were no freeways to sanitise the entry into the city. So, we passed through what seemed hours of slums, beggars, lepers, vagrant animals, stagnant open sewers and stenches to arrive at our hotel. All along the way our car was besieged by beggars trying to push their arms into our car for coins or food. I was numbed by this misery, which was alien and repulsive. I have never been back to India, and perhaps this memory has had a long-term impact. I want to, but somehow time slips by.

I guess you landed on your feet with accommodation? Singapore was still a treasured part of the British Empire so the official residence was probably pretty smart?

Good guess. The Australian Government had bought an old colonial mansion in Dalvey Road in Singapore, called Glencaird, under the shrewd advice of Alan Watt, Ralph's predecessor in Singapore and one of Australia's most senior diplomats. Alan had previously been the head of the Department of Foreign Affairs in Canberra and would have known my father well as a fellow Rhodes Scholar and as a colleague working on the ANZUS Treaty project before Ralph was posted to Switzerland.

The house itself was enormous, and was located on a big block in one of the best areas in Singapore in the Orchard Road district. There was a debate between Ralph and Canberra as to whether this property should be sold before the Harry family arrived in Singapore because of its value and because Ralph was junior to Alan. Just as well the decision went Ralph's way, because in the '90s, the block was subdivided, part being sold commercially for a huge profit and the balance being rebuilt as a splendid ambassador's residence and chancery.

The result for the family was wonderful as well, because the house was not only prestigious, which suited my mother and was indispensable currency in Singapore's rigid colonial hierarchy, but also provided space, comfort, a grand piano and a park for me to roam in as I liked.

Switching schools for you would have been hard, though? People don't often understand the anxiety kids have in moving into a new social environment.

You're right, Jimmy. The change of school was more intimidating and distressing than the shift from Canberra to Geneva, and I remember the tears and sleepless nights well. A heavy social shock. I hated this transition and expressed my unhappiness often in the early days.

I was put into a school run by the British Army that was largely populated by the children of the British military establishment. This was the Pasir Panjang Junior Army School. It was part of a network of military schools in Singapore that continued to support the presence of the British military until its withdrawal from the region in 1971.

I was unlike any of the British Army kids in look, accent, background or interests. Under the influence of fried rice, curries, coconut, ice kachangs, mango, durian, lychees, mangosteens, star fruit, sugar cane, fried chicken, peanuts and sweets, my weight ascended and my silhouette became rounder by the day.

So, how was daily life at Glencaird?

It was different to Geneva, where we had a small apartment and some normality. In Singapore, not only was our house fit for royalty, but we also had servants, including a Chinese butler called Ah Fong, who took an instant dislike to me, a cook, two maids, two gardeners, a security guard known in Malay as a Jaggah, and a Malay chauffeur named Daoud.

All meals were served in the main dining room, which adjoined a suite of reception rooms and Ralph's office. We served ourselves from platters at the table in the colonial way. Only the bedrooms and Ralph's study were air-conditioned; the rest of the house was cooled by large, cream ceiling fans that never stopped turning. You could always hear the gentle swish of the fan blades and smell the faintly acrid scent of the motors working. When breakfast was over, I would be delivered to Pasir Panjang by Daoud in the official car, another large black Humber.

It was accepted that exposing children to heat was bad, and so school ran from seven a.m. till around one p.m., when the Humber would once again sweep me back to Dalvey Road.

I would always pester Daoud to stop off at Malay kampong shops so I could stock up on marbles, Malay sweets, bike inner tubes for my many shanghais, and kites. I was guilty on some occasions of launching missiles from the Humber in the direction of other cars, with embarrassing results. Malay and Chinese drivers were unimpressed by the sight of a small boy flicking objects at them from inside a large official vehicle.

Daoud would sometimes allow me to sit on his lap and take the steering wheel of the Humber on the way home from school. He was a great mate and I loved him. He would always dress in a heavy Malay sarong and khaki long-sleeved drill shirt but was always cool as ice. He and all our other Malay servants took our family under their wings and treated us like their own. The Chinese were less welcoming. I would often visit the Malay servants' quarter on the grounds of Glencaird and there would always be some nuts or an ice kachang to be had there.

At the conclusion of Ramadan, our family would be invited to their Muslim feast to celebrate the end of the fasting period. We would join our friends in their gorgeous formal clothing and sit down with them for a cup of tea and sweets. This generous and warm relationship with the local Malays was a good influence on me, though my parents were wary of it and seemed uneasy about me spending too much kampong time.

How did you get on at school then?

I was considered posh by the army kids because of the car and Ralph's position, which I'm sure I boasted about unbearably to my fellow students, but I can't remember any regular sledging about it, although of course it was hard to make friends with kids who all lived in army housing estates far away. I remember trying to interest Dorothy in having classmates over to play and not receiving much encouragement.

Overall, though, my school experience went smoothly. I was now on the way to being large and strong, so I found myself playing soccer for the school team in the back row; I could throw the cricket ball further than anyone else; and I was a fair sprinter and fast swimmer. School work was easy and I continued my piano studies with a young red-headed nun in a convent music school chosen by my mother.

I also fell helplessly in love, for the first time, with an English girl at Pasir Panjang who didn't know I existed.

Were there other distractions from the colonial life?

There were. My parents had to run an official life, which meant they attended many diplomatic functions and entertained often.

Glencaird was a popular venue for the official community because of the beauty of the house and because my parents were good hosts. For me, it meant a large supply of nuts, salt crackers, fizzy drinks and leftover canapes that were stockpiled for official use. We kids would sit on the stairs as the glamorous guests arrived and wonder what was really happening.

In those days strict dress rules applied despite the heat and humidity, so attendance at official functions could be a serious trial.

Dorothy made me attend French conversation classes and it was perhaps as a result of this that my accent and vocabulary, if not my conjugations, mostly stayed with me. Ralph gave me a junior encyclopedia, which I devoured. I learned to make boomerangs and fly kites, I became a bat and cockroach assassin, I crashed away happily on the grand piano and continued to thrive on adventure and disobedience.

There were many unfortunate incidents where my sense of adventure overcame what little judgement I had; I'll mention one. Like all small boys, and perhaps because of my militaristic school in Geneva, I loved anything to do with guns, explosives, war and uniforms. Having found a recipe for gunpowder in my new encyclopedia, I decided to go into manufacture. I was a good saver at the time and had a few Singapore dollars. I approached Daoud and asked him to drive me down to a nearby chemist shop, which he did, unaware of my real intent. I asked the shopkeeper to sell me bags of sulphur and sodium nitrate, which she unwisely did. All I needed then was some crushed charcoal, which was easily available from the kitchen. In fifteen minutes I was back at home, undetected, with enough ingredients to create havoc. To cut a long story short, my gunpowder did the job and I managed to detonate a full ink bottle on top of my bedroom dresser, which destroyed the dresser and could easily have set fire to Glencaird. How I was not seriously injured I don't know. Ralph and Dorothy were, of course, shaken by this, the blame for which was impossible for me to deflect.

I can't remember what the punishment was, although it must have been substantial.

So how did you find Singapore society at the time?

Relentlessly class-conscious and snobbish.

Although we belonged to the Great British Family, we were treated as third-rate, being colonials. So, the Australians in Singapore stuck to themselves mostly.

But we did receive invitations to set-piece British Empire events like the Queen's Birthday celebrations at dawn on the Padang. This event was little different to what you would have experienced in Delhi a century before: the sweeping arrival of the Commander-in-Chief, Far East Military Command, who was always referred to as the C-in-C, a frightfully important looking general in pressed khaki with big red sashes and a wall of medals; the appearance of the Governor-General in shining white cottons and white-plumed helmet with a gleaming brass chin-strap; a march-past of locally garrisoned Gurkha troops; and a pretty but extremely stiff garden party.

We attended the dawn Anzac Day service at the Kranji War Cemetery, were admitted as members of the whites-only British Tanglin Club and ate chips and tomato sauce on the lawns by the swimming pool at weekends.

We spent holidays in Malaya in the traditional cool hill stations of Fraser's Hill and the Cameron Highlands during the hot season. Because of the recent communist terrorist insurgency in Malaysia, we had to drive through white safe zones and avoid the dangerous red zones of the country.

Being a patriotic individual, Ralph bought one of the first Australian Holdens exported by General Motors to Asia. This was an uncomfortable and unreliable car but we resigned ourselves to the torment of driving in it whenever we went on holiday.

We shopped at Cold Storage, drank English ginger beer and creaming soda, ate Indian cashew nuts and were herded into British safe havens during the increasingly violent communist riots.

There must have been some entertaining characters who passed through your house?

We did often have important VIPs to stay at the residence. I can remember having conversations with Sir William McKell, a Labor politician who had been Australian governor-general from 1947 to 1953 and before that premier of New South Wales; Sister Vivian Bullwinkel, a highly decorated nurse in World War Two; Sir Roden Cutler, a VC winner who became governor of New South Wales; and Tom Critchley, a pioneer diplomat who served as the Australian high commissioner to Malaysia from 1955 to 1965. Tom was a great bloke who was interested in war history. One time he came to stay he had with him some film footage shot during the fighting against the Japanese in Malaysia during World War Two and showed them to us one night using Ralph's projector. These were precious opportunities, and I can remember raining questions down on these poor people at every opening.

You still would have had a lot of time to fill in because of your parents' commitments?

My life was lonely at times. On school days I would get home at around 1.30 p.m., have a small lunch on my own and then have to look after myself till my parents turned up from their various commitments. I would do my homework on a large second-level terrace as the afternoon deluge of rain would come down, leaving the garden drenched and steaming. I would read, play the piano, practise throwing my boomerangs or firing my shanghais or roam around the neighbourhood.

At nights after dinner I would usually sit outside the main front door with the Jaggah. I'm not sure what we would have spoken about but I became very fond of him and he treated me wisely and kindly. I once made a spear to which I lashed a small knife. He saw that, especially in my hands, it would be dangerous and it soon disappeared.

I became a better than average swimmer at the Tanglin Club and, despite my unstreamlined proportions, I won many club races.

I had many friends, mainly made through my mother's efforts. We played at each other's houses and compared our fathers' cars as though we were chauffeurs gossiping while waiting for their bosses. I became a smart marbles player, and the bag containing my collection grew to the stage where it was hard to carry.

I was introduced to boxing and learned how painful it was to be punched on the nose which, because of my impatience, happened often.

I appeared, appropriately, as Friar Tuck at the annual Tanglin Club fancy dress ball. Virginia went as Maid Marion.

I went exploring the sites of the great Singapore riots of 1956 which were triggered by the government suppression of Chinese communist organisations. I collected spent tear gas shells and rubber bullets, although my collection was rapidly seized and destroyed by the authorities. The whole of the island was under curfew, which of course didn't apply to me. I remember visiting Ralph's office with him in an armoured car through a completely deserted city.

News of the 1956 Games in Melbourne travelled our way in film and photographs. We saw newsreels of our glorious athletes and the sporting battles between the USSR and the occupied countries of Eastern Europe. The Cold War was a rivalry which filled us with anxiety and which we thought would go on forever.

Melbourne

And I think your next step was Melbourne?

Well, much as I loved the freedom of Singapore, eventually, the music had to stop. In 1957 the family moved again, and you're right, to Melbourne. Ralph had been chosen to become the head of ASIS – the Australian Security Intelligence Service – the CIA equivalent, which was then based in the St Kilda Road army barracks. The appointment was sanctioned, and perhaps suggested, by the Minister for External Affairs R. G. Casey. Ralph was then forty.

It seems that at the time he was some kind of protégé of Casey's, who had had a glittering career that included membership of the British war cabinet during World War Two and the governorship of Bengal in India. Casey had been to Cambridge and had worked in British military intelligence, and would have been aware of Ralph's time at Oxford. If my suspicion that Ralph connected with the British intelligence establishment while he was at Lincoln College is right, Casey would also have been aware of this.

An appointment like that would not have been made unless Ralph had already become an intelligence insider and was known favourably to the CIA and MI6. This is consistent with my belief that he was inducted into intelligence in the UK as a student and had stayed close to it in his early years in the Department of External Affairs, and in Switzerland and Singapore.

The Australian Government believed that other intelligence organisations, including the Russians, had infiltrated ASIS during the war and that its senior management was unreliable. So, Ralph's main job was to reconstruct the organisation along more modern lines and to get rid of the old guard and any suspect elements.

One of his senior staff members and closest colleagues in Singapore was Gary Woodard. From 1970 to 1973 he was the first head of the National Assessments Staff in the Joint Intelligence Organisation in the Department of Defence. So it's likely that Gary was already in intelligence in Singapore with Ralph.

We flew once again by Super Constellation to Sydney via Darwin and on to Essendon Airport on a dark and rainy winter night in 1957.

Just after our take-off from Darwin, I was looking out my window and saw that one of the Connie's engines had burst into flames. The crew managed to douse the fire but after a fuel dump we were forced back to Darwin. Because of the unavailability of spares or a replacement aircraft we cooled our heels at a Darwin hotel for several days before being able to get under way again.

I was then ten years old. In Melbourne, we had been booked as a family into the Cathedral Hotel, a dour grey-blue and beery six-storey pub on the corner of Swanston Street and Flinders Lane, while Dorothy scouted around Melbourne's eastern suburbs for rental accommodation.

How long did you have to stay in the Cathedral?

I think we were there for maybe a couple of months, but it seemed forever. There were no two ways about it: the place was an unlovely, two-star, down-at-heel pub with ancient accommodation upstairs and a roaring bar trade downstairs. These were the days of the six o'clock swill when all pubs were forced to close at six p.m. Being on Swanston Street, we were bang in the middle of the route followed by workers on their way to Flinders Street Station from the city. They would all pour into the Cathedral bars at five p.m. after work, clad in their fawn gabardine overcoats and grey hats, to down the maximum number of beers possible by closing time. The barmaids would line up hundreds of full pots at around 4.45 p.m., and hundreds more at 5.59 p.m., which would all be belted down by 6.10 p.m., when the bell rang and the doors closed.

The other famous swill hotel was Young & Jackson, which lay diagonally opposite the Cathedral on the corner of Flinders Street and Swanston. I remember looking south down Swanston Street at Y & J from an upper window of the Cathedral, and you could see men ferrying armfuls of full, frothing glasses to-and-fro above their heads in the crush inside the packed bar during that crazy sixty minutes.

Jimmy, do you remember the famous painting by the Australian artist John Brack called *Collins St., 5p.m.*?

I remember John Brack, but I can't really remember the picture.

Well, it shows packed columns of grim, grey men with gabardine coats and hats slouching down Collins Street on their way to the swill, against a depressing yellow background, looking trapped and unhappy. My experience of the swill crowd was the opposite – the racket created by groups of mates pouring into the pubs seemed to me a song of delight, as these men prepared for the precious, abandoned hour between work and wife.

John Brack, who's now thought of as one of Australia's finest modernist painters, was the art master at Melbourne Grammar at the time and I remember seeing him work on his Collins Street painting at our art centre at lunchtimes. He was an alcoholic who died only a few years later.

The Cathedral was always full of the smell of stale booze and cigarettes, but it had one priceless virtue: a 22-inch screen TV – that's less than an eighth of the size of a normal screen these days – set up in the Ladies' Lounge on the second floor, which we were allowed to watch for an hour each night after homework and dinner.

It was here I became trapped by my lifelong TV addiction. We watched mainly American shows – *Bonanza, Zorro, Annie Oakley, O.S.S., The Lone Ranger* and *Perry Mason*. There was some live TV, including *IMT,* or *In*

Melbourne Tonight, a variety show hosted by Graham Kennedy and Bert Newton. This was regarded as suggestive and thus unsuitable for kids, but I stole glimpses now and then and couldn't see what all the fuss was about.

I would usually go down to the lounge in the mornings before school and turn the TV on to watch the test pattern or just the transmission snow. All TV watching was under the control of the manageress of the hotel, a Miss Reichstein, who had violent red lipstick, smoked unfiltered Turf cigarettes and coughed constantly. I soon learned the benefits of being pleasant to her. Now and then I could coax another fifteen- or twenty-minute reprieve, which made the day a success no matter what else had happened.

We had no idea what Ralph was doing in Melbourne. We knew he worked in the St Kilda Road army barracks in something vaguely related to his diplomatic work and that was enough to keep us happy.

While the family was still in the Cathedral Hotel I walked down Flinders Street toward the docks one afternoon and wandered into Hearn's Hobbies, which sold serious toys like model trains, radio kits, Meccano (an early version of Lego), and parts for building balsawood planes propelled by rubber or micro combustion engines. The idea of building a model plane made instant sense and it wasn't long before I bought one and began carving, splitting and glueing my first balsa model together on a glass-topped table in the Ladies' Lounge at the Cathedral, much to the dismay of the hotel cleaners who were left with the job of removing the wood cement from the glass.

This was at about the same time as the launch of Russia's – and the world's – first artificial satellite, called Sputnik, which seemed unbelievable. I used to go out into Swanston Street in the evenings when Sputnik was overhead to see the bright new Russian star speed by.

I tested my planes and their rubber band engines in the lobby of the hotel. They flew well but collided with residents too often for my own good.

Was there any social life for you and the family at the hotel?

A bit. Our hosts were the owners, John and Eileen Carlson. They were kind to our family and often invited us to their table in the dining room for dinner, which meant that we didn't have to pay for our meal. John had a bad limp that I suspect was due to a war injury – I can remember his RSL badge and the kindness he showed toward veterans on Anzac Day. He was a gruff man but was easier when he decided to have a drink. He put on a fancy lunch on Virginia's thirteenth birthday, which I remember well because it was the first time I'd eaten an oyster. I had mine with a delicious traditional pink cocktail sauce and I still refuse to eat oysters served with vinegar-based dressings.

So, did it take long for your mother to find you a house?

Not long. Despite the slim allowance that the administrators of the Department of External Affairs would have provided, she found a pleasant red brick Edwardian house at 12 Mercer Road, Armadale, near Lauriston Girls' School, which my sisters enrolled in. The house was in a good area and it was large and comfortable. It had been split into two sections, one of which we were to live in. The other, smaller half was inhabited by two old ladies, one of whom was named Miss Maud Telling. The other's name I can't remember. They were grumpy and impatient and I didn't like them except when they let me watch TV in their rooms on a Sunday evening. We were set-less.

I remember Mercer Road for its brutal summers, when the roar of cicadas was at full blast every afternoon and evening; and its winters when the only form of heating was kerosene-burning stoves and brown coal briquette fires that stank and covered everything in fine orange dust.

There was a large garage at the back of the property where I stored my bits and pieces.

Mercer Road was a place where I did a lot more growing up and where I started to figure out that the real shape of the world was unexpected and challenging.

Your folks decided to put you into Melbourne Grammar around about then?

Pretty much as soon as the family landed in Melbourne. MGS was Ralph's decision. It was a reputable and successful establishment and one of the two oldest and most prestigious boys' schools in Melbourne, the other being Scotch College.

It would have been natural for Ralph to choose Casey's old school, Melbourne Grammar, as my home for the next eight years. He would have understood the need for a strong relationship base for anyone wanting to be a part of the then powerful conservative political establishment, which was based in Melbourne. This understanding, as well as the academic and social reputation of the school, was enough for him. He may have felt that if he'd had an establishment background it would have been useful to his own career.

It was an important decision for you, wasn't it? For me as well.

It decided most things, as it would have for you, like where I grew up, who my friends were, the sport I played, my emotional, academic and professional development and my political preferences.

When the family left Melbourne three years later for Canberra, Ralph decided to leave me in Melbourne as a boarder, but took my sisters out of Lauriston and put them back in Canberra Girls Grammar. In doing that, he accepted a financial burden, which for him and the family was great.

Ralph applied for my admission to the Melbourne Grammar preparatory school, called Wadhurst after a small English village in East Sussex, and soon I was on my way with Ralph and Dorothy to be interviewed by the headmaster, Thomas Plummer, known to the boys as Thos.

Wadhurst was located at the intersection of Domain and St Kilda Roads in South Yarra, then a quiet and low-rise location that looked out over the Melbourne Domain toward the Shrine of Remembrance.

Despite my loud and probably over-confident presentation, I did well enough to be given a place. I remember Ralph taking me on the No 8 tram to the school on my first morning in Grade 5 C, with me clutching a new brown Gladstone bag containing a pastie wrapped in paper for lunch.

What class did you go into when you arrived?

The fifth form-my master was an Englishman, J. F. T. Copleston, who was on exchange from the smart Dragon Preparatory School in Oxford, and was also a resident tutor in Perry House, one of the two boarding houses at the school. He was a smallish, dark and balding man with glasses but commanded the attention and respect of the boys because of his clipped and sharp manner, but also because of an old sandshoe in his desk drawer he called Samson, which was used to beat uncooperative boys.

The Melburnian, the annual school magazine, noted me as the only salvete – that means welcome in Latin – in Wadhurst for the 1957 year. I can't remember exactly when I was enrolled but I think it was in term one. I was in Wadhurst from 1957 to eighth grade in 1960. My prep school memories are many, too many for this story, and I'm not certain what happened when. But I'll mention a few.

The school was divided into houses, which formed convenient sporting and administrative units. I was in Cain House, with light blue colours. Unlike houses in the senior school, which by tradition had acquired flavours of one sort or another over the years like sporty, academic, socially superior, or loser, the Wadhurst houses were middle-of-the-road.

And how did your settling in go?

Not bad actually. Several features of prep school in Melbourne were clear, which you would understand well, Jim. Sporting success was essential. Second, the ability to fight, shove, wrestle or intimidate was helpful. Third, having wealthy, socially important, or well-known parents to give one a believable air of entitlement was important. Academic performance was last.

I was lucky on most counts.

I had continued to grow rapidly and was now strong and tall for my age. I had become a fast swimmer in Singapore and, in Melbourne, left my swimming opponents at school and interschool level well behind. I could also jump and run unexpectedly fast for a boy of my weight. Everyone wanted me on their side in tug o' war contests. In a decision that did no harm to my street cred, I was barred by our marvellous Danish PE master, Sven Nissen, from boxing other boys in the gym because I was judged too dangerous. I could hit a cricket ball a long way and was a fair wicket keeper. So, because my mates coached me well in the art of playground fighting, I was off to a good start.

Ralph showed little interest in helping me develop my sporting skills. He would come along to swimming meets occasionally when I was winning. When eventually I found sporting interests that really did suit me, no one was more surprised than he.

The fact that I had led the easy life of a diplomat's son gave me a touch of reflected glamour that people thought was interesting.

I decided to learn the violin, as well as the recorder. I played in the school orchestra and I still have pressings of the joint concerts we staged with Scotch College and Xavier College in 1958, which sound truly dreadful. My violin master warned me that I would only turn into a decent player if I practised regularly, which I didn't do, and it wasn't long before I lost interest.

At around this time, an American film was shot in Melbourne called *On the Beach*. This was a dramatisation of a novel by Neville Shute, a post-apocalyptic story about nuclear war. This was the first Hollywood production to have come here, and it was the talk of the town for months. The male lead was Gregory Peck, an A-list actor at the time. His son Carey came with him and was put in my class at Wadhurst. He became an instant school celebrity.

Tell me a bit about life with the family at Mercer Road.

The Mercer Road house was fun. We stayed out of the way of Maud

Telling and her companion, so it was almost as though we had the place to ourselves.

Our neighbours weren't too forthcoming, and in any event Dorothy, in her way, decided they were not worth knowing, especially those on the south side, the Havyatt family. She thought the Havyatt boys were delinquent and we were told to steer clear. That didn't deter me, of course. There was a large and productive fig tree just over the Havyatt fence and I realised the need to make friends with the boys to gain permission to visit for harvesting purposes. The older boy was also an outstanding forger of banknotes. I don't know whether he ever tried to pass one of his creations but they seemed flawless to me, and his enterprise magnetic.

What about your mates at the time?

Just around the corner lived the boy who became my best friend for a couple of years, Malcolm Cleland. Mal was in my class at school. We hung out on the tram on the way home most days, and no afternoon passed without a visit to the lolly shop on the Mercer Road corner, where Malcolm and I had perfected the art of nicking sweets. We were never caught despite the burglary of many items.

Malcolm introduced me to a furniture factory in High Street where he had been befriended by a couple of the French polishers, and before long we were part of the team and making bits and pieces of furniture and earning surprised praise from our parents for our work. Quite why the management allowed two boys to wander about a dangerous shop making things unsupervised is a mystery, but it might have been to do with the fact that the boss was looking for apprentices, who could start at fifteen, and perhaps he thought we had potential.

Inevitably one day I drove a chisel into my left wrist and nearly did myself in, but I was back again before too long and no one seemed to care. No one had heard of occupational safety – that was far away.

I learned to French polish using shellac and methylated spirits. We used to apply twenty or more coats to get a good deep shine. It needed patience and I applied myself in a consistent way.

One of our favourite games was cracker fighting. In those days anyone could buy bungers – or crackers – up to the sixpenny, which was the size of a large sausage roll and could wreck a solid letterbox. We wrecked many. We would stockpile bungers and make large mortars on stands at the furniture shop powered by bike inner tubes that would throw them fifty metres. On the agreed day two teams would assemble on a vacant lot and lob these things at each other to see who could explode one closest to the enemy. I copped it many times, being slower than the more experienced boys, and it hurt. But the excitement and the laughs made it worthwhile.

Coming home on the tram was a celebration. It was always crowded with boys. There was a conductor whose job it was to collect fares and issue pastel-coloured tickets, one colour for each destination point. Sometimes an inspector would hop on and check your ticket. If you were caught without one, having saved your money for an extra lolly, you made the inspector's day and the drama was considerable. We were safe because we carried concession cards for a whole term. But when the shining bright white pillar of the Malvern Town Hall came into view the world was suddenly good and the afternoon stretched endlessly before me.

So did you develop as a swimmer? I remember the excitement in Australia with the success of our swimming team in the Melbourne and Rome Olympics and how so many Aussie families were trying to turn their kids into swim champs.

My father decided when we arrived at Mercer Road that, as I had shown speed as a swimmer, and because it was just after the Melbourne Olympics, when the Aussie swimmers were on top of the world, my talent should be tested and that I should join the scores of thousands of children who now were, in most cases pointlessly, patrolling the training lanes of the Olympic swimming pools that had mushroomed throughout the country. So, Ralph took me for testing to the Malvern baths, where one of the more famous swimming coaches in Melbourne was the resident trainer. His name was Crawford.

The plan also had to do with Ralph's belief that a swimming program would help me regain a more acceptable profile.

My test was successful, and before long I was labouring up and down the training lanes of the Malvern pool. This extended the period in which I was able to swim well, but eventually physics called me to account – my competitors grew taller and leaner and I got taller but not leaner, meaning that when I had to make a choice between swimming and wicket keeping, swimming was easy to abandon.

How do you remember your relationship with Ralph around then? You would usually see a father becoming a strong mentor and friend when the son begins to grow up.

I think Ralph thought that his example was all I needed. There were no fireside chats or on-the-run bits of advice. It was more a process of detachment as Ralph became busier and more preoccupied with his work. He came to the Malvern baths now and then to check my training. One evening he was in the changing shed with me as I took off my swimming togs. Why this night was different I don't know, but he looked at me with unconcealed dislike and began to abuse me for being fat, saying that there was no reason for him to be spending good money on my training if I didn't have the discipline to manage my body weight. I was badly hurt. I felt I had let him down and was cast out in his eyes and therefore had no hope of gaining his approval, or my approval of myself, again.

There were some figures in our Melbourne period who were more kind. One was a colleague of Ralph's from ASIS. His name was Vic Barr and I think he was one of Ralph's more junior staff members. He was interested in me and after I became a boarder at Melbourne Grammar he and his wife would sometimes have me to stay for a weekend at his house in Burwood. I remember him taking me to the MCG to see the 1959

Grand Final between Melbourne and Essendon, who were celebrated rivals in those days. He had a wonderful rich laugh and was willing to try to answer my endless questions.

Another was Dorothy Lansell-Smith, the mother of a good school friend. Her husband had been a prominent real estate agent but had died from an African fever he caught on a hunting safari. She also invited me to stay at weekends when I was a boarder. Dotty was keen to introduce my mother to her Melbourne friends and to involve us in the St John's Toorak Anglican Church. Dotty was a true eccentric and a believer in the benefits of what we now know as organic foods. One of her favourites was a porridge made from millet, which I was forced to eat. She also preached the benefits of drinking large quantities of water. She was well ahead of her time there. She spent her spare time chasing recently widowed men but they were all too sensible to become involved with her.

I was asked to present the eulogy when eventually Dotty died, well into her nineties. I hope she thinks I gave her a decent send-off.

What about hobbies?

Well, I revived my aircraft factory at Mercer Road. I had begun making what were called sailplanes, or large gliders. I pestered Ralph to come with me to a local park to launch them. It took me weeks to get him to come.

Electronics were a big buzz. Many of my mates had crystal sets, which were crude radio receivers that didn't need any batteries but which needed long copper cable aerials strung up in the air – usually on the roof – and had to be listened to through big, heavy earphones. The reception was always garbled and faint, and the stations often weren't well separated, but I loved having a kind of window to the outside world and something to listen to secretly at nights. My aerial stretched from the garage to the house. Whenever we went on trips, which wasn't that often, I would always take it down and then in whatever motel or holiday house it was, I would string it up by winding it to-and-fro between light fittings, towel rails and door knobs.

I wanted to build more reliable and powerful radios, so I convinced one of the technicians from a local radio shop to give me a design for a simple valve radio. He made me a chassis from aluminium plate and sold me the components I needed to assemble the unit, which Ralph wrapped and gave me for Christmas. Soon I had an efficient and selective receiver with a volume control at my command.

This launched a period of addiction to all electronica – telephones, Morse units, galvanometers, PA systems, oscilloscopes. I worked with the first transistors – a huge leap forward because they only required low voltage current, they were small and they generated no heat.

And how were your relationships with Penny and Virginia going around this time?

Penny and Virginia did well at Lauriston. Ginny was then, as she is now, much loved for her sunny character, her kindness and her beauty. She attracted attention from boys from the right schools immediately. She was invited as a fifteen-year-old to the Melbourne Grammar Boat Race Dance to celebrate the Public Schools Head of the River rowing races. Ralph refused to let her go. There were storms for a week before he relented – mainly my mother's doing, I suspect. But it was mean to have refused her and I wondered at the time why he wanted to take away something so innocent.

One bonus for me was that many of Ginny's school friends, some of whom she still has, would visit Mercer Road. I was fascinated by these creatures. They were mysterious, unreachable, inexplicably exciting and paid me no attention.

Penny was a bright, capable girl, full of life, mischief and fun. She was an excellent student, had many friends and adapted easily to life in Melbourne. She and I were friendly rivals but I was aware that she monitored my sometimes eccentric and sometimes unlawful behaviour and that there was always a risk that I would be reported to the authorities. She continued to excel as a game player and could beat me at most things.

My father had made a dismal effort to teach me what were then referred to as the facts of life in response to a cache of lively poetry he discovered in my schoolbag, but the connection between what he stumbled through and the real meaning of what I experienced when the Lauriston girls were floating around the house remained obscure.

Did you have much to do with your grandparents?

Not really. My mother's parents were never discussed and I had no contact with them at all. Ralph's parents lived in Launceston and were pensioners, so they found it difficult to spend much time with us. We didn't have a conventional, close relationship with them, but they would sometimes visit us in Mercer Road. If it was Christmas, my grandfather would approach the question of my present unusually. He thought that even small gifts were an extravagance and would lead children to believe that some things in life were free. Not surprising for a man who had to lead his family through the Depression of the '30s. So, he would sit me down and conduct a general knowledge test on the basis of a penny for every correct answer. No correct answers, no present. He was a classics scholar so I did learn some Greek and Roman mythology from him. He also taught me the old Greek alphabet, which I can still remember. But I could see where Ralph's inwardness and self-discipline came from.

There must have been more good memories of Melbourne for you?

Singing was one. The Wadhurst choir was compulsory but provided access to senior school productions for junior boys, especially trebles like me. I sang in Gilbert and Sullivan's *Trial by Jury* and *The Mikado* as a female chorus member, and in "The Ballad of Tubal Cain" by Henry Russell; I adored the costumes, grease paint and alluring Merton Hall girls.

Wadhurst boys helped the Senior School Chapel Choir on special occasions but I wasn't interested in becoming a nerdy chapel chorister. I remember one concert where I was asked to sing a solo; I was overcome by nerves and blew the song. A sign of things to come.

Ralph's library included his large collection of his Launceston Grammar School prize books in a prominent place. They were smartly bound in deep navy blue leather with gold embossing. I read one or two of them but they were the kinds of titles that not many schoolboys in the 1960s would have been interested in: translations of French classics, Dickens, Jane Austen, Shakespeare, poetry and philosophy. My tastes were more low-brow at the time. I preferred Jennings and Derbyshire, Kingsley Amis, Biggles, war history, the development of science and technology, and art. I won prizes most years, and was proud to receive them, but I was never able to match the imperious rows assembled by Ralph.

My life, however, while confusing and often painful, was still full of friends, scrapes, interests and lessons. I was full of energy, ambition and curiosity, and making a mark.

How long was the family in Melbourne?

When my father's job at ASIS was done in 1960, after about three years, he told us that he had been asked to return to Canberra. This was our fifth move in a little over ten years. At least, this time, we would be moving back to the family house in Tennyson Crescent.

I've mentioned that my parents had decided that I would be left in one of the boarding houses at Melbourne Grammar to complete my education. I was eleven years old and in Year 7.

My life has benefited overall from the decision to base me in Melbourne but boarding school wasn't all hearts and flowers.

I know. You boarders were made to lead a life that I couldn't have. That's why I tried to get you out of there as often as I could. I wonder why your folks couldn't have seen that coming?

They just had no idea what the conditions were like and really had no way of finding out.

One of their assumptions was that the boarding school would "make something" out of me and that even though the life would be disciplined and maybe even harsh, that was a price that might need to be paid to turn me into someone responsible and hard-working. Did I emerge more wise, tolerant, responsible and compassionate? I emerged feeling less confident, less loved and less sure what path I should follow in life. I might have been more independent because I had to make many decisions that I otherwise wouldn't have had to, at least not on my own. But better equipped for life? No.

I did benefit, I know, from the academic and sporting quality of the school, from some of the friendships I made, and from the general kudos in Melbourne of being an alumnus of an elite institution. But it was hard yards.

Why was that?

Many reasons. There was the general misery of being institutionalised and the often cruel and random treatment the system delivered. Also, boarders found it difficult to find a group of steady mates because parents of Melbourne boys had to go through some fairly inconvenient hoops to arrange a weekend exit for a boarder and they just couldn't be bothered. More of that in a minute.

As importantly for me, this was where I and my family parted company. While my parents were in Australia, I would usually rejoin them in Canberra for the holidays, but it was as though I was a boarder at home. By the time all of us had settled down as a family unit it was time for me to go.

When Ralph was on post overseas, which was most of the time during my adolescence, I was able to see them only once every two years. The policy changed to once a year when I was in Year 12. There was no allowance for family travel after I went to university. Ralph found it financially impossible to pay for visits himself so I spent all holidays thereafter looking after myself.

The fact that I was absorbing more than my fair share of the family's slim resources in the form of school fees sat heavily on me. After my parents returned to Canberra I had no grounding, no home, few permanent friends; both the worlds I inhabited were temporary.

What was Perry House really like?

I remember well the day I was dropped off for my first term.

Perry was in the grounds of Wadhurst, the preparatory school at the junction of St Kilda Road and Domain Road. School House, the other boarding house, was part of the main building complex and near the chapel and main sporting oval. Its culture was agricultural, tough and conservative and it regarded Perry boys as nouveau and weak.

The two establishments were in reality little different in structure and tone. They were modelled on the boarding houses of the English public schools – hard, disciplinarian, dominated by senior boys, sports oriented, unforgiving, and for many, lonely and unsympathetic. There was bullying of new students, rigid and often petty rules, a guilty-till-proven-innocent culture, no free time, corporal punishment, few opportunities to stay out at weekends, old and uncomfortable furnishings including horsehair mattresses and army issue, worn grey blankets, drab lino flooring, poor food, no heating and no sensitivity to individual problems.

Australia in 1960 was still deeply conservative. The general standard of life in the English public schools had probably become more advanced and humane than was Perry House then. News, and especially changing customs, arrived in the colonies slowly.

I was frightened for quite a while. I took with me for comfort and status my latest radio set, which was a jumble of wires, earphones and batteries in a crude box. It was quickly vandalised by other boys and had to be scrapped.

I learned the routine soon enough but there were many low moments because of the loss of my family and the difficulty of communicating with anyone. I couldn't afford the pay phone and it was dominated by older boys anyway. So, the only alternative was letter-writing.

Letters from my parents were like the diaries and photos of my grandparents: just the detail of activities and movements, mostly professional in Ralph's case, that to me and my sisters meant little. Certainly not likely to comfort or inspire a boy stuck in a gulag like Perry. The foreign stamps on the letters may have impressed some of the boys, but they spoke of my isolation. We were ships in the night.

Weekends were never welcome. The Exeat system was hard to navigate as you know yourself, Jim. It required a written application to the housemaster and a long and nervous wait for approval, and was only available twice per term.

My parents left Melbourne without having made many good friends, because Ralph was too busy, and because, in the way of old and conservative societies, they were seen as temporary and without family money. My mother used every means to induce those she did know to invite me to stay, but in most cases, they did it through obligation to my parents rather than because of any interest in me. At least until my sporting life began, I was usually one of the not-well-connected rump that rattled unhappily around the school while other, more privileged boys were whisked away on Saturday mornings in their parents' Jags and Mercs.

There were some happy exceptions. But, particularly in my early years, life could be slow and quiet.

There must have been some distractions.

Sometimes we were fed crumpets and honey, which in a sea of culinary mediocrity I looked forward to. The usual fare was almost criminally unhealthy: bacon and eggs swimming in fat; lamb's fry; meatloaf; white bread, butter and jam; rice pudding; junket; grey lamb; hamburgers; kidney pie; tripe; mashed spuds; jam rolls, and so forth. Not a vegetable or a fresh piece of fruit to be seen.

Occasionally there would be a weekend movie in the Wadhurst hall. And there was table tennis but the table was usually dominated by others.

That's all I can remember. Otherwise, you made your own amusements.

Were you ever attacked or hazed?

No. I was seen even at an early stage as being a risky proposition to mess with. But being noticed, a different thing, I found easy, because of my size, my forthrightness, my ability, my willingness to take risks and my waywardness.

I remember stories I heard from other boarders about how tough life could be for younger boys especially.

Bad memories here. Perry was largely run by the older boys, many of whom were in a repeat Year 12. This was called second year matriculation. It existed as a kind of gap year in which students, having already completed Year 12, would come back for another year to take up a different range of subjects, spend a bit more time on sport, try to gather wisdom, and form the ruling class from which the school captain and his prefects would be chosen.

These senior boys were deep-voiced, burly, testosterone laden and in many cases cruel. In the boarding house, they were demigods. They were responsible for the enforcement of a disciplinary system that the masters rarely interfered with. After dinner and an intemperate quantity of port in the dining hall, the housemaster would usually retire to his study or bed, leaving the senior boys to do his work. There would usually be a junior duty master available, but the prefects seldom referred anything to him for consideration.

A large foolscap book with Dickensian marbled covers was kept in the house captain's study in which to record what were called warnings. These were rule breaches. The rules were mainly trivial. Infringements included: making a bed untidily; having unpolished shoes; talking back to masters or prefects; reading or eating after lights out; being late for dining hall; not wearing clothes that were precisely in accordance with the manual; contesting the justice of a warning; but also, more serious offences such as swearing, smoking, telling dirty jokes or writing profane poems.

Any boy receiving more than two warnings in any two-week cycle was required to serve a prefects' detention on a Sunday morning. This lasted for two and a half hours, and included a short cleaning detail, followed by a carefully-monitored and endless cross-country run, followed by sprints and exercises designed to bring the miscreants to complete physical exhaustion. Most boys would be dehydrated and ill. Worse than the physical punishment was the stream of abuse and humiliation that the prefects would inflict.

I know than caning was a feature of the disciplinary landscape at our school, and it was well-known that the boarders got the brunt of it. So being who you were, I suppose you copped a fair amount?

In spades. Any boy receiving more than three warnings in a two-week period would be caned. Canings were conducted by the prefects at night after lights out. Just as the candidates were dozing off, the harsh dormitory lights would be turned on, and the chosen would be dragged out of bed and marched down to a study, where they would line up against a wall in the cold and bleak corridor outside the study door.

Everyone would be terrified, and many in tears. Then the house captain or one of his deputies would open the study door and summon the first victim. The door would slam, followed by muffled shouting as the prefect would read out the warnings and admonish the boy. Then came the sickening whistle of the cane and the sharp crack as it met the boy's buttocks. One. Two. Three. Four. Sometimes six. The boy would emerge trembling and in agony, massaging his arse furiously. There would sometimes be blood seeping through his pyjamas. The next boy in line would be summoned, the line-up would shuffle down the passage, then, eventually, it was done.

The cane they used was the real thing: long, heavy and designed for assault.

Consider that some of the victims were eleven or twelve years old. The trauma and humiliation was extreme.

Did you experience beatings often?

I was caned many times, and it lives with me. There are still times of stress when my posterior aches with remembrance.

It was assault, pure and simple, which seemed incomprehensibly disproportionate to the offences, mainly alleged by prefects out of dislike or boredom, never capable of review. Today, masters and senior boys would be prosecuted for this.

In Solzhenitsyn's *The Gulag Archipelago*, he analyses how the Russian state refined to a sharp edge the techniques of denunciation, arrest and interrogation of political enemies. He describes the important advantages provided by night arrest, including the dazed and helpless condition of the victim; the absence of witnesses; the terror inspired in the other residents of the victim's house or apartment. It is chilling that similar techniques should have been used both in the Gulag and in the boarding house of a respected and prestigious Melbourne school, but not surprising given that the intent was identical: maximum fear and confusion, minimum resistance, lack of scrutiny.

The fact that I recall this in such detail, and am affected still after so many years, speaks to the trauma.

Parents were distantly aware of the possibility of corporal punishment but could not have known about the barbarity of the process in its detail. The concept then was that the masters acted in loco parentis, that is, had received delegated parental authority over their children. It's hard to believe that parents ever envisaged a strong and intemperate eighteen-year-old beating an eleven-year-old child.

The school authorities woke up in a rush as the liberal winds of the '60s blew through even the sclerotic Australian educational establishment, because by the time I went into Year 12, caning was a thing of the past – in 1965 it was as though it had never happened.

But it happened to me. And it happened to many other young people in Perry. The thing that was destructive for me and others was the arbitrary and unappealable nature of the alleged offences and the brutality and public humiliation involved.

Of course, we never discussed this among ourselves: one of the boarding house norms was that anyone complaining about these punishments was a sissy and what you had to do to remain sane and unremarked was laugh them off.

So how did the system affect your general attitudes?

I was stridently against the system and I was seen to be such. I know now where my adult sensitivity to injustice and my impatience with coercion comes from.

Boys are competitive. They don't like orders and they're programmed genetically to seek dominance and independence. Repression and lack of parental warmth at home didn't help. By contrast, some schools, especially ones as conservative as Melbourne Grammar, liked responsibility (meaning compliance and obedience) and would act instantly and harshly against anything that looked like revolt, including unexpected initiative, determination or courage. Those qualities are ones the wiser schools of today encourage rather than incriminate. Naturally, being proclaimed an outsider, or unusual, invited institutional death, with all the guilt and self-punishment that went along with it.

By the time I emerged into Year 12, I was typecast as outside the mainstream. Although I was seen as a leader in many areas, including class work, sport and music, I was never a candidate for school or house captaincy. In one of Headmaster Brian Hone's annual reports, he assessed me as having every talent, adding the fatal words, "except judgement". To his credit, he offered me my second Year 12, financed by the valuable Marian Flack scholarship, to see whether the penny would drop, but it did not.

I also think, though, that having been provided with so many experiences and so much stimulus as a young boy sharpened my ambition and appetites. I had a hard time managing these within a conformist school structure, but my life has been enriched by a keen understanding of the possibilities of life.

You had a reputation for being bright and adventurous, along with the rebelliousness. How did you progress academically at school?

My academic progress through school was good. I was interested in physics and pursued it with honours through Year 12, but didn't try especially hard in chemistry or advanced maths. I did well in history, politics, French, economics and English, mostly to first-class honours level, with a couple of state top five finishes, a Commonwealth Government university scholarship and a Trinity College scholarship. I was a solid member of the Upper Sixth Form, the group of twenty or so academic leaders in Year 12.

I took on the role of caterer for the Upper Sixth Form meetings because it gave me the chance to eat food I liked rather than having to suffer, yet again, the product of the school dining room kitchens. I cooked respectable pastas, risottos and pies, surprising most of the nay-sayers, most of whom were jealous toe-the-liners.

So what were the things that really got your attention in those days?

I was much more interested in music, sport, girls and pubs in my last couple of years, so although I prepared reasonably diligently for exams, I was no swot. Sport and music were my saviours.

As I swept through puberty and adolescence, I kept growing quickly and by the age of fourteen was over six feet tall, and six feet four inches by the end of Year 11. There was a corresponding improvement in my height-to-width ratio so that by the age of fifteen I had a figure resembling the acceptable. My strength also developed rapidly so that by then, all but the most ambitious boys steered clear of any physical confrontations with me.

As you know from what we talked about earlier, I loved music and could sing. I had also become a reasonably competent pianist by the time I went to boarding school, although because of a dislike of practice on my own, and perhaps some laziness, I abandoned formal instruction when I was fifteen.

I also acted in the annual school plays. One role was King Henry VIII in Bolt's *A Man For All Seasons* and another, Oedipus in Sophocles' *Oedipus Rex*.

Your musical interests went way beyond the standard conservative school stuff, didn't they?

Perry House was where my real introduction to music happened. When I look back on how my musical interests and knowledge developed, I and a few others were way in front of our peers and were pushing boundaries.

Dan Robinson was a smart, sociable and very funny bloke who always looked at life with scepticism and irony. He was one of the few boarders who could see what a fraudulent and ugly system Perry was and wouldn't have a bar of it. He looked way further down the road than I did and was a loyal friend as well as an inspiration.

His parents had given him a portable record player, which we listened to constantly. It sounded tinny and didn't keep a constant speed, meaning recordings often warbled. But it was good enough to allow us to play jazz records from the '20s and '30s, including Jelly Roll Morton, Sidney Bechet, Louis Armstrong, Josephine Baker, Bix Beiderbecke and King Oliver. Bechet was a special favourite and we played "Wild Cat Blues" and "Kansas City Man Blues" all the time.

Dan found a recording of a band called the Clarence Williams Blue Five, which included Bechet and Louis Armstrong, and also some of the tracks recorded by Bechet after he went to live in France toward the end of his career. We also played country blues and folk: Big Bill Broonzy, Memphis Minnie, Lawrence Lane, Woody Guthrie, Pete Seeger, Sonny Terry and Brownie McGhee, Blind Lemon Jefferson and Muddy Waters. This was a heady diet for someone like me, brought up on *My Fair Lady* and The Ray Conniff Orchestra. It was a new world to escape into, far from the drudge and menace of a boarding school life.

I was hearing about sadness, booze, drugs, addiction, fallen women and racist persecution for the first time; and I understood that musical talent could be found in the most underprivileged people from the most dire lives, and that you didn't need to have been taught at a conservatorium or to be a proficient music theorist or have the blessing of some white haired maestro to make beautiful, haunting and challenging music. There were people who were supremely talented from nowhere and devoted to a craft that had nothing to do with anything I'd experienced before. And it was somewhere that no one from the world of Perry House or the school wanted to go: it was ours and ours alone.

Of course, Dan and I were seen as odd for admiring what was seen in Melbourne in 1960 as distinctly bohemian musical tastes. This made no difference to me: it was what and where I wanted to be.

Then along came early '60s pop music!

It was an amazing time, wasn't it? Just after I began walking through those doors with Dan, while I was on a Scout hiking trip in Tasmania, I heard my first Beatles song on a tiny trannie. The jangly guitars, the perfect harmonies, the youthful energy and abandonment was glittery, tribal and exciting. There had been rocker bands with electric guitars before but they were seen as thuggish, Hells Angels types.

When I got back to the boarding house, some boy had pasted a photo of the Beatles with their mop-top haircuts on his study window. When I saw this, and connected the photo with the music, I knew that this was a tidal wave that would sweep over everything and everyone.

Dan bought himself a Spanish guitar and began to take lessons. He had great talent and more, he practised hard and soon turned himself into a decent folksinger with a repertoire of Australian, Irish and American traditional songs. He went on post-university to join a rock band called the Wild Cherries where he developed a serious alcohol and drug habit that almost killed him. My concentration on rowing didn't allow me to lead a life of late nights, clubs, alcohol and all the other '60s paraphernalia.

This also spared me from smoking, which would have taken hold for sure had I not been training.

I was interested in electric guitars and borrowed one from a Chinese boy from my year called Andrew Geh. I learned the basic chords quickly and often jammed along to Cliff Richard and the Shadows, the Beatles, Gerry and the Pacemakers and the other UK-based beat bands that were blooming in the wake of the Beatles' success.

Was there any other source of music education for you?

Many. At about this time, with a bequest from the Myer family, the school built the Myer Music School in Domain Street, not far from the main grounds. I negotiated the right to practise in the rehearsal rooms, but we discovered a large collection of vinyl records that the Myer family had donated to the music school. The reproduction equipment in the listening room was excellent and the collection included blues, jazz, folk, Latin and other material that we spent hundreds of hours, many illicit, absorbing.

Dan and I took up the double bass at the same time in Year 10. We played in the school orchestra and smaller ensembles for concerts. He and I also played together in the music school, sometimes blues and ragtime, sometimes pure jazz improvisation. Our bass teacher was a Mr Morton, then a first desk bassist with the Melbourne Symphony Orchestra. Dan did better than I did – I didn't practise, mainly because of sports commitments, which Dan didn't have, and because, as I mentioned earlier this afternoon, I had difficulty with music reading and preferred to play by ear. Morton put up with me though and he loved coming to the orchestra's performances.

Dan was a well-known figure at school, wasn't he. Did you keep up your relationship with him?

Dan left the boarding house when his father moved to Melbourne in 1963, in my Year 11. Dan's father Sos bought a house in Domain Street, opposite the school. He adopted a more and more liberal and underground lifestyle as his folk singing developed and he started to play in some of the smaller coffee houses around South Yarra. I spent weekends with him and enjoyed the crowd of musicians, singers and artists that would drift through the house looking for a beer or a meal. These people made up a decent proportion of Melbourne bohemia at the time, including Asher Bilu, Adrian Rawlins and Roger Scales. This was when Bob Dylan first broke on Melbourne and I guess Dan was seen as some kind of Australian Dylan – young, talented, handsome, committed to his singing and art. Dan's parents were hands-off and didn't pay much attention to what we did, so we spent most of our time in the local pubs drinking flagon red and in clubs with our other friends.

Saturday mornings were always a treat. That was when Sos would make his weekly pilgrimage to the Victoria Market and to Jimmy Watson's wine bar, where he would buy gallons of cheap red and white wine, sherry and vodka, vegetables and other provisions. Saturday lunch was a loud and long celebration where I was introduced to the joy of friendship and sharing around the dining table. This had never happened in my family. I didn't know that this was the way most people lived.

On one of my weekends out late in Year 11, we went to the smartest beat club in Melbourne, called Pinocchio's, one Saturday. A band called The Flies was playing Beatles covers. I couldn't believe the intensity of the amplified sound, especially the bass, and how the band sounded pretty much like the Fab Four.

I think that's when you must have started to think about starting a band yourself? I remember a couple of school dances where you and a couple of other guys were featured.

Hearing The Flies did it. The following Monday I convinced Andrew Geh that we should start a band up. We recruited two day-boys, Peter Eddy and Guy Adamson, to be lead guitar and drummer. I would play bass but I didn't have an instrument and I knew there was no hope of getting any financial support from Ralph. So, I would tune down a standard guitar and play it through Peter's amplifier, and for performances, hire a separate amp from Allens Music Store. We called the band The Four Knights.

Our repertoire included covers of Shadows instrumentals, Cliff Richard songs, surf music, Beach Boys, Beatles, Merseyside tracks from Herman's Hermits, Gerry and the Pacemakers and Petula Clark, Billy Thorpe and the Aztecs, and the Kinks. We played mostly at house socials, school dances and parties and were auditioned by aspiring managers and producers. We didn't cover the Rolling Stones – they came along later than the other bands, and their pure R&B music wasn't something we could copy easily. Chuck Berry-style riffs were harder than they looked and needed a big bass sound, which we didn't have, plus a gnarly solo singer, which we also didn't have. The essence of emerging rock in those days was big amplifiers and heavy bass.

Practice was always a problem – we had no transport and it was hard for me and Andrew to get away from the boarding house without sponsorship. Our interest in the band was deeply frowned on by the housemaster and on a couple of occasions I was late back after rehearsal, which brought great wrath down on my head and did my reputation amongst those in authority no good. Being in a rock band wasn't the same thing as being in a choir, or a brass or even a jazz band: It was seen as working class, a bit dirty and very much not the done thing.

It was rare for someone like me, who was an established sports and academic figure, to crossover into what was seen as a nonconforming and dubious activity. But it was a huge amount of fun and might have developed into something interesting in a different world.

Can you tell me something about how your musical tastes developed during your life and how you've kept your musical interests up?

A big subject!

My love of music in all its forms has stayed with me as one of the moving forces and refuges in my life. It was launched by my mother.

She was my guide, my supporter, my critic and the creator of my tastes. Whenever I listen to music, or think about it, or book a performance, or play an instrument, I think of her and wish she could be here to see how the world has changed, and how I have changed.

She gave me my first record player, which she bought in Germany when she lived there. It was a Dual portable with detachable speakers which, for its time, produced fine sound.

I had a few LPs when Mary and I married, which I played regularly at our first apartment in Wattletree Road. I had become a fan of Haydn and I would listen to his symphonies at weekends, often tearful at the beauty, simplicity and grandeur of his compositions. I also had recordings of Creedence Clearwater, the Beatles, Bach, Beethoven and Mozart, the Rolling Stones, Sly and the Family Stone, Chick Corea, Linda Ronstadt and Pink Floyd.

I began collecting records, which I continued to do till the advent of the CD in 1982. I started buying used and new vinyl again as it came back into vogue in 2000 or so, and I now have many records. The collection is a mix of classic rock, jazz, pop and classical.

I was always a reproduction nerd. I've kept upgrading since the 1970s and I now have a system that includes a Linn Sondek LP3 turntable with Naim CD and amplification, Linn speakers and two Naim subwoofers.

Like everyone, I use music streaming most often now because of its quality, diversity and ease of use.

I wonder whether I'll ever be able to catalogue my vinyl and CDs, much less listen to all of them, but I do keep trying.

I can still turn on good music and find myself in another world. I don't spend enough time playing my instruments – I'm not good at organising my time to allow that, but I need to keep trying. I've learned how to record music digitally using Garage Band, so maybe I can do more of that too if I better structure my time. Overall though I have to recognise now that I can't get done all I'd like to and that I have to make hard choices and learn to be happy with less.

How do you feel about live music?

I love it. I sit down at the end of every year and try to pencil in the diary with performances. In 2024 Donna and I went to the Adelaide Writers and Arts Festivals after years of indecision and stayed with friends. Finding the best performances is always a bit of a lottery at festivals but we did OK.

One musical gem in my life has been the Sydney International Piano Competition. Virginia has been connected to the competition since its inception in the '70s and has been chair of the board since 2018. I've been a keen follower and went to Sydney in 2024, her last year as chair, to watch the finals and keep Virginia company. It was a happy and charming experience. She gave a speech as the board's representative in the Opera House concert hall immediately after the awards were announced and did so with quiet dignity. She was much feted during the post-award celebrations and will leave the board as a successful and much-admired director. Well done, Virginia.

So how would you describe your current musical taste?

Varied, extensive and curious. I hoped to attach an inventory of my recording collection to this, but that may not happen. I love the classical repertoire for the most part, but I don't listen much to the avant-garde or atonal, like Arnold Schönberg, John Cage, Pierre Schaeffer or Philip Glass.

Bach is the transcendent genius to my ears; to hear him well played by sympathetic and devoted artists like András Schiff is a joy. His melodic invention, restraint and the phenomenal complexity of his counterpoint is bewilderingly beautiful.

Jazz, especially bebop, and particular artists including Gillespie, Coltrane, Jamal, Shearing, the New York Jazz Quartet, Nina Simone, Monk, Chet Baker and Ornette Coleman, has always captured me.

The greatest names in popular music for me were Warren Zevon, the Byrds, the Steve Miller Band, Dire Straits, Boston, the Stones and Beatles of course, Pink Floyd, the Who, ZZ Top, the Bee Gees, Crowded

House, Hendrix, David Byrne and Talking Heads, Sharon Shannon, the Whitlams, the Ramones, Ian Dury and the Blockheads, Dylan, Paul Simon in his many incarnations, and Velvet Underground. I know I've missed plenty of names there.

I haven't had much joy from more recent pop, my age obviously being a factor, which I've found repetitive, over-sampled and often harsh. I don't like rap and hip-hop. But there are some modern standouts including Lady Gaga, Pink and Adele, who do cross boundaries for me. Taylor Swift means little to my ears. So, while I haven't explored every corner of the musical universe, I know a lot of it.

My hi-fi system is located on the way to my office and if I turn it on as I go by, I know I'm feeling happy. If I don't, I know I need to do something about it.

Out Into the Wide World

So your school experience ended in 1965. How did you feel when you left the boarding house?

My end-of-school feelings are mixed, Jimmy. I probably shouldn't have spent the additional year at school. It didn't expand my academic horizons, or any other horizons really.

I was happy to be on the move at last, but of course uncertain about my future. I was enrolled in the law school at Melbourne University and Trinity College where some of my school mates were headed, so at least I knew where I'd be during the next four years. But it was like being a caged animal released into the wild or a prisoner leaving jail: packing up the slender detritus of my school years was sad. There were other blows. My parents didn't come to any of the events that marked my transition, like my final school assembly, my last chapel service, my last Perry House dinner. But by then I didn't expect it.

I also knew that there were mates I'd never see again. I did maintain some contact with Dan after I left school but our lives were going in a different direction then, so it was just a matter of time till the mateship fizzled out. Dan and his Wild Cherries guys had a reunion concert every few years and I always tried to get along to see him play. By then he and the band were tired and frayed and it was never a good experience.

The misplacement of leaving was soon behind me though, as I had to go to Canberra immediately after the numerous traditional at-home leaving parties thrown by wealthy parents of friends, to attend

Virginia's wedding to Martin Braden. I then hopped a plane to rejoin my parents in Brussels for the summer – the first time I had seen them for too long a time.

I was, finally, on my own two feet.

Did you stay in touch with the family while you were at boarding school?

As I said earlier, contact was occasional and real family stopped after boarding started. Relationships need to be nurtured and in order to be nurtured, they need common causes and common interests, and regular face-to-face contact. As time went on, those connections didn't flourish, meaning that the substance of my family relationships became diluted and repetitive and backward looking. The reality was that all of us had invented and lived separate lives by the time I left school. I would never have thought of calling Virginia or Penny up for a cuppa or a meal together. What would we have talked about? Luckily for me, my relationship with Virginia has grown and deepened since my divorce and we are now great mates and share much of life together.

Do you think you benefited overall from being left in Melbourne?

I did miss a male mentor, but this would probably not have been greatly different had I lived in Canberra with my parents, given my father's professional commitment and unavailability.

Boring as it is to say, the scars of the early lack of attention and love in my life remained, and I am still, in my seventies, trying to understand their impact. But this would not have been much affected had I stayed with the family. You can take my efforts with these recollections as evidence that the quest goes on, although no bitterness or resentment remains.

I'm grateful to my parents for having turned me into a Melburnian. There is no question that it helped my academic results, enriched my friendships and provided more opportunity than I would have had otherwise.

Your attendance at Virginia's wedding in 1965 and the trip to rejoin Ralph and Dorothy in Belgium must have been a wonderful experience for an eighteen-year-old just released into the world?

Virginia's wedding was delightful. She was a truly radiant bride but I'm sure she felt the absence of my parents. If ever I resented my father it would have been then. There must have been a way for him at least to have got my mother to Australia but it didn't happen.

Belgium was full of growing-up experiences. Ralph was the Australian ambassador. Belgium was a kingdom, with a flourishing royal family and a nobility not much different in style to the one in the UK. So, when he was called to present his ambassadorial credentials, in the form of a mandate on parchment signed by Queen Elizabeth, he was escorted to the palace by a guard of mounted cavalry.

Ralph and Dorothy had chosen a large house in the Avenue du Chili, in which I was given a comfortable room on the top floor. It was furnished in a grand, Louis XVI style with much marble, gold leaf and shellac.

The house was equipped with domestic servants and a chauffeur available at any time to whisk us to this shop or that event.

Dorothy immediately began a training course for Penny and me in Belgian etiquette, which we would find essential at the many parties and weekend visits we would make during the holiday. The most important gesture for a man was the baise-main, or kiss to a woman's hand, as a replacement for a normal handshake. This had to be executed daintily, with minimum pressure, eyes fixed on the recipient, bowing slightly, but on no account to involve actual contact between the lips and the hand. There were also the conventions of greeting in French, how to sit correctly, how to manage food from a serving platter to one's plate and how to sip wine politely.

We shopped at fashionable malls, dined in style at fine restaurants and attended several diplomatic occasions, including a tremendous commemoration ball for the 150th anniversary of the Battle of Waterloo and a New Year's eve black tie dinner at the residence of the British Ambassador, where the women retired, gracefully, to allow the men to smoke cigars and drink port as had been done at such dinners for hundreds of years. We had been trained to dance Scottish eightsome reels, which we performed at midnight. We were also invited to weekend parties by Belgian industrialists interested in investing in Australia, attended show-jumping competitions and went for long drives in the country.

My mother organised a party for the young children of diplomats and friends at our house where I fell in love with an heiress but was crisply discouraged by her mother for the obvious reason that I had no money. And Australia could have been Mars.

We also went back to Shonried in Switzerland to ski as a family. Somehow Ralph managed to re-establish contact with Madelaine Frautschi at our old chalet, and we booked to stay there. Of course, with the growth of the ski industry and a lot of hard work and Swiss frugality, the family had rebuilt the old chalet and so we didn't need the cows to heat us from below anymore. Ski equipment was much safer and smarter, and grooming of runs was common, so the experience was a delight.

I had grown up and I was a strong presence on the slopes. Madelaine was interested in my progress and took me often for informal lessons on tougher terrain. She taught me to prepare my skis properly, to assess the conditions carefully and not to be frightened of pushing my skiing envelope.

It was easy for me to make friends in that carefree place. I struck up a conversation with a couple one day, an American journalist from AAP and his strikingly lovely Italian wife. Soon I was skiing with them regularly. Before they left the village, they invited me to stay with them in Rome on my way back to Australia. She was captivating and I had no hesitation, because of her, and because I'd never been in Rome before. My Roman visit was everything you could wish for – delicious pasta in sun-filled piazzas, my first fresh, crisp and exuberant Italian wines, my first taste of crazy Italian traffic, monuments, galleries, cathedrals and the melodic, up-and-down Italian language.

We swore to stay in touch, knowing we never would.

The Japanese have an expression, "ichi go, ichi e", which was taught to me by a Japanese lawyer I met much later in life.

Ichi go, ichi e can be translated as, "once, a meeting," and "as in this moment, an opportunity." What this is meant to tell us is that each meeting, everything we experience, is a unique treasure that will never be repeated in the same way again. So if we let it slip away without enjoying it, the moment will be lost forever.

For many years I believed that my lawyer friend, who was about to return to Japan, was telling me that our friendship was once-only and could never continue because our lives were destined to travel along much different lines. That made me sad.

Now I know this wasn't what he meant. He was telling me how much he valued and would treasure our time, not dismissing the possibility that we could remain friends. I wish I had realised that earlier.

Did you go anywhere else around Europe?

There are two side trips I remember. You need to recall that this was a time when I would wake up dying to be up and at the world: I was eighteen and bulletproof; I'd spent years in an unlovely boarding institution and the freedom was thrilling.

I was keen to learn about European art, so I visited different parts of Belgium to find special paintings, structures and sculpture. I organised a series of day trips to Bruges, Ghent, Liege, Saumur and Antwerp by train – easy to do because none were more than a couple of hours away and my French was good. My main targets were the sculptures of Michelangelo and the Flemish school painters Jan van Eyck, Rogier van der Weyden, Hans Memling and Hieronymus Bosch. I also visited some of the better-known Flanders World War One battlefield sites around Ypres including Hill 60.

And the other one?

Well, it was a kind of initiation. Ralph and Dorothy knew a wealthy French couple who had a lovely, traditional apartment close to the Arc de Triomphe in Paris in the Avenue Friedland and arranged for me to visit them for a week. I wasn't at all sure what to expect but Ralph told me in clear terms that I was to behave myself and that the main aim of the visit was to improve my formal French and get to know Paris.

My hosts had a daughter of around twenty-five who, I was told, would also be there, and that she would arrange some evening outings. Intriguing. Ralph handed me an envelope of cash just before I left to catch the train, telling me how generous an allocation this was and that on no account would he send any more if I overspent. I had no clue what things cost in Paris but figured, incorrectly, that I'd be covered against most contingencies.

I duly arrived at Avenue Friedland and met the family, including the somewhat attractive daughter who, from the get-go, I caught staring at me intently, although I wasn't sure what her intent was. Let's call her Marielle.

Ralph's friends were true to their word: all communications were in highly formal French, during which I was constantly corrected because of my slangy grammar and Swiss French accent. Swiss French, they said, was bastardised and I must listen to them very carefully to ensure that I eradicated all those low-brow intonations from my speech, or else be ignored by Parisians.

On my first night, Marielle took me to the Comédie-Française, an historic playhouse like the Shakespeare theatre in Stratford, which performed the works of Molière, Racine and Corneille. She suggested that we dress formally, as Ralph had suggested I bring a dinner jacket. I can't recall the play but I had trouble following the seventeenth century French. The theatre was perfect: enormous, built in the grand manner, soft, dark and plush.

After dinner we went to a small restaurant in the Latin quarter and it was then I realised my supply of cash was already under stress. The problem was this was a very Parisian place, hard to get into and so more than usually expensive. In spite of all that and my gathering anxiety about bankruptcy, the meal, and the evening, were charming.

The next day was solid touring on my own, which I loved. I saw the Louvre for the first astonishing time and unlike today, where it's jammed, I was able to see the exhibits I wanted to. I visited the Orangerie, several modern art museums, Montmartre, Notre Dame, La Tour Eiffel.

Then that evening, Marielle asked me whether I'd like to go to a Parisian boîte, meaning night club, to have a drink. It was becoming clear more and more that the family was connected because you needed to be a member, and if not, inspected carefully before admission – like Studio 54 became in New York except that this was on a much more intimate scale.

Although I was a hick at the time, I knew enough to understand that this was a place where French rock and arts royalty gathered, and Marielle pointed out several well-known stars including Johnny Hallyday, Sylvie Vartan and Mireille Mathieu. And I was buying, at astronomical prices, drinks for Marielle and myself, and by the end of a brilliant evening, I was broke.

The next day I had to call Ralph for support, which he provided with exceptional reluctance, but I was able to take a young American woman, arranged by Marielle, to the movies the next night without incident.

I still remember this passage with appreciation but embarrassment as well, of course. It was one of the things that convinced me that I'd never take a job that would put me under financial pressure. And one of the reasons I find myself over-generous to others: so they have no reason to feel any financial discrimination or awkwardness.

Law School and Trinity College

OK, so now you're on the way back to Melbourne after your idyll in Brussels, which by the way, I reckon you were lucky to have.

I agree with you, Jim. The Brussels stay was wonderful in every way, but finally I had to board the plane home to Melbourne to face real life. I thought it was the end of diplomatic privilege, but there were a couple of later experiences that allowed me to revisit that world.

I've asked myself whether the unearned luxury of the diplomatic life changed me, and whether I'd become arrogant or haughty or entitled as you might expect. I don't think so. I lapped it all up but I didn't believe I was entitled to it and it didn't turn me into someone obnoxious. You're welcome to disagree.

One thing it did do is heighten my fashion sense. I collected a wardrobe in Belgium that was middle-of-the-road there but that in Melbourne looked super-modern and classy. Even though I had a less-than-slender figure, I was happy to dress on the edge of acceptance. I wasn't unwilling to turn heads, especially female ones, and to be known for it, although not for the first time it presented me as different and unconventional, not Melbourne.

So now you're in law school and Trinity College. How was your induction?

I can't remember where I stayed before uni started. Maybe I came back just in time for O week – orientation week – where freshmen were invited in to look at the university, explore their faculty, be recruited by all manner of societies and causes, and drink. I think that was it, and that Trinity took in we first year low-lives early to give us refuge and some sense of stability.

I remember O week perfectly. The awkward meetings with old school mates whose lives were certain not to fit with mine anymore; getting to know Naughtons Hotel opposite Trinity College, which was to be a comfort and haven in my uni years and well beyond; the embarrassment of trying to get talking with women; the exhilaration and fear of freedom and responsibility; the scent of '60s anarchy and revolution in the air; and the depression into which I plunged when I was shown to my first quarters by a tired and rude porter. Many of my school mates had been given cars but for me this was an impossibility.

You remember that I was a non-resident at Trinity when you were there so I have some idea what it must have been like to live in. I remember that college facilities were a bit grim in those days, weren't they?

Indeed they were. The place was divided into wings where you stayed according to strict seniority rules. I had been allocated to Clarke's, on the northern college boundary. The room was in every way but name a cell. It would have measured perhaps three metres by two; it was dingy and dirty, with scuffed lino floors, a bed with a creaky and sagging wire base, a stained horsehair mattress from the '40s and a battered chest of drawers with a cold water tap and sink next to it. There was an ablution block fifty metres down the hall with open showers, stained sinks and chipped and stained dunnies.

Next stop was my study, on the second level of the same wing. Same situation: cold, hard and empty. I had no money for furnishings or carpet so that's the way the room stayed.

My study mate turned out to be a boring and cheerless individual with whom I spent as little time as possible.

One thing I did manage to finance was an old but still workable radiogram of 1940s design. I used it to play the few records I had, including the incomparable Cream, and to listen on short-wave to Ashes cricket broadcasts from the UK, which got me through many a night of study.

Was it hard to settle in after the early days?

I don't remember it being a problem. I was independent after years of looking out for myself so it was a familiar process. Sport helped. It wasn't long though before I began to meet some more interesting people and form friendships that would last, in some cases, for life.

You remember I was put in the college rowing eight as soon as term began, which meant training and dinner with fellow oarsmen most nights. Having come from Melbourne Grammar where the sport was organised and rowers had to show respect and at least give the impression of trying, college rowing was anarchy. We boated out of the Melbourne University Boat Club (MUBC), an ancient and smelly shed on the Yarra full of dust, rubbish, rats and dirty, discarded towels and singlets.

The season was less than four weeks end-to-end, so training was frenetic, and generally crews became slower rather than faster. Our coach was Chester Keon-Cohen, who had a reputation as a formidable MUBC stroke but whose method was long on shouting and short on patience. Two of the senior members of the crew, Bill Stokes, whom I knew as a relative of MGS friend Lawrence Stokes, and Ian Galbraith, would regularly arrive drunk and stop the boat to spew after a few minutes of training. They were fond of telling the freshmen the number of ounces of beer they'd each consumed during the day, which would be more than 200, or in excess of twenty standard pots. It was obvious that we had no hope, and so it proved, when Ormond College stroked by Peter Nicholson beat us in the heat by three lengths.

But it was worth it for the post-boat race piss-up, a truly memorable night, where oarsmen and hangers-on would visit the other colleges one by one to finish off their barrels.

In those days, a party would be classified as a niner, meaning a nine-gallon keg, or an eighteen or some cases more. Much honour was to be had for being the one who drank the last beer drawn from a particular barrel. No one drank from glasses. You were expected to have a handle, meaning a pewter pot, which would lie in state on your mantel or windowsill from one occasion to the next.

Did you get into much strife with the College authorities?

Ian Galbraith, my crewmate of alcoholic disposition, often recruited me to raid the college kitchens for post-pub suppers and on one occasion we were caught astride a high kitchen window by the college porter Sid, which meant an appearance the following morning before the warden Robin Sharwood. We were hungover and he was bored, so it was a quick and painless encounter, but from then on I made sure to stock food from Hall before any major social event.

Other than that, I went through Trinity essentially at peace with the administration.

In those days, you had to wear a black academic gown to Hall, where meals were served, and there was a start time but you weren't frowned on if you were late – it was just that the food ran out pretty quickly.

I had some great Trinity mates. Ian Alexander had been with me in Perry; he was very bright and doing first year medicine but turned into a ferocious drinker. I'd be in my study doing something and there would be a bang on the door:

"Who's that?"

"Alex."

"Sorry mate, but I'm tied up at the minute."

"No you're not."

Reluctantly... "What did you want?"

"Wanna get pissed?"

"Thought you'd never ask."

That would be the end of that day.

Alex was also one of my companions during the pass and honours course that Melbourne Uni students would attempt. A pass was drinking one seven-ounce beer at every pub from the uni down Swanston Street to Flinders, Flinders to Elizabeth and up Elizabeth to Nortons, all in less than ninety minutes. It sounded easy but there were twenty-four pubs along that route then and it was all we could do to finish. We found ourselves in some dingy Carlton house after the event more dead than alive and managed to make it back to the college the next morning. We ceased to have any interest in the honours course.

I became friends with several Ormond College inmates, including Peter Nicholson, Ross Robson (who later became a Victorian Appeals Court judge), Bob Cann (who became a wealthy Perth architect and property developer) and the cricketer and MGS head Paul Sheahan. We would meet to drink and listen to music at the Ormond Beehive unit's common room. Our favourite band was the Animals and our favourite song, which seemed to summarise the temper of the times, "We Gotta Get Out of This Place". Peter soon formed a relationship with the daughter of the Ormond warden and had moved her into his unit and was rarely seen thereafter.

I was finding my feet fast and beginning to adjust to a new, looser and more challenging life.

There was a bit of an ex-MGS ex-GGS flavour to the Trinity residents, wasn't there, but there was a decent mix of blokes from a lot of other places. Did you find it hard to work things out socially?

My core mates were from MGS and Scotch, guys I knew or had competed against at school. But because I spent a lot of time out of the college doing rowing training I wasn't as tight with as many as others were. My besties were Ian Alexander and Rob Buchanan, who went into law practice after a long period working as a labourer in France and doing loads of drugs. For a long time we didn't do much except go to movies and drink. Rob was a car nut and had a lovely old MG TC, and Ian bought a Triumph 650 Bonneville motorbike, which he fell off all the time and almost killed himself once. He sold it to buy his fiancée a wedding ring, and sure enough their marriage lasted about a year, so he lost the wife, the ring and the bike in one hit.

So did the college break up into groupings at all?

Yes. There were roughly four: the swots; the theologs, who were members of an Anglican theological training centre established within the college, almost 100% of whom were gay and who led frantic and risky social lives; the bohemians, who dressed in beads and kaftans and were stoned most of the time; and the regulars who didn't care to affiliate with much, worked reasonably hard, listened to the Beach Boys, the Beatles and Bob Dylan, played billiards and snooker, made the owners of Naughtons Hotel wealthy and played kick-to-kick footy on the oval. I was closer to them than any other group although I dined regularly and exhaustingly with the more convivial theologs, usually at the Clare Castle Hotel in Carlton.

I didn't know really what it meant to be gay but I soon learned. Several of my MGS mates came out in college, which in those days was still a dangerous thing to do. Even though the university was tolerant, society as a whole wasn't and employers weren't either.

There were several quite brilliant gay Trinity men whose later careers were damaged by prejudice. The theologs were the most expressive and reckless gay men; somehow their access to vestments, incense and crucifixes, and the '60s notion of no limits, bred the most drunken parties and the hottest affairs, which were all public. A number of them subsequently converted to Catholicism. I always wondered what attracted them. Maybe it was the more voluptuous church-wear or the Latin.

But you had to buckle down to learning at some stage I guess.

I was hard-working for a time. I attended most of my first-year lectures, given by some profs who were excellent and some who were hopeless.

I didn't warm to law as some did. Another way of putting it is that law didn't become my home or my church. I found some subjects interesting but many boring. Whenever I think of administrative law my vision goes grey. But my background and family expectations, and my dislike of controversy meant that I saw myself as well and truly stuck in law. Imagine if I'd announced that I'd switched to music or fine arts – it would have been a bloodbath.

First-year law was like a Formula 1 testing circuit at the beginning of a season. No one knew who would do well and who wouldn't. People you thought would shine didn't, and people you thought slow would become high honours students for no obvious reason. Legal aptitude was, to use another sporting analogy, like golf – you either had it or you didn't. No matter how hard some people worked, they might get some lower honours but they would never top classes.

How would you assess your own performance?

Remember what I was saying earlier about you being my honesty man? Don't forget that this was the '60s, where you felt your obligation was to be socially progressive, to be experimental, not to be of the establishment and not to appear too career oriented. I spent a lot of time reading, thinking, watching progressive movies, listening to edgy music, going to concerts, figuring out women, attending demonstrations, photographing for the uni magazine *Farrago*, raising cash pumping petrol, as well as trying to maintain a top-level rowing career. So there were many ways to spend time doing anything but work.

There was one exam per subject per year in November, no assignments during the year, no checking of lecture attendance, no progress monitoring, so you could do nothing for two and a half terms and then give it a mighty crack.

I did some work in first year but I didn't elect to go into the honours stream, which I could have done, but it involved extra lectures that rowing prevented me from attending. In second year, 1967, I spent nearly four months training and racing overseas with my St Catherines four and arrived back only a few weeks before the exams and barely scraped through.

Third year brought reasonable honours, and in final year I had a collection of firsts and high seconds and finished quite high up in the class list, so better than I deserved.

In terms of aptitude, I would say I had it but I didn't enjoy or embrace it. I was never destined for the High Court Bench.

In the end it didn't matter that much because if you were a graduate from Trinity it was easy to find Articles of Clerkship at a good firm, unlike today when everything is so competitive.

Did you find college to be a success for you?

College was pretty much as it was meant to be: food, accommodation, work, independence, women, mostly well-chosen friendships, fun and exposure to a much broader cross-section of ideas, music, politics, people and racial and ethnic difference than school offered. I never fell out with the college authorities, I got on with my fellow residents and I was reasonably well-regarded, I think, although I'm sure there were times when my anxious self would surface and that would ruffle the composure of some social occasion or other. Like I'd been at school, I was known as a talented and somewhat confronting outlier.

There were times, as there had been for me as a school boarder, when I was lonely, or if not lonely, solitary. I had to look after myself. I arranged all my travel, holidays, clothing, books, communications, sport, excursions, training, diet, work and relationships. Contacts with my parents were thinning out as well. Dad had been posted from Belgium to West Germany by that time so Canberra as a refuge was unavailable.

My allowance from Ralph was reasonable but not generous, so I had to work during term as well as during holiday periods. Pumping gas was the most flexible and best paid work during term, when you could do night shifts. In those days every car was filled by an attendant; these days, none.

I also took on serious jobs during my uni vacations. These included truck driving; working as a builder's labourer digging piling caissons on the site of a new city office building; being a tobacco salesman in

Damman's, a well-known and fashionable tobacconist; working as a cement mixer operator with the piling company then known as Frankipile; and winding up with a period as a piano salesman in Allens Music Store in Collins Street. I got that job because initially I was hired as a delivery labourer on an Allens truck, and one of the managers caught me playing a piano in the Allens warehouse during my lunchbreak and he offered me a sales job. I spent a lovely three months trying to seduce mainly old ladies into buying a piano. I also knew how to manage the documentation of credit arrangements known as hire purchase, which seemed beyond the capacity of Allens' other employees. This was a whole lot easier and cleaner than being on a truck or working in the building industry.

Overall, college was a good platform for my tertiary study and gave me more campus time, more connection with the uni community, a broader network and some life structure that I would not otherwise have had. I'm grateful to my father, as I was for the MGS experience, for giving all those possibilities to me.

The Sixties

Was there anything exceptional about having been to uni in the '60s?

Well, it deserved to be fabled. It was a unique and fascinating time, when so many ideas were pouring forth, where there were social asymmetries, divides and schisms everywhere, like parallel universes.

Because the '60s thing began to make itself noticed seriously just as I walked in the uni gates, it seemed normal in a way – the questioning, the experimentation, the breakdown of institutional respect and order. It seemed the way I would have expected universities and students to have been. But life was radically changed, in ways that were sometimes superficial and sometimes serious. The bush didn't change much, but the cities did.

The kind of experience that students would have had, say, in Paris or London or New York was of course different and sharper than ours. Those unis invented all the now well-known social movements that created the chaotic and the envied, but to some degree mythical, '60s student lifestyle.

In the US you had the hippies, yuppies, Students for a Democratic Society, Black Panthers, Weathermen, Timothy Leary psychedelics, Haight–Ashbury, communes and especially the broad and multi-layered anti-Vietnam War movement. Music from the US, played constantly here, was similarly resonant of the counterculture, drugs, free love, eastern mysticism and rebellion. In Paris in 1968, students literally captured the city and created one of the most serious political crises in the history of

France. It was mostly about personal independence and hatred of the political elites.

Students challenged university administrations in the US and Europe over curricula, teaching, grading and admissions. This had never happened before and boards of trustees and vice-chancellors responded with fear and ineptitude. The changes made in response were startling. When I became a student at the University of Virginia in 1976, the impacts were clear. There were formal, published reviews of professors' performances; exams could be taken at any time and unsupervised under an honour system; affirmative action programs for Black and underprivileged students were in place, students found themselves on advisory boards and course content became softer and more socially oriented.

So where do you think all this came from?

The prime drivers of the ferment were an intense desire for change driven by distaste for a stifling and borderline criminal political establishment, and a newly aggressive and courageous press.

There were '60s philosophers whose writings became emblematic of the time, like Marcuse, Leary and McLuhan, but although I tried to understand them I couldn't, and pretty much no one else could either. So, there were many pots boiling over at the same time, and it was hard to see what made sense and what didn't.

Lyndon B. Johnson, US president from 1963 to 1969 – the heart of the period – was uniquely unqualified to respond: he was an old-time Texan Democrat-fixer, who had a good heart and worked hard for civil rights but escalated troop numbers in Vietnam to mad levels and lied about most things to do with the war. It was the war, and the depiction of the war on TV particularly, that exposed the corruption and dishonesty of the political class, rather like the Covid pandemic has done in this time. The exposure of this fallibility by the newly aggressive media created a feedback loop that at one time, when mixed with breakdown of law and order in Black neighbourhoods, looked like bringing the US close to social breakdown.

Just before my 1967 rowing crew left for the US, we received an invitation to race in Chicago. Although we were only dimly aware of this at the time, that summer, known as the "long, hot summer", saw the most violent and bloody urban rioting that had ever occurred in the US. During that summer, 158 riots erupted in urban communities across the country. Most shared the same triggering event: a dispute between Black communities and police that escalated to violence. During those convulsive months, the massive social unrest resulted in 83 deaths and 17,000 arrests. In Detroit, which experienced the bloodiest of the uprisings, there were 43 deaths, 7,200 arrests and more than 2,500 buildings looted, damaged or destroyed in five days of rioting. The managers of our team decided that the risks we faced going into urban Chicago – the site of the even bloodier riots of 1968 – were too high and the invitation was declined.

Some of these ideas and organisations drifted here in diluted form, and some took root powerfully, like the anti-war movement.

Demonstrations were regular on most Australian campuses, but on the whole I would say that our lives were less affected than those of our US and European cousins because of distance, time and slow communications, and also because Australian students as a whole were simply more conservative and slower to understand what it was all about.

Everything has changed now, hasn't it, in media, communication, Artificial Intelligence, political campaigning.

Yes. People today have no idea what it would mean to be without social media as an information resource. Everything today is immediate and nothing is accountable. Then, you had to read the paper, or listen to the radio news, and think. You had a chance to form an independent view free of social media sledging, wokeness, correctness and all the other pernicious apparatus used by social controllers. People would have been horrified by the idea, for example, that the views of sensible men could be cut down by accusations of male toxicity, or that anyone could be de-platformed.

How about the phrase Dylan used in "Ballad of a Thin Man" where he wondered how much Mr Jones really knew about what was going on around him. That question summed up the origin and strange beauty of the '60s in one line. It alone justified Dylan's Nobel Prize.

I do, and it was the way we all felt. Dylan in many ways was our voice and the distiller of the temper of the times. I think it would have been a lesser age without him; less separate, less clear, less satisfying.

Absolutely. But can I say a bit more about the music of that time? I've told you something about the '60s experience in describing our rowing adventures in 1967, and I mentioned music and some of the bands I liked. Music and the '60s were inseparable. They were each other in a way. There had been music and musicians who were popular before, like Frank Sinatra or Billie Holiday or Louis Armstrong, but never before had there been anything like the Beatles. They were loud, good looking, funny, prolific, brilliantly musical, lovable and seemingly inexhaustible innovators. They introduced an era of fun, fashion, style and adoration that had never existed before. They created the conditions for an explosion of other, wonderful bands and solo artists, and that in turn allowed the creation of the Woodstock rock festival, the recorded music industry to mushroom, the insane and groundbreaking design that went into covers, ads, film and TV, music journalism, the concept album, rock musicals and the propulsion of the political and artistic counterculture. *Sgt. Pepper* can claim to have been the most startling, original and unexpected collection of music in history. All of that allowed us to separate ourselves from the older generation who, clearly, would never understand what was happening.

To me, the current mania for artists like Taylor Swift is hard to understand: I find the music repetitive and dull; it can't be compared to anything produced by, say, the Beatles, or the Who, Rolling Stones, Pink Floyd or

Queen. It's like watching surfers ride waves created by a machine: pretty, perhaps, but anodyne, riskless, manufactured and predictable.

Good to get that one off the chest, Jimmy.

Did you worry about the Vietnam draft then?

Not as much as I should have. It was one of the flashpoints for the anti-war folks of course. I took a simple approach. Many of my mates ran to join the Citizen Military Forces or the Air Force or Navy Reserve, and committed to years of training and attendance as a way out. I simply let the draft happen and luckily my birthday marble didn't drop. Home free. I'm not sure what would have happened to me as a draftee with Ralph in the Embassy in Vietnam, but as it turned out, I didn't need to worry and nor did he.

Overall, the tight-arsed and uncompromising Australian conservatism from which I suffered so much as a child and schoolboy did a lot of dying during my four uni years. So, I am forever in debt to my US and European student counterparts.

When Donna and I lived in France on and off in the early 2000s, we met several men and women who claimed to have been on the barricades in Paris during the 1968 student riots, which froze Paris for months. They were former communists/unionists and spent most of their time worrying that the government would take away their pensions, which were princely and had vested at an early age, not much over fifty. Anyway, it was there that I saw how much time had stripped away their fervour, their radicalism, their belief in equality. They were just old men and women, like me, dreaming of a time, long lost, when they challenged the world. For me as a graduate of that time, to see them so reduced was a disappointment.

And what was the feeling in your guts about it all, when you were in the middle of it?

I was happy. You must have been too, Jimmy, because you went through it as well. Suddenly everyone over forty was listening to us rather than us to them. Ideas about society, the media, politics, discipline, music, celebrity, the value of experience, governance, the possibility of young people succeeding in any environment, education and especially politics were changing fast and we knew that the world would never be the same.

No one believed government leaders because of the Pentagon Papers released by Daniel Ellsberg, the revelations in the US press about the brutality of the Vietnam War and the perfidy of Richard Nixon and Kissinger. I decided that most of my professors were not worth listening to, so I refused to attend lectures in most of my subjects in my third and fourth years in the law school. It didn't seem to affect my results much either way. But it did give me more time for reading, going to see movies and Naughtons Hotel.

Did you develop any bad habits as a freshman?

Well, of course I did. I experimented with soft drugs now and then, mostly because of music, and occasionally psychedelics, but because I was training most of the time I had to be careful. Nothing much else really, apart from alcohol. I developed a liking for short sweet mini-cigars, which in those days you could smoke anywhere, but that didn't last past first year.

My relationships with women were off-and-on. Until Mary came along in 1968 I had had no regular partner. Having been a boarder at school where there was little contact with women other than a highly regimented dancing class and no one to counsel me as to how to treat the opposite sex, my approaches to women were ignorant, uncomfortable and largely unsuccessful. So, I had never understood what girls looked for in blokes and how to deliver it. I fell in love now and then but I believed that I was unattractive, and this coupled with my anxiety convinced me that women would never naturally gravitate to me. I learned years later that they were usually interested but immediately saw my barriers and diffidence going up and decided not to waste their time. Later, in my thirties and forties, I was often pursued and sometimes stalked, by women of different ages, which took me entirely by surprise.

Intermission

"Jim, it's getting late and I've trespassed on your goodwill too much for one day. Let's visit the winery and the cellar, and find ourselves a good port."

"Would love to," Jim says.

"And we can talk about more important things, perhaps."

Jim and I walk slowly down the hill from the house to the winery shed where Donna's brother Darren built me an above-ground, insulated and cooled wine cellar. The garden looks soft, alive and mysterious at this time of night, and we can hear deer honking up the hill. I swing open the cellar door and Jim looks around with shining eyes. It's Aladdin's cave to him.

"Interesting!" Jim says. "How many bottles have you got in here?"

"Around three thousand and, unfortunately, climbing. I'm a tragic. I can't help myself. My cellar is a bit like my life – the collection has been opportunistic and not especially well-planned! But a delight to be in anyway."

I decided to make gin about six months ago without knowing anything about it really except that the aim is to generate a mix of flavours that complement each other and taste good with tonic and citrus. So, I bought 100 litres of 90% proof pharmaceutical grade ethanol and some packs of botanicals, and started infusing and mixing. I've never liked commercial gins, which I often find hard and bitter; the more fashionable and expensive the harder they are to drink. So I decided to use familiar aromas that would be recognisable, different and pleasing, like vanilla, lime, rose, blossom, coriander and of course juniper. I gave it a pale violet/rose colour and, lo and behold, it was delicious.

I grab a bottle of gin and we wander back to the house. Wombats rustle around at the edge of the forest. We go back out to the terrace with a couple of big glasses, some slices of lime, ice and a few bottles of Fever Tree tonic. By now the stars are out and the Southern Cross is blazing. The skies clear toward the end of the year; the Milky Way runs north–south, and Sirius and Canopus are directly overhead, with Orion slanting a bit north-west and the Southern Cross forty-five degrees to the south-east.

"Seriously good drink, Johnnie," says Jim after a big swallow. "Never tasted a gin like that before."

"Take a bottle with you when you go. I'd like some feedback."

"How about two?"

We start chatting again about not very much, and try to identify a few constellations. I've always been interested in the universe and how it ticks. How the system of planets works, why night skies change the way they do, when the solstices and equinoxes are, how the earth spins in a wobbly way and how time is affected by mass and altitude as Einstein thought but no one believed until caesium clocks were invented. So I look at how the spot where the sun sets changes during the seasons, and I know exactly how far south and north of west the setting point reaches because the back-lit tree line is like a fine graph, and I think about how early civilisations would have been able to predict seasons.

"These evening skies always absorb me," I say. We're lucky that Melbourne lies directly behind Mount Victoria and we don't get as much light pollution as other close-to-city places would. The sunsets are always bright and the cloudscapes are always sharp in clear weather.

The trick is to suspend time and just let the beauty of what we see sink in. I can't do that as much as I'd like because I let my head get filled with rubbish and I let myself be captured by my mobile phone or something else useless. But I always try.

"More gin?"

After one last glance at the burning sky, we drift back down to the lounge with an old port. I'm not sure how long Jimmy's going to last because he's slowing down now. Then I see Jim's eyes closing and I realise that it's over for today.

"Jimmy, come on, mate, time for bed. We can have another crack in the morning."

"Yep, I'm done!" Jim says, wobbling to his feet.

I walk him down the long gallery that joins the lounge to the rest of the house, and show him to his room.

"Get up whenever it suits you, mate."

Jim walks up to me and puts his arms gently around me. I'm speechless. It's the last thing I expected.

"I enjoyed that," he says. "Thanks for telling me some of your secrets. More tomorrow, I hope."

***

The next day dawns bright and hopeful. Our bedroom is on the east side of the house so I'm usually up with the sun. Like the western skyline, I know where the sun rises at different times of the year and I always look out to make sure it's in the right spot.

I wake Jim with a big cup of New York breakfast tea, which steams because even in October it's cold here in the mornings.

Then I pull a side of bacon that I smoked a few days ago out of the fridge, some eggs from a farm just down the road and a loaf of fresh sourdough. It's not long before the bacon's sizzling and spitting in the pan. Jim wanders into the kitchen looking a bit untidy. I sit him down and hand him his breakfast, which he devours.

"Beautiful, Johnnie," he says. "Makes me want to get back to the yacht. I'm going to get cleaned up and I'll see you up in the lounge in a few minutes?"

When he's finished his makeover and seems comfortable, we look at each other and grin.

"Right," Jim says. "Where were we? Is there anything we need to add to the story of uni days?"

"Not much, really," I respond. "When I walked out the college gates I was wistful, knowing that this wonderful period of freedom and achievement was about to be replaced by real life, but at the same time I was impatient to get on with things and become important and wealthy. I had walked into Articles of Clerkship after what seemed a cursory interview, and Mary and I had decided to get married, so my life seemed well organised."

The Big, Bad World

So, what happened to you after you left college?

I rented a small apartment close to Mary's family apartment in Kooyong Road, Armadale where I spent not much time because I had clandestinely moved in to the family apartment, where Mary and I lived with Mary's younger sister Ann. There was a fair amount of dodging and weaving to be done whenever Ken and Bridie McKenzie came to town, but overall it was a good arrangement, especially as I earned almost nothing as an articled clerk.

One memorable privilege in summers in those days was accompanying Mary to events at Kooyong Tennis Stadium. Her grandfather had bought permanent seats in the stadium when it was built and these seats could be transferred by will to family successors. We spent many happy times at Kooyong at the Australian Tennis Open watching epic matches over the Christmas/New Year period. We were also allowed to use our seats for all the other events that were staged at Kooyong, which included concerts by the Rolling Stones, Elton John, the Who and Simon and Garfunkel.

Most of my spare time was spent training for rowing and rugby, helping with the eternal wedding preparations, seeing my mates, taking photographs and working.

One of the special times was dropping in to a pub in the city, called Mulcaheys', which was owned by an older Mercantile Rowing Club member, after training on summer weekends. Our crews would go out on blazing afternoons with no water (this was seen as weak), no hats (hats were seen as even weaker) and no sunscreen (this was seen as verging on stupidity because your oar handle would become slippery).

Anyway, around twenty of us would pour into the pub parched and exhausted, and down three or four pots in fifteen minutes, whereupon the evening would light up and finish who knows where or with whom. Great days indeed.

The Law

How were your early days in the law?

Long winded. I was engaged in 1970 as an articled clerk, or trainee, by Corr & Corr, an upper tier commercial law firm with around twenty partners that had a strong practice in consumer credit, which meant financing arrangements for small businesses, for vehicle and equipment purchases and for property development. The firm usually acted for the finance companies, in many cases bank subsidiaries, because one quite brilliant partner, Simon Begg, had devised a way of circumventing the imposition of a state tax on lending, which made the finance companies more profitable.

The firm itself was located in the old Argus newspaper building in cheap and gloomy premises – grey lino on the floors, ancient desks, cubicles constructed of chipboard and chicken wire glass.

What sort of flavour did the firm have?

Well, it was respected but not by any means an establishment firm that could ever expect to win major industrial and banking clients, or populate the boards of listed companies.

I discovered that the partnership had a pronounced Catholic flavour and was openly antisemitic. My fellow clerks were Alan Myers, who had graduated top in the law school in my year – he was an old Xavier college boy who became immensely successful as a QC and investor; Charles Sweeney, a somewhat spiky man, whose father had been a Bankruptcy

Court judge, who also became a QC and editor of the *Australian Law Journal* and was also an old Xaverian; John Telfer, a highly intelligent Old Melburnian whose professional history I haven't followed; and me.

My initial assignments were unspectacular: research into tax and stamp duty legislation; debt collections; securities enforcement; and the arrangement of credit transactions. I caught the eye of Simon Begg and he began to unload his documentary work in my direction, which gave me a practice base.

I became a senior associate after a couple of years but it was clear that partnership was a long way away and that the old Xaverians had the inside track, so I began casting around for other jobs.

The truth was that I was bored, underpaid and over-ambitious, and that a consumer credit firm would never have kept me happy. I flirted with the idea of joining the Department of Foreign Affairs to follow Ralph but the idea didn't last long when I looked at the public service pay scales.

Did you move to another firm?

No. I had been urged often by my rowing coach Hubert Frederico and my crewmate Paul Guest to go to the bar. I thought about it carefully, because I did have the gift of the gab, I was a good analyst and a risk-taker and I was happy to work hard, but I knew that anyone with any kind of anxiety issues shouldn't consider it. In any event, I wasn't completely happy with the idea of being a sole practitioner either, because if you weren't working you made no money. Plus Mary was now pregnant with my late daughter Sarah, earlier than I had expected.

One day I spied a newspaper advertisement by a group called Dominion Properties, which had been founded a few years earlier by a man called Lloyd Williams, which wanted to recruit an in-house lawyer and was offering twice my salary and a free car. I didn't do my due diligence all that well, but I found Lloyd an attractive and charismatic individual and the business interesting. Lloyd was fast becoming a Melbourne corporate and social identity with a passion for bloodstock and horseracing. He is now the owner of an enormous stud at Mount Macedon; he founded Crown Casino with Kerry Packer and has won eight Melbourne Cups.

I know Lloyd and Dominion, but they sound very much off the beaten track for conservative you.

You're right, but Dominion was just outright fun.

I looked after all of Lloyd's legal issues in conjunction with Nicholas Holt of Rigby & Fielding, one of the sons of former Prime Minister Harold Holt. The relationship with Nicky was always uneasy. He was worried about the loss of revenue I would represent to his firm, and I was worried about his attempts to cut my lunch. But we got on well in the end.

Who were Lloyd's mates at the time? If memory serves me right, he had a kind of eastern suburbs rat pack?

He did. Lloyd was the consummate people person. He had a loyal retinue of male and female friends including Michael Prentice from the building family, Jonathan Edgar from the real estate family and Gabor Hubay, a Hungarian architect/designer. They formed a watertight business and social group. The Caroline Street South Yarra office would empty out into Maxim's Restaurant in Toorak Road at around 11.30 a.m. every Friday, and Lloyd would hold court there amidst great ceremony and at vast expense until all hours. I was a young and green drone to them and so was never part of the Friday revelry, but Lloyd gave me an open account at Hermann Schneider's excellent Four Seasons Restaurant in South Yarra to make up for it, which I used hard and often. He also gave me a new Triumph 2000, which, for someone who had never owned a car, was a dream come true.

How did Lloyd make his money? I know he was a controversial figure in Melbourne who had a reputation of being smart and uncompromising. I think he was an old Xaverian as well?

He was. He made his initial pile by buying up historic homes on big properties around Toorak and South Yarra and turning them at light speed into brick apartment blocks; their ugliness raised many a blue blood hackle. He then moved into larger commercial buildings, many of which are still standing. One of his secrets was developing a great friendship with Bruno Grollo, who was a bricklayer by trade and turned himself into a contract builder for Lloyd. Bruno built almost all of Lloyd's apartments and got his start in Australia from that work.

Lloyd had a superfast mind, a deep knowledge of human psychology, an uncannily successful negotiating style and great capacity to innovate.

It was a bit feast and famine. When lending conditions were easy, the business was easy and vice versa. Lloyd was caught out building a partly un-permitted apartment block at Pasley Street, near Fawkner Park, and was forced by the local residents to demolish it, to his chagrin, but this was one of his few reverses.

The Dominion office was in Caroline Street near Toorak Road, and one of the tenants was the Turkish consulate. One day to my surprise I received a hand-delivered invitation to join the Turkish consul for lunch. I know of no reason why this might have been forthcoming but, in the spirit of adventure, I accepted. I joined the consul in a nearby restaurant, expecting him to be accompanied by others from the consulate, but it was one-on-one. Less than ten minutes after we sat down, the consul's hand found its way to my upper thigh, which informed me immediately that seduction was the aim of the encounter. So, with what I hope was an element of grace, and trying to maintain my composure, I excused myself and returned, amused but still surprised, to my office and safety. I realised that in such situations, due diligence really was required, which since then I have always attended to.

The end came when Lloyd began to groom me as his ambassador to a number of regulatory agencies which didn't suit my career ambitions, so I resigned after around a year and started to look at job ads again. This would have been at the end of 1973. But I wouldn't have missed the experience for anything. Lloyd and his boys were a hoot, led a mad and rich life and revelled in their ability to offend the establishment and make piles of money without working too hard. That would never be me, but it was inspiring to watch.

So what was going on in your personal life at this stage?

A mixture of things. After Mary and I were married, we continued to live in the McKenzie's Kooyong Road apartment, officially this time, for a few months while we decided where to live.

While we were there, I received a bad knee injury playing rugby for Hawthorn Rugby Club, which I used to do for winter training. The injury took many weeks to recover from. I needed a reconstruction, which was a rare operation in those days. My surgeon was Howard Toyne, who had been Australia's Olympic team doctor. Although the size of my scar suggested an agricultural technique, the knee healed well and to this day it works better than the other one. I was warned that I would never ski, play squash or lift weights using my legs again, but I did all three well afterward, and I credit that success to the gradual rehab that the next season of rowing allowed me to do.

One scary discovery I made during this convalescence was that I had high, at times dangerously high, blood pressure. I think this was partly the stress involved in trying to manage a competitive career, but I suspect also that all I could see in front of me for decades was grinding professional work and family responsibility. I could also see even at that early stage that life with Mary wasn't destined to be easy but with everything else that was going on I didn't give it much conscious thought.

In the latter part of 1972, we found a pretty unit at 240 Wattletree Road to move into. The big decision was whether we would spend $25 a week rent on a one-bedroom unit or $27.50 on two bedrooms. We chose the two. It was our first taste of independent married life and the place where I founded my wine collection. We had received many gifts of wine for our wedding and Ken McKenzie bought discounted wine for us through Younghusband, for whom he worked at the time, so the cellar prospered.

We commuted to Melbourne for a time in Mary's Morris Oxford. Mary worked for BHP Petroleum as a receptionist at the time and we were keen to save a deposit on a house.

Then in late 1972 we bought our first house, a small red brick '20s bungalow in The Grange, East Malvern. The price was an astronomical $17,500, for which we received a first home-buyers' grant from the Commonwealth of $1,000, meaning we had a few dollars with which to do some cheap renovations. The house hadn't been touched for many years; when we were pulling up the old carpet for example, the underlay was '30s and '40s newspaper, which we should have kept but didn't. We took out a loan of $10,000 from National Mutual on condition that we also bought a life insurance policy. I lay awake for weeks wondering how I could ever pay it back.

The job of taming our block, which had become overgrown over the years, fell to me. I laid Hawthorn brick paths, built a concrete slab outside the rear entrance, made flower beds, planted flowers and shrubs and a Tasmanian blue gum outside one of the front windows, hung wallpaper, built bookshelves and cupboards and painted.

The family lived at The Grange for fourteen years, during which all of our children were born. One major renovation designed by our Echuca architect friend Greig Carter was completed and the roots of many friendships and community activities developed. We sold in 1986 to move to a larger, much more modern house in Knox Street East Malvern; it ran into Bourke Road opposite Central Park, which had been part of the original Royal Melbourne Golf Club. But I would say that our times at The Grange were the happiest we had: the children were a delight, we were well-integrated into the local community, my work was interesting and rewarding and the sky was usually blue.

OK, you've resigned from Dominion Properties. Where to after that?

A year at Dominion was enough to convince me that going back into a mainstream law firm wouldn't work. Corrs had been boring and stiff, and

I couldn't see myself working for finance companies all my life.

This was the time when the mining industry in Australia was blossoming with the development of Hamersley Iron, Comalco, and Bougainville Copper by the Rio Tinto Group subsidiary in Australia known as Conzinc Riotinto of Australia, or CRA. CRA was advertising for lawyers because the then MD, a brilliant ex-McKinsey partner Rod Carnegie—he had been appointed to the job at the unheard-of age of thirty-seven and had extensive US experience—believed that companies should have their own legal staff.

So I applied for a job in the legal department of Hamersley Iron, but my application was intercepted by the new CRA Group General Counsel Robin Chambers. He pulled rank on Hamersley and I joined his four-man legal team shortly thereafter.

The Rio Tinto Years

So began a diverse, rich and fulfilling twelve-year stay at CRA. The group is now known by its original UK name, Rio Tinto.

How did the experience compare with what you'd been doing?

It was a new life and a new professional departure for me. It was a mining group and so its structure was based very much on line-management theory, and it was also bureaucratic because it had its roots in Broken Hill's Zinc Corporation and New Broken Hill Consolidated, which had been merged to form Australian Mining and Smelting Ltd or AM & S. There were rules and procedures for everything, and non-engineering, non-operations people were looked down on by the real employees; if you happened to be of Broken Hill birth, you were what was called an A Grouper, like a Brahmin in Indian culture, and regarded as the real fabric of the company.

This was a group under youthful management with ambition and determination to be big and important everywhere with no limits. It was then one of the largest listed entities on the ASX and in bitter competition with BHP, Western Mining and Mount Isa Mines for growth in a battle it was winning. And, crucially, Carnegie and Chambers wanted the internal legal team to do everything.

So I guess you were being exposed early on to deals you might never have seen in private practice?

I was. I found myself advising on huge transactions with multiple partners in all corners of the world. The work involved close contact with senior management and their foreign counterparts, senior bankers and market advisers, and when needed, the senior partners in Australian and international law firms. I also was regularly attached to delegations of various sorts that transacted business with global partners, mostly in mineral sales and corporate acquisitions. For a time I lived beyond my real level of competence but I made up ground quickly.

Did you spend much time in Japan?

My earliest experience of that was being made part of the early missions to Tokyo selling Hamersley iron ore. Unlike today where iron ore generates rivers of cash, then it was a marginal business that depended almost entirely on the goodwill of the great Japanese trading companies like Mitsui, Mitsubishi and Marubeni, who represented the Japanese steel mills, which were still opaque and traditional in style and not much used to dealing outside Japan.

Our meetings with the trading companies in Tokyo would always be conducted in huge conference rooms that were stifling in summer and icy in winter. The team leaders would be placed at the centre of a big table opposite one another and the remaining members would be seated in precise order of seniority down to the table ends. Of course, I would be well down the table.

Negotiations were slow and boring, because everything said by one leader would need to be translated, then the response translated, and so forth from nine a.m. to five p.m. every day. Sometimes the missions would last several weeks, but they were always successful. The Japanese believed firmly that their relationship with Australia was valuable and long-term and that they stood to gain from putting as much Australian iron ore as they could under contract for the future.

The relationships that grew up during that formative time have proven to be durable and valuable, because Japan and Australia are now best friends and have a vast commercial relationship.

When this was happening in the early '70s, the Japanese people were still disliked by many older and more senior Australian business leaders, and if you had taken one into the Melbourne or the Australian Club then your reputation would have been seriously questioned.

Did you make many friendships during those times?

I did. The younger Japanese in Tokyo were keen to establish close relations with their western counterparts because they believed in the principle of friendships developing into important alliances as the years passed and seniority grew. So, every night, I and my younger colleagues would be entertained lavishly in the Ginza and other lively parts of Tokyo.

We would be taken to small and very expensive sushi restaurants and tempura bars that we would never have been able to visit without powerful Japanese friends. We were often entertained at the traditional inner-city walled mansions of the great trading companies where it was as though we had been transported back in time hundreds of years; and we were taken to endless mama-san bars, pachinko parlours and sumo wrestling matches. What a time, and what a life.

I received Christmas cards from my Japanese friends for many years after I left Rio Tinto.

Can you give me a snapshot of the other kinds of work you were doing with Rio?

A few deserve mention.

I was involved at different levels in the mining agreement between the WA government and Hamersley Iron, and most importantly, in the regular battles over Hamersley's secondary iron ore processing obligations, its royalty arrangements with Lang Hancock, environmental management and industrial relations.

Early on I was responsible for the administration of all of Rio's mining leases at Broken Hill. This involved collaboration with the Broken Hill survey department and the fabled Chief Surveyor George Dalby. I visited George many times but I could never persuade him to go to the pub or any place where there might be blue collar staff – he was white collar and intensely proud of it, and intensely conscious of the unwritten but iron-clad law that no white collar man should ever fraternise with blue collar men, especially not at pubs.

I worked with the brilliant John Falk on reconstructing Rio's solar salt interests in WA and setting up the first sales office ever established in Tokyo by any western mining company. Eventually we succeeded in persuading the trading companies that salt needed to be re-priced to market after decades of suppression, and a suite of new sales agreements was entered into. My association with John was relatively short-lived because he injured his head badly when he fell off a ladder at his home in Malvern and was no longer the same person intellectually.

I was part of the team that bought the US aluminium interests of the Martin Marietta Corporation, and the team that established the Woodlawn lead and zinc mine in New South Wales.

Did you spend much time in South-East Asia?

Yes. I advised the manager of Rio's tin mining operations in Malaysia, the magnificent Englishman Jim Champion, on his new dredge developments and his tin sales contracts, which took me to Kuala Lumpur and Tokyo often. His wife Molly, the memsahib of memsahibs, took a shine to me and I was invited to stay at their substantial house whenever I was in KL. Jim was a mad keen squash player and he would organise sessions every day. Luckily, I was a better player than he was but if it hadn't been for the masseurs at his club, who unlocked me after every game, I would barely have been able to walk. Jim was a great and kind mentor who would sit me down whenever I became impatient with authority, which was most of the time, and counsel me to get over the rough ground lightly. If I have any wisdom now, I can thank Jim for knocking some sense into me then.

Jim was also a fine judge of Asian cooking, particularly Chinese. We enjoyed many a long and voluptuous dinner together. It was also through Jim that I met my great mate Chris Long, who then worked with Rio in Jakarta looking after the group's minerals exploration program and was later transferred to Singapore.

So how were you seeing your career developing at this stage?

It seemed as though I was well-regarded albeit junior in CRA. I was lucky because Rod Carnegie had rowed at Melbourne University and also at Oxford although in one of the worst eights ever boated by Oxford for the boat race and he was aware of my rowing background. Rod and I were part of a team that went to the US at the inception of the Woodlawn Project at the invitation of St. Joe Minerals to settle the price of CRA's buy-in to the project. Ralph obliged with a dinner at his residence in the rarified environment of Beekman Place that included Rod – which couldn't have done me any harm – and Rod included me in all the negotiations that ensued, in which he was comprehensively out-manoeuvred. So, I was on his radar.

I often was asked to visit Hamersley in Western Australia. At the time, CRA and BHP jointly owned a fleet of Grumman Gulfstream aircraft through an entity called Associated Airlines, which we would use for flights to the West and PNG. The aircraft were small and very fast. Often, Carnegie would be on the same flight but as soon as he got on board he would disappear into a blizzard of newspapers and briefing notes and not emerge until we landed. He was keen, it seemed, to avoid any human contact with lesser employees. His fellow travellers always understood that Rod was the philosopher king whose word was law and that he could do what he liked.

Lawyers weren't supposed to show initiative, but I was a problem solver and had some significant successes in moving stuck transactions forward. One morning I was invited to Rod's office for reasons that weren't explained. I was as nervous as hell but when he sat me down it was clear that he had heard about me in dispatches and wanted to inspect me firsthand.

"Thanks for coming to see me, John, good to put a face to the name."

"My pleasure."

"I wanted to touch base because I've heard some good things about you, and I wanted to tell you that you've been doing some fine work. You seem to be on a promising path in the company." Rod continued, saying that they'd looked at my analysis of our relationship with the WA government under our iron ore agreements and thought that we really understood them for the first time. "You've got some good things going for you, you're smart, you seem sensible, it looks as though you're interested in a career in the company." Then came the pitch: "It's probably time for us to look at getting you out of law and into management because my sense is that that's where you really belong."

"Rod, that's very generous of you, but I'm not sure Robin Chambers would be too happy about that!"

"You let me worry about Robin."

I was certainly interested in the idea and I sincerely appreciated the offer. He shifted the conversation to small talk about rowing and our kids. But this was an unheard-of encounter that in some ways was a complication; it became known and I could hear guns being loaded and cocked all around me.

There must be some stories you've tucked away about those years that people would like to hear?

Many! Being on the road in exotic places with a relatively open expense account did involve some entertaining happenings. In those days managements were not too worried about expense formalities and there were many examples of excess. Some executives maintained Tokyo apartments that were not always used for regular purposes; one fabulous friend and high spender when travelling would always transit through Zurich even if the final destination was New York, because he liked a particular restaurant, and so forth. Corporate life now is much less colourful.

Chris Long and I were sent in search of investment opportunities for Rio in the late '70s to Indonesia, where Chris was posted at the time. We spent six glorious weeks wandering through Java, Sulawesi, Sumatra and Lombok. We were both interested in Indonesian textiles, antique Chinese trade ceramics and pottery and so quite a bit of the trip was spend trying to unearth treasures of one sort or another. We visited Central Sumatra as part of a visit to the Asahan Aluminium smelter. Chris was an outstanding networker and knew an eccentric American who had been a chopper pilot in Vietnam during the war but who had settled in Sumatra to avoid returning to the US. Chris hired him to fly us around Sumatra and he was indeed a magnificent pilot. On our return from one trip I was watching the fuel gauges anxiously because there was a big headwind and I realised that our situation was touch-and-go. There was no way we could have landed in the Sumatran jungle beneath us. We did land eventually, on fumes. Our pilot informed us that we had something like thirty seconds of flying in the tanks. Our dinner that night was particularly joyful.

On an early visit to Tokyo, I was attached to an iron ore delegation made up of experienced, tough and mischievous executives. One day after work they took me to what was called a "mama-san" bar. These were famous and diabolically expensive institutions usually owned by a clever woman. How they attracted clientele I'm not sure, but expense account Westerners seemed to love them. As the evening wore on, the Hamersley men slipped away one by one until the last one patted me on the head, handed me the bill and walked out. It was a set-up. The bill was for US$8,000, which in the mid-'70s was a terrifying amount. By the grace of god I was carrying an unlimited AMEX card and it covered the expense, but the real question was how I would ever be able to explain this to senior management. When I was back in the Melbourne office and had lodged my expense claim, I was summoned to the office of the Hamersley

MD Russ Madigan. I knew I was about to be sacked. But after hauling me over the coals angrily, he burst into laughter and said "John, this is what these guys do to anyone visiting Tokyo for the first time: you've been had! Just be smart enough not to let it happen again." He signed the expense account, and I exited, wiser and very relieved.

That gives me a good taste of what Rio life would have been like then: the Wild West!

Nicola Harry, 1992.

Michael Harry, 1996.

Donna Harry, 2006.

My father-in-law, Tommy Brittain, 2006.

Max Lindsey, Balnarring, 2015.

Donna's cousin, Jenny Farrell, Sydney, 2008.

My brother-in-law, Ken Woolley, 1993.

My groomsmen (from left to right) Stephen Gillon, Martin Braden, David Douglas and David Bishop, 14 December 1970.

At the gate of La Romanée-Conti vineyard, Burgundy, 1992.

During a motorbike tour with Ian Mackie, Northern Victoria, 2022.

With David Douglas at our Victorian Rowing Association Hall of Fame induction, 2015.

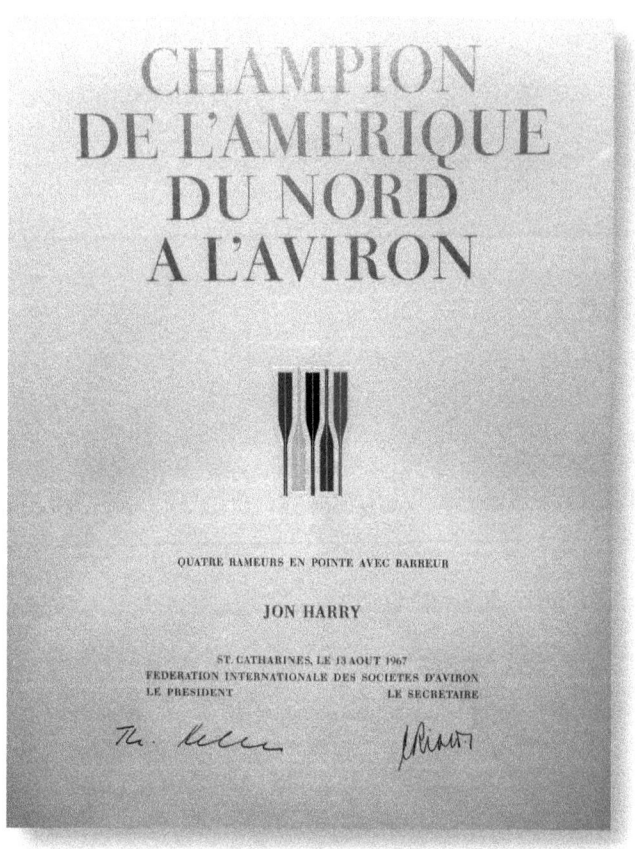

Championship certificate, North American Rowing Titles,
St Catherines Canada, 1967.

Rowing Hall of Fame certificate, 2015.

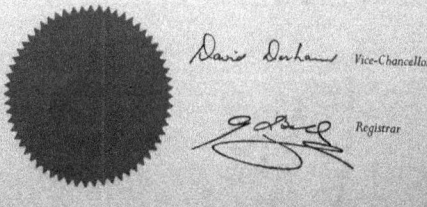

LLB certificate, 1970.

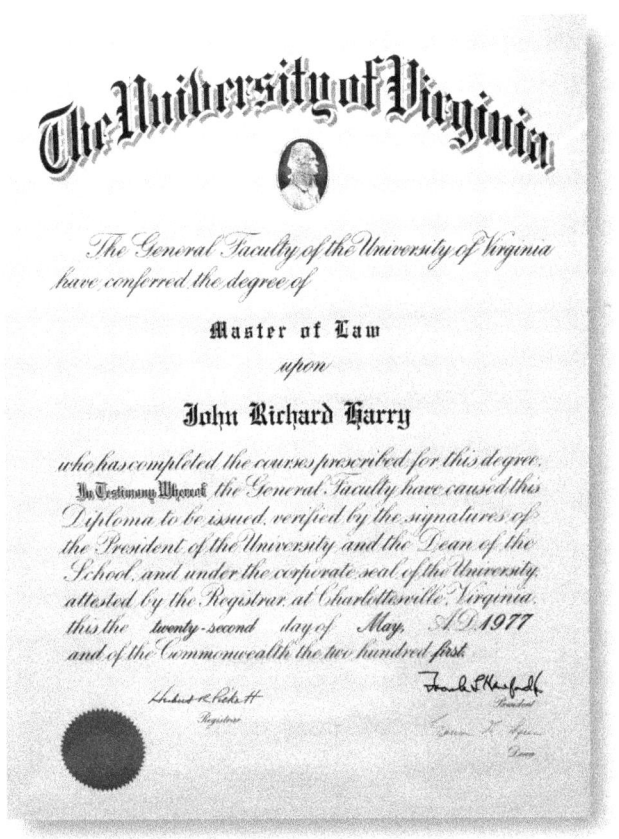

LLM certificate, University of Virginia, 1977.

With my mother-in-law Winsome Brittain,
7 December, 2023, Melbourne

With Donna at our wedding in Queensland, 2 May 2005

The author, Egypt, 2021

The University of Virginia

I know you did some study in the US early on in your career. Maybe we should take a sideways step to look at that?

Good idea. It was a landmark experience for me and also Mary and my children, and quite separate from anything else I did at any stage in my life, really. Testing and formative. I came out of it with great respect for the US, its belief in freedom and generosity, and its sense of obligation to share the benefits of US culture and, to use a somewhat old-fashioned word, civilisation, with the rest of the world.

I find it sad to reflect on how much the social and political structure of the US has become so much more cynical, polarised and violent since I was a student there. All of us know about the fractures displayed in American society in the '60s and early '70s – student uprisings, racial rioting, the betrayal of Nixon and Watergate – but no one then could ever have imagined a time when a US president in the person of Donald Trump would lie persistently and deliberately, would fraudulently contest legitimate election results, would encourage a mob to go to the US Capitol for mayhem and murder, would joke about the attempted far-right political killing of the husband of the Speaker of the House.

I had been thinking more and more about taking a post-grad degree because I'd never had any respite from work in Melbourne and I wanted to test myself in another system and, of course, burnish my CV.

One big issue was whether I should go to the UK or the US. I loved the idea of rowing at, say, Oxford, although I was getting to the end of my sporting career. But this wasn't a major influence. I decided that the quality of education at a good US law school would be superior, and the received view at the time was that, at least in Australia, a US LLM was viewed more highly, so I concentrated on the US option.

I know that US university fees are enormous today and probably would have been then. Was that a concern?

It was, of course, because we had two children and Mary was pregnant with our third, so we didn't have much spare cash. But I thought that I might be able to find a scholarship and maybe persuade CRA to give me a stipend of some sort to make it possible.

So I applied in early 1975 for a generous scholarship offered by the AT&T Corporation, which then owned and managed the whole of the US and international Bell telephone business. The scholarship was for foreign students wanting to study in the US and was administered by the Fulbright office in parallel with the Fulbright scholarship program. I was primarily interested in studying the regulation of deep seabed mining in international waters, which had only recently emerged as a technical possibility and had been a much-debated topic at the third UN conference on the law of the sea, which began in 1973 and concluded in 1982 with the signature of the second United Nations Convention on the Law of the Sea.

I was awarded one of two scholarships offered to Australians. The terms included all tuition and a living allowance. So, I was off and running. I then applied to the University of Virginia School of Law, which had just established the Center for Oceans Law and Policy, for a place in its graduate program. I was accepted into the law school and invited to become a fellow of the Center with financial support, so everything had fallen neatly into place.

So what was CRA's response to the news?

My boss Robin Chambers was supportive, but he told me that he would keep my position open only if I returned pretty much straight after

I graduated. I did have in mind that I might try to work with a Wall Street law firm for a few months, especially as Ralph and Dorothy were likely to be in New York for at least another year, and it would have been good to spend concentrated time with them, which we hadn't done for ever. So, I applied officially for leave of absence and it was granted.

We then packed up our Melbourne life and boarded the big 747 for New York to stay with Ralph and Dorothy while we made arrangements to go to Charlottesville 150 or so miles to the south in Virginia. My parents' apartment was located in one of the most prestigious and expensive blocks on Manhattan – a beautiful '20s building in Beekman Place at the corner of 50th Street and First Avenue. The apartment itself was enormous; there was a cook, a maid and a chauffeur, so we were spoiled but very comfortable.

I have to pay tribute to Mary and her parents, who were unquestioning in their support, especially Mary, who agreed to leave a well-organised and familiar life to go to an unknown place knowing that I would be completely committed to my work and facing the need to give birth to our daughter Nicola without any of the support from family and friends she would have had in Melbourne.

Did you know much about Charlottesville or Virginia?

Not much. I knew that the university had been founded by Thomas Jefferson in 1819 and that the original university buildings were beautiful examples of pre-Civil War Southern architecture that now have UNESCO World Heritage protection. I also knew that the university was one of the first in the US to be created explicitly as non-religious and to offer a broad program of liberal arts and scientific subjects. I was aware that the law school was nationally ranked and exceptionally sought after, meaning that my class would be full of super smart students and that a demanding year was in front of me. Even though it was a very important period in my life, I tend not to reminisce much about it because it was traumatic and evokes memories that have marked me in some unpleasant ways.

To this day I have nightmares about being lost and unprepared for my US master's law exams. I guess this is a kind of PTSD that will likely always be there in some form.

There were many loose ends to be tied up before we could go south, including the purchase of a car. I found a bright red Fiat 124S for a reasonable cost, which served us well throughout our US stay. It was a bit Italian and a bit sporty, and not particularly roomy. On the trip down to Virginia, we managed to jam in two adults, two young children and three large suitcases. When Nicola arrived things were even worse. And getting out of downtown Manhattan in pre-GPS days was a nightmare, but before too long we found ourselves humming down the interstate and then onto the gorgeous country roads that took us through emerald green country Virginia, surely one of the world's most lovely places.

So, what were your first impressions when you arrived in Charlottesville?

We were very happy with our Charlottesville launch. The university year in the US starts immediately after Labor Day in early September, so the family set off a couple of weeks before commencement to organise a house, meet the folks from the Center for Oceans Law and Policy and finalise my induction process with the law school, including selecting courses.

Charlottesville sits at the base of the Blue Ridge Mountains, which are a part of the Appalachian chain that runs from Washington DC to Tennessee. Summer in the Blue Ridge is deep magenta, airless, hot and humid, and so it was when we arrived. I remember the heavy magenta haze that blanketed the mountains to our west as we made our way through the countryside. This area is populated by wealthy Washingtonians and New Yorkers who have bought into the myth of Virginia gentility and who own manicured, white-fenced farms and horse studs where they gather to play at weekends; but also by the original and mainly poor Virginia small farmers who live in the hollows and peaks of the mountains and for whom life is socially and genetically inbred and has barely changed in three centuries.

We stopped at a service station for petrol and food on the way down. The accent of the attendant could have been from Alabama – thick and guttural. As Australians we're used to minute differences in accents over long distances. Not here. The Mason–Dixon line was razor-sharp: we were in the Deep South just after crossing the Maryland/Virginia border.

We were met on our arrival by some law school people responsible for greeting incoming foreign students, who had organised temporary accommodation for us. They settled us into a faculty house in southern Charlottesville, which was unglamourous but welcome because of the work we still had to do.

Did it take you long to find your own house?

No, it was quick and easy. The population of a university town is mobile and it wasn't long before we spotted an advertisement for a lovely old white clapboard house in North First Street, near the city centre, owned by the professor of Spanish at the University of Virginia. This location was around fifteen minutes from the law school. The professor, a Mr McGrady, was about to go on sabbatical in Madrid for a year and the timing for us was perfect.

His wife Maria was Spanish and she took an immediate liking to our children; Mary's late pregnancy also helped, so before long we had signed a lease and were moving in. As well as the house, we were lent the family Kombi van, the professor's jugs of wine, and his enormous gun collection, including pistols, silencers, ammunition-making kit and a long guide to local hunting opportunities. My first task was to lock the guns up safely after a detailed search of the house, which revealed a number of hidden weapons including a heavy revolver in my bedside drawer.

It seemed that everyone was curious about us because we were Australian. We received early and sincere invitations from our neighbours John and Susan Pezzoli, who became and still are treasured friends; from the head of the Center for Oceans Law and Policy John Norton Moore; and from Ed and Margaret Good from the placement department of the law school, whose kids became and have remained great mates of our own.

Was it long till Nicola was born?

No. She arrived on the 9th of October at the Charlottesville General Hospital barely five weeks after we arrived. It was hard for Mary because I was inundated and trying not to collapse at the law school, but she got through everything OK and in the US manner was tossed out of hospital after a couple of days to settle Nicola into North First Street.

Our experience at the hospital was chilling, however, because racism was still deeply entrenched in Virginia society, as it was in most parts of the country in 1976. Mary was placed in a segregated ward for white women only. The ward for Black women was next door. These women were, to say the least, expressive during their labours, but the nursing staff not only barely attended to them but were also repeatedly abusive and insulting as the decibel count grew. It was easy to understand that it was one thing to have a suite of racial equality legislation on the books in Washington and an entirely different thing to eradicate real-time racist behaviour.

We had a similar experience when we hired a Black woman to help Mary with domestic tasks when she arrived back from hospital. On her first day we invited her to sit with the rest of the family for lunch and she was so shocked she could barely speak. She had never shared a meal or any social occasion with foreigners before, and it was weeks before she seemed to be comfortable with us.

So how did you feel about being chucked headlong into a strange environment like Charlottesville?

It was weird, really. There were big differences in the way people behaved, for example, which surprised us. On the one hand, people were welcoming and warm, but quite reserved and formal. Terminology was different, manners were different, supermarket offerings were often unexpected, politics and sport were different. There was much learning to do. At the law school, the students and faculty were amazingly bright and connected, and I got the feeling sometimes that Australians were seen as too relaxed to be serious academic competitors. In fact, even though the academic burden was intense, the ability to plan, to see the big picture and not just the detail, to cope with time pressure, to be realistic – all good Aussie qualities – were essential to success. This is boasting, but I had amongst the best results in the graduate class and was fully competitive with the best of the US students. That was a considerable surprise to me and, I gathered, to most of our American friends.

So what was the structure of the master's course?

Master's students had to take any subject mix they chose to make up one full year of the Juris Doctor (JD) degree required of the regular US students. In addition, I was required to complete a research monograph for the Center for Oceans Law and Policy – I'll call it COLP – into a deep seabed mining topic. Intelligent planning of workload and course difficulty was essential to survive. As one example, I chose to do corporations law and not securities regulation, which I knew would be highly complex and black-letter, and so excessively time-consuming and, from a grade point average viewpoint, dangerous.

I worked every day and night except Saturday afternoons, unless the UVA basketball team was playing. Ed Good had found us season passes to UVA games at University Hall and I rapidly became addicted to the sport, which was phenomenally popular, so I indulged whenever I could. I still follow intercollegiate basketball during what the Americans call March Madness – when the NCAA championships are conducted. UVA was a member of the Atlantic Coast Conference, then the most respected university league in the US.

Speed-reading techniques were important because the volume of material to be absorbed on a daily basis was sometimes in the hundreds of pages. In the early weeks I was frankly drowning and terrified but gradually my assimilation and analytical speed sharpened up and I began to feel less under siege and more balanced.

The law school itself was a beautiful modern complex in its own precinct in the university grounds. Classwork was essential because UVA adopted the Socratic method of teaching developed initially at Harvard in which the professor would generate continuous dialogue by firing questions at the class and demanding answers. It took me some time before I screwed up the courage to speak up and when I did, the whole class looked around to inspect the person with the strange voice and accent. The answer was adequate if not penetrating.

By the time I sat the final exams and handed in my final papers, I believe I was at my academic, and perhaps intellectual, peak.

UVA from its Jeffersonian beginnings adopted an honour code that applied to all student conduct. The basic principle was that any honour violation—no student shall lie, cheat or steal ...—should be reported and that any accused student should be tried by students, and if found guilty be expelled. That principle was expressed in the context of exams by a system that allowed students to collect exam papers from the law school at any point during a particular time window, write their answers whenever and wherever they wanted within the designated period, then drop them off again at the law school. After a lifetime of hot and tense exam rooms and gruff invigilators, I found this almost unbelievable. I wonder whether this beautiful idea has been corrupted by electronic communication and social decay.

I'm exhausted! But did you get any opportunity to look around the Charlottesville area and get to know the East Coast of the US any better?

There was a winter and a spring break during the academic year, which we did use to do some looking around. We were also given a few days over Christmas, which we spent with Ralph and Dorothy in New York.

We visited the Outer Banks of North Carolina and Kittyhawk, where the Wright brothers had their first flight, and Ocracoke Island, which had been a refuge for pirates and where the residents still spoke a strange blend of old English and modern American. We went to Pennsylvania Dutch country to see the Amish people, to West Virginia, down the Blue Ridge toward Tennessee and south to some of the great Civil War battle sites, and of course to Washington DC. Then after graduation we went on an extended car trip south, west and north to New York where we rejoined Dorothy and Ralph as the summer was coming to a close.

What other memories do you have of your UVA experience?

The winter. There was snow on the ground from November to March and that year was the coldest for something like fifty years. It was below zero Fahrenheit on many days and Chesapeake Bay froze over. You only went outside in those conditions when it was absolutely necessary because of the bulky clothing you had to pull on and off, the treacherous ice on the roads and footpaths, the risk of frostbite and hypothermia. It was hard to start a car, every car window iced immediately when you got in, pipes burst and your heating bills were enormous.

The faculty. These men were the best in the country because of the law school's reputation and tenure was hard to gain. But they were humane, generous and courtly people who went out of their way to help the graduate class with any problem because they knew how hard a task it was to go from zero to full academic pace in weeks, as we had to. The dean of the law school invited the graduate students for drinks once a month and other faculty members would always join him.

The music. I got to hear a lot of bluegrass, country and blues that I wouldn't have listened to otherwise. I found Boston, the Eagles, ZZ Top, the Steve Miller Band, Lynyrd Skynyrd, Steely Dan, Tom Petty and the Ramones, mostly courtesy of my wonderful neighbour John Pezzoli.

The campus changes of the '60s. UVA may not have been the most radicalised campus of that era but its voice was loud enough. There were students on the university and law school councils; the relaxed exam system I described had been installed; every semester a review by students of the faculty was undertaken and published; the admissions criteria for students had been widened to include affirmative action admissions based in whole or part on racial and underprivilege factors. Anyone who believed that the '60s revolution as it applied to universities was a temporary phenomenon was wrong. Black and Latino students were common in my time, although there were mutterings occasionally about their performance.

Now it appears that the conservative majority of the US Supreme Court, in an action brought against Harvard and the University of North Carolina, is likely to outlaw affirmative action once again. We are seeing the tip of the destruction that will be brought down by the conservative court stacking undertaken by Trump.

Sounds an amazingly full experience for one year. These days, years disappear before the end of January! Is there any way you can sum it up?

I always thought that my experiences in rowing crews were as concentrated, sharp and fulfilling as anything I would experience, but I was wrong – it was UVA. Recalling this time with you has brought back a taste of the tension, exhaustion, exhilaration, adventure and fulfilment I was given. The fact that AT&T, the COLP, CRA and the university would provide such a gift to someone they didn't know for reasons that were uncertain with an outcome that wasn't measurable speaks of decency, kindness, trust, honour, hope and in the end, love. How else to explain it? How to explain to social media trolls or destructive journalists or Trump supporters that a world without these qualities is hardly worth living in? I doubt that I'll ever not be sad at the leakage of these norms from the fabric of the US. If this story is one of ups and downs, Jim, this thought is definitely a down.

New York

So, into the Fiat and back to New York?

Yes, with three kids under five representing, in the words of Zorba the Greek, which the really old people reading this may recall, the full catastrophe.

I had applied to Sullivan and Cromwell, a white shoe New York firm par excellence, for a year in residence as a foreign trainee, and once again to my amazement I was accepted. I had also been offered a shorter internship with the less prestigious but much more eccentric New York firm of Coudert Brothers through Drew Quale, with whom I took an international banking course at UVA. Since CRA were less than enthusiastic about a second full year of absence, I decided on the shorter option, which they agreed to.

The six extra months in New York were wonderful but the Coudert experience wasn't. I was treated like any other young lawyer and worked long and hard, and it didn't take me long to decide that I didn't want to practise law in a large New York firm; the New York partners saw Australians as somewhat savage and agricultural, and unlikely to be partner material.

We inhabited the Met, MoMA, the Manhattan art galleries, the uptown restaurants, Broadway, jazz clubs and the Apawamis golf club in upstate New York where Ralph was a member. Ralph had also arranged for us to take over the Beekman Place apartment of the Dutch UN Ambassador who was away on extended leave, together with his domestic staff. Spoiled wasn't the word.

By the spring of 1977, the family was on its way back to Melbourne for the beginning of the next chapter.

Photography

Johnnie, why don't we take another detour and leave the career stuff aside for a while?

Not so exciting, is it? Maybe we can talk about photographs?

Fine. I notice you've got photos on your walls – all yours?

Mostly.

So how did you get interested in pictures?

I'm not sure how I was drawn to photographic images, but it was early on. I'd always been interested in art and I would always try to find galleries and museums when I visited somewhere new. I was a mad fan of Michelangelo and chased his sculpture and painting all over Europe. It was super realistic and had a strongly emotional and plastic quality. How could a man look at a block of marble and visualise an image inside it in three dimensions, then have the persistence and control to reveal it chip by chip? The idea of the Renaissance – applying passionate curiosity and scholarship to the rediscovery and re-creation of classical art, resulting in art that was, while in a sense classical, completely new and beautiful – was entrancing.

I was always making things – compositions on the piano, radios, chemical compounds, alcohol, stories, pottery, bits of carpentry, model airplanes, bombs, cakes, billycarts – so when I was drawn to photography it seemed natural to get involved. Ralph, as I mentioned, was a keen home movie maker but never a still photographer.

I also found great photos disturbing: real but not real; not a depiction of reality but something strange, new and willing to tell their story from a unique viewpoint if you could master the metalanguage. I remember the sickening images taken during the Hungarian Revolution in November 1956 showing the thousands of Hungarians slaughtered by Russian tanks that arrived to suppress the freedom movement, the bodies scattered in the streets, newly covered in lime, and the desperate mass migration over the borders of Austria and Yugoslavia.

I had never seen a picture of a dead person before. Many of those refugees found their way to the West, including Canada and Australia. A Hungarian rowing mate of mine, Martin Tomanovits, now dead, guided his mother and sisters over a tough mountain route to Austria after his father was killed – it was a bad winter and the family suffered – and finished up in Melbourne.

Then there were the famous pictures of the water polo match between the Russian and Hungarian water polo teams taken at the 1956 Olympics showing swimmers from both countries being hauled from the water, streaming with blood, as the young Hungarians tried to take revenge for the Russian atrocities. I wondered how the photographers got themselves in a position to do their work and how much courage they would need to be working literally under gunfire.

I could see the potential of photos for making art and I wanted to try. The family had an old still camera and I would save up for rolls of film and use them up on subjects I thought might be interesting rather than documentary. I was accused by the family of wasting money. I didn't draw or paint, so this seemed a good starting point.

Did Ralph and Dorothy show interest in what you were doing?

No. I would have been hard to guide, they would have been legitimately busy, and their nineteenth century vision of parenting was that mentoring and encouraging a child's interests wasn't part of their role. It was best that I found my own way because that way I couldn't be deflected or frustrated.

Because you were a boarder it must have been a difficult interest to pursue.

In fact, being a boarder with lots of weekend time on my hands was a help.

I discovered that the school had a small darkroom under the stairs in the schoolhouse building, and it wasn't long before I was spending winter afternoons learning how to develop and print black and white images. I don't have any of those now – they were badly processed and wouldn't have lasted long. But watching prints emerge in the developing tray was magical, thrilling even. I thought, well, the world is now open to me and I can portray it in any way I like at any time I like.

Did you keep the interest up at university?

It kept up with me rather than the other way around. I just didn't feel comfortable without a camera close by. Pictures had become a compulsion. I didn't feel the need for other people to like what I was doing, although of course I was pleased when they did. I also never saw myself being recognised as a great artist or becoming a professional or exhibiting. I'm sure that was partly my lack of self-confidence. That might also explain a little of why I wanted to get behind a camera all the time – to hide, to find something that I could use as a social prop – because as I told you, and you knew well, I was uneasy company then. I found most social occasions exhausting; people would hear about me and my background and get ready to meet a big, athletic and confident person. When they met someone quiet and watchful, you could see the surprise in their faces.

I'm trying to organise a retro exhibition of my work at the moment and the idea terrifies me, but why not now?

I guess equipment became a thing as well?

You always think that a better camera will make you a better photographer. I knew it wouldn't, because some of the greatest photos ever made have come from primitive gear, like the war reportage of Robert Capa, who used old and primitive cameras, or Henri Cartier-Bresson. But I was always keen to buy the next shiny thing and I was forever in and out of camera shops.

I can't remember what sort of camera I had at school but when I arrived in Trinity College I managed to scrape together enough money to buy a Pentax Spotmatic; it was Japanese and one of the earliest single lens reflex cameras made. I thought it was beautiful. I told you earlier that for a while I took photos for the university magazine *Farrago* but it wasn't particularly glamorous or fun. I tried hard to cultivate art photos and portraits. The pictures are obvious and clunky but I was having a crack at least. One of the valuable parts of having a camera in hand was that many of the things I did and the people I met in those early days, especially family and rowing, are preserved: I have hundreds of good negatives from the mid-'60s onward whereas most of my friends have just a few blurry and faded colour prints in dusty albums.

After Mary and I moved into our first apartment, I decided I needed a better camera. In those days, the camera of choice for press and street work was the Nikon F. A mate of mine, Paul McSweeney, was going to Japan so, without consulting Mary, I asked him to buy me one. It cost me around $200, which at the time was a fortune and I was justly reprimanded for dedicating two months' rent to a camera when it should have been saved for our house deposit.

I became interested in the idea of DIY and started to wind my own film and make my own development chemicals. The results were fair but you couldn't replicate Kodak or Agfa, which is what I mostly used. I also spent a lot of time visiting exhibitions and going to swap meets with other cameras weirdos to find accessories.

Darkrooms were always a problem. I had to improvise constantly, and it wasn't until our house in Knox Street was renovated in 1990 that I finally was able to build one. That was where my best analog work was done. By then I owned my first Leica – a lovely brushed-chrome M3 double action unit with a gorgeous 50mm Summicron lens, which I supplemented with a 90mm Elmar that I bought on a visit to the US.

I spent many happy hours working in that darkroom and became a good developer and printer, having been a devotee of Ansel Adams. His three books of instruction, called *The Negative*, *The Camera* and *The Print*, were my bibles. The big messages were visualisation, tonal control and documentation. I was also experimenting with 2 ¼ x 2 ¼ inch format cameras. I had several over time but the first was a twin lens Mamiya, followed by an ancient Rolleicord. The gain in quality was enormous but these machines were not for street use. They were too big and too slow.

One incidental benefit of having my own darkroom was that when I was working I couldn't be interrupted. Many were the afternoons that I shut myself up out of harm's way to spend quiet time.

Overall I would say I'm a camera nut. I've collected six Leica M series cameras: one M3, two Digiluxes, one M6, one M8, one M9 and one compact. I also have two R series SLRs plus a Rolleiflex and a Hasselblad, and all the lenses and other paraphernalia that goes along with them. My first Digilux and my Hasselblad were given to me by Donna who has always supported my photographic madness without reservation.

I recently bought a Fuji X100V fixed focal length rangefinder to simplify and automate, and although I've taken some pleasing material with it, its image quality isn't in the same league as, say, my M9.

Are there any photographers who've grabbed your attention more than others?

There are. It's actually quite a long list. I tend to like artists who work in the Ansel Adams F64 mode, by which I mean the ones who, whatever is being depicted, pay close attention to image quality: sharpness, depth of field, full tonal gradation and richness of print colour. The pictures of Adams are mostly variations on a landscape theme; technically, they're complete and beautiful and many of them are heroic and magnificent, as well as serene.

The pictures of Robert Mapplethorpe, by contrast, have an entirely different perspective; there are portraits, there are flowers, there are flags and other social ephemera, and then there are his homoerotic works, which are as disturbing as they are dazzling.

But in the case of both men, technique is fundamental; the works of both draw as much from film and paper as seems possible; they are spectacularly immediate, rich, open and enveloping; clear masterworks from consummate craftsmen. In one sense they are figurative, but in another and much more important sense they are anything but figurative. They open a window to the observer that offers intimacy and inspires awe; you know the surface of their pictures is representative but you also know that the representation is staged in such a way as to convey something different, a construct of the mind of the author that is, to borrow a phrase from an exhibition blurb that long ago locked itself in my brain, mysterious, dense and true.

Do you read photographic critics or philosophers?

I try not to. Most photographers don't like to use words to describe their work. Susan Sontag, a well-known American critic, author and aesthete, has been a prolific commentator on art and literature, and among other works, produced a short book called *On Photography*. Although the book was popular and in some quarters admired, to me it's an exercise in unfinished intellectual pyrotechnics that skips from idea to idea without producing a core narrative or an understandable central viewpoint.

Her work, like some of the other serious writing on the subject, is to me like an exposition on politics: speculative, internally contradictory, confusing and dogmatic; is it really insightful to say that photographic images are mere fragments of a whole and seek to elevate the banal to the status of beauty? Or that photography as a medium is corrupted by its use as a commercial tool? Or that photography collapses our sense of scale? Some of her ideas are surprising, but is this commentary useful to individuals trying to understand the medium? Not to me.

One of the most famous and artistically certain American photographers, William Eggleston, not only refused to write about photographs but refused to be interviewed about them. He was a magnificently quirky and self-confident man who made some of the greatest images of the age. I would sooner look at them than read Sontag any day.

What captures me is the fact that individual images can be so powerful, in contrast to movies, which fade from my memory like autumn snow; and that they can seem ordinary at first but with observation grow into objects that entice, amaze, humble, sadden. I feel the same way about them as I feel about a Michelangelo statue: how on earth did that conception occur? How did this man or that woman dig a thing of such power and beauty from the raw material of the universe? If my optimism about the human race ever sags, I pull out a book of great photographs and dream.

A third artist with whom I fell in love with early on is the Hungarian André Kertész, whose work is less precise technically than, say, Adams or Mapplethorpe, but as honest, evocative and sympathetic. He was famously modest in describing his work, when he said something like, in taking photographs, I reshape and walk around my subject until it is arranged in a way that pleases my eye.

I'm also much moved by the great Americans Walker Evans, Robert Capa, Richard Avedon, Diane Arbus and Edward Weston, the German-Australian Helmut Newton, the Englishmen David Hockney and Bill Brandt, and the Aussies Bill Henson, Max Dupain, Olive Cotton, David Moore and Frank Hurley. And lots of others.

Are you still photographing as often and as intensively as you used to?

No, sadly. I think that's mainly because I've allowed my time to be invaded by the Wild Fire wine business, by the complexities of running a vineyard and farm, and by my commitments to old mates who need help. And I've been consulting to my old rowing club about some cultural and disciplinary problems they've been having.

I've found that writing this memoir has only moved when I've gone away somewhere quiet to work. So it is with photographing – I need more time and commitment and more printing. Printers don't like being neglected.

But I've nearly finished the first two of the series of photobooks I'm making – colour and monochrome. The last two volumes, portraits and places I love, are less developed but I've collected many of the images I mean to use. There is an interesting dilemma – do I add commentary to each image or not? If I were a professional I wouldn't, based on what I've just said, but because these will be companion volumes to my memoir, I might.

We have a butler's pantry in Iona that was designed with analog processing in mind, and I still have a substantial store of unexposed film and chemicals, but with everything else happening these days I have trouble getting down to it.

How do you see your own photographs?

The questions I ask are: are they pleasing to my eye, or not? And do they look at their subjects with fresh eyes and emotional intent? Do viewers resonate with anything when they look?

In some cases, I like them and I see something distinctive in them. They are often concerned with quiet places, small figures, shuttered windows, closed doors and spare geometry. The folks who've read my book to this page wouldn't be surprised by that. I titled my first photo volume *Outside In*. I'm on the outer fringe, looking at the comfort and security of the inside, wanting to enter but uncertain how.

When I see a negative or a print that's pleasing, it's like a door opening – it admits me, it excites me, it gives me hope that there's something about the way I see that's just me and no one else.

It sometimes saddens me because I don't know what's going to happen to my archive. And it makes me feel guilty because I could have done with more attention and more discipline.

Are my images pleasing to the eyes of anyone else? Some people, I think. If I do stage an exhibition I think it would be well-received. Too late, of course, for me to develop any kind of following but maybe I'll also create a website to do some easier display and see what happens. One of the problems of the modern world is that everything that does anything, be it a computer, a camera, a piece of sound equipment, a refrigerator or a phone, has a huge inbuilt system that needs to be learned and managed, otherwise the object can't be used to best advantage. So much to remember! So I'm wary of embarking on anything like a website development because I know how much work it would represent.

Have you collected photos as well?

I haven't bought many originals, but I have a large collection of photobooks and I still buy photographic book collections regularly. I hope they're kept together and cherished when I'm gone.

What do you plan to do with your camera collection?

One of the difficulties of any collection is deciding where it should go when you can't use it anymore. I have some ideas. I know that older film equipment is becoming used and loved more and more, just like vinyl records. I'm sure that between Donna and me, we'll work out a solution.

I'm looking at a photo of your kids on that wall over there – they seem happy and relaxed, as though they've just come out of McDonald's. We haven't talked much about them, have we?

OK, this was 1987 and at that stage Sarah was fifteen, Pip was thirteen, Nicola was eleven and Michael was five.

Sarah arrived in 1972. Mary's pregnancy was reasonably smooth although she was extremely ill in the first couple of months. We had just taken possession of our first house in The Grange, East Malvern and the house was upside down when Mary went into labour because some renovations were under way. After Mary's call I shot out to collect her and delivered her to the Mercy Maternity Hospital in record time.

I was lucky, because husbands were only just being allowed to attend births. We had a kindly GP called Peter Brew, who agreed to me coming in, although the hospital midwives made it very clear they thought this was a bad idea! I had done all of my prenatal training and I thought I was ready, but when the action started, I confess I had a couple of very wobbly moments. Mary did a superb job after a tough labour, and all of a sudden we were three. An overwhelming if daunting experience.

The families were overjoyed, as we were, that the next generation was on its way.

I had a very late and alcoholic night and was woken by my alarm early the next day. It took a few minutes in my poor state to realise that I had agreed to attend an early work conference that day with none other than the senior partner and because I was late I had to scramble to get into the car and get on my way. On my arrival at the office, I was horrified to see that in my haste I had suit trousers and jacket that didn't match-that the senior partner would view as an outrage to him and to the clients. When I turned up in the conference room he immediately noted my crime and said to me in a venomous voice "Mr Harry. You are undressed. Please take your seat at the end of the table and do not move or stand up or speak or do anything else likely to attract attention to your pathetic state." Well, I survived in the end but it was a close shave.

Pip was also born at the Mercy two years later almost to the day. My memory is that the delivery was quicker but that Mary developed some medical problems including high blood pressure.

Nicola was born in Charlottesville another two years on, again close to the dates on which Sarah and Pip had been born.

So, by the end of 1976, we were five.

Edging Away from Law

OK, so back to the career track?

The family came back to Melbourne from New York in 1977.

I returned to the legal department, where General Counsel Robin Chambers starved me of interesting work to re-establish what he believed was a respectful attitude on my part, even though my UVA law school results shook him. I resolved to leave law once and for all and soon I was invited to join the Rio minerals exploration division full-time as negotiations manager; I agreed to leave Robin, much to his chagrin.

My work for its general manager, John Collier, whom I had worked with successfully as a lawyer, was one of the most fascinating experiences of my life.

The division's job was to find more Hamersley Irons and Bougainville Coppers, and also step out into pure gold, industrial minerals, oil and gas, uranium and coal. There was an ample annual budget of, in today's terms, AU$1 billion-plus.

It was an operation not unlike venture capital, where a big player like Rio would seed prospective exploration ventures brought to it by third parties, with the right to buy a controlling equity slab cheaply if anything was found. There was also an internal exploration team that would peg tenements and geologically assess them.

So, how would you describe the exploration experience?

It was the first time I'd done anything other than lawyering. Not having to report to Robin Chambers, a talented but controlling man, was a big plus, and my switch signalled to my superiors of which there were a depressing number of layers that I wanted to be in the management mainstream. The engineers and geologists usually were first in line for senior production positions, but Rod Carnegie had demonstrated that people from the finance side weren't barred from the upper echelons.

My job was to check titles and local foreign investment regulations where the projects were located outside Australia, negotiate joint venture terms with those third parties on the most advantageous terms possible, and document the ventures in a bulletproof way.

In the dying days of the Whitlam Labor government, a restrictive foreign investment policy was introduced in the form of the 1975 Foreign Acquisitions and Takeovers Act. This prevented foreign corporations, including CRA, from acquiring majority interests in Australian mining tenements without government approval. After complex negotiations between the mining industry and the government, an Australianisation policy was introduced to allow foreign corporations to be viewed as Australian: if they reduced their foreign ownership content below fifty per cent over time, then they would be allowed to acquire Australian assets.

A large part of my new job was working out how CRA should navigate this policy transition to be able to continue to acquire rights in Australian mineral tenements and develop CRA business. This involved much liaison with Canberra, and on occasions, direct contact with Paul Keating, who had become the shadow minister for mineral resources and energy when Fraser defeated Whitlam in late 1975. It was obvious from the first meeting that Keating had an excellent mind, worked hard, knew his brief and was destined for high office.

I guess the travel load was high?

It was mad, really. I was away one week in two, all over Australia, South-East Asia, Central Asia and South America, and met some of the most able and decent men in the business, as well as some of the industry's greatest knaves. Because I was seen as young and inexperienced, the knaves and the party boys would always try to skin me, but generally speaking I gave a good account of myself. Remember that in the 1970s, mining fraud was everywhere because stock exchanges weren't regulated as they are now, and founders often injected worthless tenements into listed structures, then pumped and unloaded them for a profit before the house came crashing down. So we had to be careful about our counterparties.

I loved the able and honest ones. My favourite was Jaime Ongpin, for many years the CEO of the Benguet Corporation, then the biggest mining group in the Philippines. I met him in 1979 to discuss an exploration joint venture with Rio. He was maybe thirty-five at the time and greeted me and the idea of a Rio alignment well. He was a wine lover, and once he learned of my interest, he invited me to his holiday home at Baguio, a cool mountain resort and university town, to the north-east of Manila, to sample his very substantial wine cellar and speculate about the global mining industry. Jaime was conservative, super smart, ethical and well educated, having graduated with an MBA from Harvard. He was from a foundation family and was violently anti-Marcos; he became embedded in Corazon Aquino's Yellow Revolution that led to the overthrow of Marcos, and then became Aquino's treasury secretary and main financial adviser.

After I left Rio, I learned that he had been found shot in his office, shortly after being sacked from the Aquino government following a political settlement between Aquino and the other Filipino oligarchs. He was forty-nine. The government alleged that he had committed suicide, but I have no doubt he was assassinated because of his unwillingness to sink into the ineradicable swamp of graft that Manila has always been. But I'll always remember his charm, his courtesy, his intensity and his profound desire to improve the lot of his country and his countrymen.

Did you have a favourite city or country?

The Philippines and Thailand, probably, but all of Asia was a delight then. Manila in the 1970s was still a charming, inexpensive and beautiful place, which I loved even if you had to check your guns in when you went into bars and restaurants. A room-service breakfast on my terrace at the Manila Shangri-La was simply perfect, from the brazenly perfumed saffron mango to the silky scrambled eggs and the pungent coffee. Now, the city is dirty, pollution-covered, grey and even poorer, and once again ruled by a Marcos. When will they ever learn?

Bangkok was similar to Manila but even more perfumed, exotic and gentle. I used to stay at the old Erawan Hotel located on the southeast corner of Ratchaprasong Intersection in Pathum Wan District, near the famous Erawan Shrine. The shrine was full of bowing and praying Thais all day and night, and was covered in incense burners, offerings of fruit and rice and a thick carpet of white flower garlands. It's hard for we westerners to have any understanding of the faith and devotion of these societies. The hotel itself was built in 1956 and was one of the first to pitch itself at the foreign tourist, even though it was Asian in every real way. The entrance was manned by courtly attendants swathed in red and black silks with glittering gold trim, and the interior and every room was covered in rare wooden panelling. Just like Manila, the city has now become choked with traffic, rail overpasses, garbage, stinking drains and rats.

I saw it at its best.

What would you say were your high points in the exploration world?

There were many adventures but the biggest by far was my involvement in the foundation of the Argyle Diamond Mine. I negotiated the diamond exploration joint venture that Rio formed with a group of Tanganyika and associated mining houses led by Ewen Tyler, and the commercial mining joint venture that was formed when Rio found diamonds at Ellendale, then Smoke Creek and finally the huge diamond-bearing Kimberlitic pipe that contained the Argyle deposits.

I was part of the team that created the first run-of-mine diamond sales contract between the De Beers organisation and Rio, without which the project would not have succeeded. The relationship stayed with me even after I left Rio, when I was engaged to advise Argyle on disputes with De Beers over diamond pricing and the eventual dissolution of the De Beers selling arrangement. This involved many trips to London and Antwerp and to the legendary De Beers headquarters at Charterhouse Street in London. All of us on the Argyle side came out of our De Beers experience wiser because of the degree of duplicity and disrespect we experienced from what we, naively perhaps, had always seen as a reputable organisation.

I was offered a flawless 1.5 carat pink diamond just after I left Rio for the staff rate of US$50,000 but couldn't raise the cash. It would be worth well in excess of US$1.5 million now but I console myself with the certainty that it would have disappeared in my divorce settlement. One of the betrayals of De Beers was that it tried for years to classify coloured diamonds as fancy and cheap because it wanted to stockpile them for itself. The smart operators who bought coloureds then have done very well.

So what did you go on to after exploration?

After a couple of years I was approached by Jim Champion, who was then running the Rio mining business in Asia, which consisted mainly of Malaysian tin extraction. He asked me whether I'd consider a management role in the Asia business, which was about to have its budget and scope expanded to enable Rio investment in metal-consuming operations. The strategic reason was to acknowledge the growth and importance of the Asian economies, and to train a cadre of Australians in how to do business in Asia. The idea was driven by Rod Carnegie, who was a deep and long-range business thinker.

My job would be to manage the Melbourne interface with the Asian business unit and to help with identifying and evaluating new Asian business opportunities.

I agreed to this immediately because I loved Asia, I had already worked there for the exploration unit under some testing conditions, I enjoyed working for Jim Champion and I could see that would be my first real, albeit small, step into the Rio management structure. I was aware that my performance was being monitored more closely than usual because I had been identified as an emerging senior management candidate despite my personality's rough edges.

Was Jim Champion a smart ally for you at that stage of your career?

In some ways yes, and in others no.

Jim's story is fascinating and too long to do justice to here. He was the first mature man to take an interest in me and my career; he became a loyal mentor; he was a brilliant Cambridge graduate and a fine squash player; he saw the Asian business landscape with clear eyes; he was a magnificent eater and drinker and his wife Molly never stopped trying to seduce me. And he introduced me to my dear friend Chris Long. But as it turned out, he was not well liked by the ex-Broken Hill mafia in senior management, which set me back in my relations with the Melbourne office.

So what were you and Chris Long up to in Asia then?

Rod Carnegie had decided that Australian companies needed to learn how to become successful investors and business managers in Asia, and therefore needed to train a group of younger executives to do the investing and managing. He also saw that direct participation in Asian businesses would provide an intelligence window to help forecast demand, prices and preference shifts for CRA. So, he launched a search for metal-consuming enterprises that could be made more efficient and profitable with CRA's capital, technology and manpower.

Chris and I became a core part of the small team brought together to study and execute Rod's plan. The mandate was broad but it included activities in galvanising, sheet painting, steelmaking, the making of grinding balls for ore ball-mill use, and hi-tech foundry and forging for the oil and gas industry.

We had modest success. After a number of tries, we found a company in Singapore in 1981, then known as Jurong Alloys, and proposed it for purchase to the Rio board. Jurong made high-integrity steel components for the petroleum industry. Carnegie and the board liked the idea and suddenly I found myself living in Singapore with the family as the new finance director of the company.

How did the legacy employees respond to that? I suspect not well.

We inherited two Australian senior managers from Jurong, and as you would expect, they were deep blue collar, tough, experienced and resented having been sold to a newfangled mining company.

They especially resented the imposition of their new finance director who knew nothing about steel, them or their business. I would, I'm certain, have played the company bigshot, rather than trying to be useful and making friends slowly and helpfully.

Of course, my new colleagues enthusiastically dug as many holes as they could for me to fall into, and I obliged them. The biggest problem was that they isolated me from information about the business. It was the old and inefficient silo model. The production manager, for example, refused to teach me how steel was made and processed into components, which just made it harder and slower to learn.

The essence of the business was the manufacture of heavy steel components such as pipe flanges, pump casings, pipeline valves and collars. This required making steel from scrap in an electric arc furnace and moulding the molten steel, followed by heat treatment for stress relief and final machining.

There were roughly 400 employees, mostly Malays, Thais, Indians and Pakistanis. It was a cultural nightmare. It was impossible to impose any health and safety standards. The arc furnace operators, for example, refused to wear boots, risking death daily when pours from the furnace took place. Factions of different nationalities were at war, and there were industrial accidents, sometimes involving large gas fires, explosions, and deaths. Customers never paid on time, marketing was exhausting and commercial control and forecasting precarious.

Was Jurong a success for you though?

Yes, overall. My immediate Rio superior was Leon Davis. He was placed in charge of the Asia business when the upgrading happened, and both Jim Champion and I reported to him.

Leon was a clever operator, with a formidable and ambitious wife. He subsequently became managing director of the Rio business worldwide, and if I had declared my loyalty to him and his career at that point, and acted supportively, who knows what might have happened. But he saw me as one of Carnegie's golden boys and as all ruthless corporate killers do, he did his best to steal my ideas, downplay my performance and scrutinise everything I did, right down to the cost of the toilet paper in my apartment.

Instead, I fell into that hole as well by trying to expose his tricks, which led to serious bad blood. I was thirty-five at the time and lacked the guile and foresight to compete with Leon.

I was also aware that if I was offered the mandatory mine site job experience, life for my kids would be harder, their schooling would suffer and Mary would be ill-equipped to deal with the demographic she would need to integrate with.

Sounds to me like you were on a hiding to nothing! So how did all of that resolve itself?

Well, another door, this time back to the legal profession, opened.

An old friend, Lachlan Donaldson, called me out of the blue to tell me that one of the senior commercial partners in his Melbourne firm, a small and prestigious establishment law office called Hedderwick, Fookes and Alston, had been sacked by the senior partner, Jock Macindoe, for insubordination, and would I be interested in his partnership subject to a six-month probation?

This was a unique opportunity. If I'd entered the firm as an articled clerk it might have taken me ten years or more to be admitted.

My Rio life was problematic, so it seemed sensible to consider this. It would bring the family back to Melbourne permanently, it had the potential to multiply my earnings many times, and it would be tenure for life in what was then regarded as the best firm in Melbourne, with the possibility of ascent to directorships on the boards of the largest listed companies in Australia.

I flew to Melbourne and was interviewed by Robin Syme and Bill Rogers, both senior partners and establishment leaders. That went well, I received an employment proposal and found myself a day or two later announcing my resignation from Rio altogether. Leon Davis was furious because he knew there would be blowback from Carnegie, and told me that I would need to find my own way back to Australia, which was a mean decision and a bitter end to ten years of hard and mainly successful work for the CRA Group.

And were you happy with that choice?

Yes, but I wondered what it would be like to return to the life of a professional consultant; I did worry about whether I'd be able to manage the transition.

I always wondered why Hedderwicks would have made me such an unusual and generous offer. Maybe it was the fact that I had a number of friends in the firm, but I did have a reputation for intellectual strength and toughness, which I felt was overestimated. I had come back from my USA post-grad experience with a 4 + grade point average (better than A) at the law school, which was rare for Australians, so a kind of myth had emerged about my capability.

I joined Hedderwicks in May 1982 and worked hard to re-establish myself as a practitioner, not having consulted since 1975. It was a hard grind. I was invited into the partnership in November 1982 and for the first time felt secure and happy in my work despite the professional experience being far from electric. The firm possessed a tight and loyal culture, the relationship among the ten or so partners was supportive and happy and the ethics of the firm were watertight, unlike the parlous standards of the behemoth accounting and legal firms of today. I was given responsibility for several banks and corporates, which, if truth be told, I wasn't fully prepared for but I seemed to scramble my way through on most assignments.

Then we decided in 1984 to merge with a slightly larger but culturally compatible firm in Arthur Robinson & Co, which had a sound mining and resources practice with, as one of its premier clients, Rio Tinto!

Arthur Robinson & Hedderwicks became justly recognised as the leading law firm in Australia for many years, until it decided, unfortunately in my opinion, to merge with the old Sydney firm Allen Allen & Hemsley in March 2001. I was a member of the merger negotiating committee and the inaugural board of the merged firm, but decided to retire in 2002 to set up Arcadis Capital, a micro-investment bank, with my colleague and friend Andrew Martin.

The merged firm is now called Allens, and has become one of four or five indistinguishable national commercial firms with none of the magic, the flair or the respect that ARH enjoyed. The final terms of merger were hard on the older partners in particular because their pensions were to be stripped more or less, and I knew that per partner profits would suffer as the new culture was built and productive economies of scale were imaginary. So, remembering the adage that no man ever became wealthy selling his time, I quit.

My partners thought I was mad, but Arcadis delivered more in returns to me in three years than I had received in all the time I had been a partner in the law firm.

One evening during a partners' retreat in the mid-90s I was drinking with the managing partner of ARH, Michael Robinson, an able but crusty and domineering individual, and I asked what he would have done if it had not been law. His reply floored me because of its frankness, but not its sentiment. I would, he said, have done something useful. I could not have agreed with him more.

Johnnie, I want you to make this quick so we can move on to more interesting stuff, but what were the highlights you remember when thinking of your legal career?

I can answer that best by saying that it would have been hard to improve my client list and my transaction experience. Remember that my contribution was necessarily seen as that of a risk manager rather than an architect, and it was hard to convince clients to treat architectural suggestions seriously even if they had merit. There were times where my advice was seen as deadlock-breaking and fundamental, especially in tough negotiations, but that was the exception rather than the rule.

I worked for Rio Tinto, BHP, Shell, Mayne Nickless, Woodside Petroleum, ACI, Cadbury Schweppes, the Bank of Tokyo, OCBC, Pasminco, the Bank of America, the Victorian and South Australian governments, Argyle Diamonds and a long list of less well-known companies. The largest transactions were in privatisation: I managed the creation of the Gandel Property Trust, the sale of the Victorian TAB, the sale of Telecom and creation of Optus, the commercialisation of the North-West offshore gas project and the privatisation of the Electricity Trust of South Australia.

My last boast is that I was regularly ranked publicly at or near the top of lawyer surveys in my fields.

There's not much to be gained by looking at any of these exposures in detail, although many of them involved political and personality clashes that businesspeople would find entertaining.

There must have been some special experiences or exceptional people you came across as a practising lawyer?

I can think of a few. Before the merger of ARH with Allens in 2001, the two firms pooled their activities in Asia as a first step toward integration, and at the same time, created a best-friends relationship in which they would share intelligence and bid for jobs jointly. The association was called the Australian Legal Group. It also included firms in Brisbane, Perth and Adelaide.

At the time, Allens had offices in London, Jakarta and Singapore, all of which were under-performing, and it was also agreed in around 1994 that ARH should buy into the Allens Asian business fifty-fifty, and that the new offshore entity, called Allens Arthur Robinson, would also jointly open offices in Port Moresby, Hong Kong, Bangkok and Shanghai.

I was then invited by Andrew Guy, the managing partner of ARH in 1995 to take up the role of Managing Partner Asia with responsibility for the existing offices and for the new office openings. I was to be based in Singapore with Mary. We decided that it would be too disruptive to bring Michael with us so he went into boarding school at Melbourne Grammar and would visit us each holiday. From his reports, his boarding house had been transformed for the better and his life there was as close to normal as it could have been. I was delighted when he was invited to be house captain, a job that his masters said he did very well. In a nutshell, I was thus plunged into a backbreaking three years of work, which involved even more intense travel into all corners of Asia. Even though there was a heavy administrative load, I still needed to develop our client base and generate better cash flow and profitability to underwrite the longevity of the network.

Then, we decided that we should open up in Cambodia to take advantage of the heavy stream of postwar reconstruction and commercial investment that had begun to flow into Phnom Penh.

There were many memorable transactions that came my way and which quickly schooled me in the way business was done in Asia, where one of the bigger challenges and risks was detecting and managing corruption. I was asked for bribes from governments and corporates every day, and arranging our engagements while not running foul of the Australian Foreign Corrupt Transactions legislation and our own ethical rules was not simple. By and large we did that, although many of our competitors casually ignored the problem.

Three Asian deals in particular stand out.

The first was a merger between a huge Indonesian conglomerate and the Malaysia Mining Corporation, which I eventually decided was designed purely to extract huge bags of cash for the insiders. After a massive amount of work my bill was still unpaid for months, so I hopped on a plane to Jakarta and sat in the office lobby of the Indonesian counterpart for three weeks until they were so sick of me that a cheque was produced.

There was one happening in that merger that illustrates well how hard it was to operate in the Asian environment. Because MMC's merger target had extensive investments in forestry and timber, I was asked to investigate whether a foreign investment approval was needed for the merger. Based on the law in force at the time, it was. To receive approval, we first needed to apply to the foreign investment authority, with extensive documentary support, for hearings to be held during a mandatory wait period and for a determination to be made after a cross-government consultative process. A year or more would be needed for this.

Here is how it then went:

"Pak Hassan, here is what your laws provide in relation to MMC's acquisition of Indonesian forestry assets." I explained the approval process and timing.

"Are you very sure, Pak John?"

"Yes, it seems clear. Here are the regulations." I provided the details.

"But we don't have the time, Pak John."

"That seems to be the case, unfortunately."

"Please wait, Pak John."

Hassan disappeared and a large and noisy motorbike started up and roared off into the distance. An hour went by and the motorbike screeched back to a halt outside the office. The rider entered the conference room and handed Hassan a yellow envelope, which Hassan opened, looked at briefly and handed to me confidently.

"Here, Pak John."

I looked at the one-page document. It was a form of consent signed by the minister for foreign investment approving the merger. It was invalid on every count, despite having been purchased for a large sum of money.

"Well, Pak Hassan, this document has been issued contrary to the requirements of the law and is therefore invalid."

"But the minister has signed, Pak John, so we will proceed."

Game, set and match.

The second deal that stood out was a hydro-electricity project in Xe Kaman in Laos, which was conceived to generate electricity for the Thai market. The project leader and our client was a crazy republican Irishman who was prepared to do anything and pay anyone to be awarded the franchise. I spent weeks on end in Vientiane in fruitless conferences with the Lao bureaucrats waiting for bribes to be assembled and for something to happen. In the end, as was so often the case, nothing did happen and my firm received an enormous fee haircut, which I complained bitterly to my client about. He informed me that he was IRA and that he was tired of my bleating. I was smart enough to stand down at that point.

The last was an assignment I received from AusAID, the entity that administered Australia's foreign aid program, to go into Cambodia in late 1994 to help with reinstating Cambodian legislation for mining and petroleum exploration and development, which had been abolished by Pol Pot as part of his destruction of the Cambodian state during the civil war. That had ended only in October 1991 with the signing of the Comprehensive Cambodian Peace Agreements (known as the Paris Peace Agreements) brokered by the United Nations. Cambodia was temporarily governed by the National Council and the United Nations Transitional Authority in Cambodia, which was then replaced by the joint government of Hun Sen's Communist Party of Kampuchea and the royalist FUNCIN-PEC party loyal to Prince Norodom Sihanouk.

The assignment also included representing the Cambodian government in managing the first international tender for Cambodia's offshore petroleum exploration acreage in the Gulf of Thailand, which was believed to be prospective and possibly the only source of a large and sustainable cash flow for Cambodian redevelopment.

My firm presented its credentials to a joint meeting of FUNCINPEC and Hun Sen representatives; the men lined opposite sides of an enormous conference table, staring murderously at each other and not in the least interested in what I was saying.

The minister then called me into his office alone.

"Mr Harry, you have been selected as adviser to the government for this task."

"Minister, we are most honoured to assist the government and we will do our best to ensure that the project has a good outcome."

"Very well. But there is one more thing."

"Yes, Minister?"

"There will need to be a contribution made by your firm on a monthly basis to assist in the development of departmental infrastructure."

"Minister, as long as the ministry issues detailed invoices under your signature for these amounts, we will advance them."

I knew full well that the invoices would be bogus and that the payments would be pocketed by the minister, but we had decided as a firm that it was not our duty to investigate the payment destination.

"Thank you, Mr Harry."

The installation of the new legislation was a relatively easy process, but the subsequent tender was a nightmare.

A tender is a process whereby a government advertises the availability of blocks of exploration acreage for oil and gas drilling, in this case offshore Cambodia, to international petroleum companies. The government documentation, which a brilliant Scottish colleague, Gavin MacLaren and I prepared, sets out the block description, the terms and conditions under which exploration will be conducted, the terms of exploitation – most importantly, the split of production between the government and the bidder, and the machinery for tendering – the timetable, the shape of the acceptance and the fees associated with the tender and award.

The next step is for the government to conduct a qualification round, which reduces the scores of likely applicants to ten or so qualified tenderers who would be entitled to lodge a full bid.

Gavin, who moved to Cambodia at around this time, ran the project on the ground, and he and I were given a tiny office in the new ministry with windows that faced south – the sunny side – with no air conditioning and a couple of useless fans. It took weeks to prepare the tender documents, steer them through the ministry, have them approved by the joint government, which because of old political enmities was close to paralysed, finalise the list of tenderers and organise dispatch. Gavin, who was still in his mid-twenties at the time, was phenomenally effective, and formed a relationship of trust with Hun Sen, to whom he became a close adviser, an amazing feat.

We were aware that outside our office, a parade of tenderers' agents equipped with large stacks of US dollars was washing through the offices of the minister and senior politicians, seeking placement on the tender list during the tender evaluation.

We were then asked to assess the incoming tenders and provide our views on how they ranked against each other.

In the end, with one or two exceptions, we were able to ensure that the awards went to credible and solvent companies. This was not a simple task.

The flow of fees from the tender process was an essential addition to the cash available to the government and assisted the rehabilitation process then under way to restore governance in Cambodia to something resembling normality.

Chevron discovered oil and gas in Block A offshore Cambodia in 2004. The government, still dominated by Hun Sen, effectively nationalised the block, which is now again under private ownership. Oil is flowing and at last, our project is delivering substantial benefits to the Cambodian people, of course after Hun Sen's ticket clip.

As I told you, Jimmy, although I was successful in this colosseum, I never warmed to it or loved it as many of my partners did. So, that's really all that needs to be said about law.

It seems strange to dismiss twenty-five years of hard labour in just a few pages, but that was the reality of consultancy: you did essentially the same thing every day, you kept the franchise in good standing and looked forward to the day it would all stop. I could talk about the culture and politics of the firm, which naturally I was involved in, but it would say nothing new about me or my life, and would seem tedious to outsiders. I can summarise those non-professional aspects of my partnership quickly: I was well-received by most of the partnership as a good lawyer and a sensible thinker about the commercial functioning of the business. My voice in partners' meetings was strong and I was regarded as someone whose views should be treated seriously. But, as is usually the case with individuals who are well-presented, successful and opinionated, I generated jealousy and sometimes ill will from the technocrats and those who had ambitions for management roles. If only these people had known that I wasn't remotely interested in formal management. I got done what I needed to in other ways.

Perhaps the only other thing worth mentioning about those years is that when my marriage began to unravel, I ceased to be as strong a contributor and my voice softened; another reason for my early exit: my course had been run.

Would you say that you'd been rewarded fairly for your efforts as a practitioner?

No. The way our old firm worked was that, subject to an earn-in period, all partners shared equally. The theory was that as long as all partners made a roughly equal contribution, this would avoid money disputes, and that if one partner struck trouble, say, with his health or his marriage, he would not have his earnings diminished, and because all partners might need this protection at some stage, it was in effect an income-preservation insurance policy as well.

As the firm grew of course, some partners became under-performers for reasons of professional failure or laziness rather than events of force majeure. So, a partner underclass evolved, which was rewarded unfairly.

Also, the more successful rainmaking partners were more obvious and less happy as our market became more open and competitive. Clients were handed down in early days, but as the impact of competition laws required more and more free contest for work, many partners found themselves underemployed while the generators thrived.

I felt no shame in gathering clients, and ran presentations well despite my anxiety, and my stature was no handicap. So, I was at or near the top of the billing tree for practically my whole time in practice. In my last couple of years, I billed several times what the next best partner did.

Although I could see that performance-driven remuneration might reduce happiness and ethical standards, its advent was inevitable. Hence my determination, eventually, to go into business outside the firm to capture, at last, an equity-driven earnings stream rather than an advisory stream, which would always be smaller.

OK. Let's take another detour. What do you suggest?

How about rally driving?

Really?

Yes.

In early 1999 I saw an ad inviting competitors to join the second London to Sydney Car Marathon. The first had been staged in the '60s and I knew of it because by ex-brother-in-law Martin Braden had been a competitor and I grew up on a diet of tall tales of that rally.

The idea was that anyone interested would form a team, acquire and equip a vehicle for long-distance driving through rough country and then spend around two months on the road in competition with all the other teams. The idea was irresistible to someone cooped up for twelve hours a day in a dusty law firm.

So, I invited my mates Tim Cecil, Chris Long and Peter Chapman to the party and against my expectations they agreed to become team members.

We duly purchased and converted a Nissan Pathfinder and had it shipped to London for the start of the competition.

The start was at Heathrow Airport after a week of preparation and trialling. The great day dawned bright and we arrived at the start to find a crowd of maybe 30,000 spectators massed around the send-off ramp. There were around 100 teams and it was immediately clear that some were better prepared than others. There were American muscle cars, Porsches, antique sportscars, 4WDs like ours and small Japanese rally cars driven by real professionals. It wouldn't take long before the pretenders and the mechanically illiterate would strand themselves in ditches, blow up their gearboxes, take dirty fuel on board or break their axles. We were unscathed: a 100% mechanical success. Sheer luck in fact.

So what route did you all follow?

Each team received a rally book that set out in sequence every inch of the way to Sydney. Every intersection, turn, bridge, underpass, border crossing and hotel was marked on an individual page with the distance between each marked point being recorded. We were equipped with a device called a Terratrip that measured and displayed the meterage we covered so in theory your navigator could, by watching the book, the road and the Terratrip, know exactly where he was. But there was ample scope for disaster: signs on the road moved, Terratrips would go out of calibration, night would fall, the navigator would doze off after a particularly celebratory evening or someone would tell a long joke and suddenly you would be bushed.

I can't recall the route exactly, but as I remember it, it was the UK, France, Alsace, Austria, Hungary, Czechoslovakia, Romania, Bulgaria, Greece, Turkey, Thailand, Malaysia, Singapore and Australia. By far the roughest and toughest sector was Australia.

I guess spending that amount of time on the road with the other crews would have been good fun?

The sheep and the goats were soon separated. Tim Cecil brought with him several good food guides that covered most of the Eastern European countries we went through and with his help we would decide nightly where we would be likely to find the most convivial restaurant. This habit became known to the rest of the crews and when we finally stopped at out hotel in the evening we would be surrounded by a mob wanting to know where we intended to go. So, every night was a party and we forged many firm and happy friendships as a result.

What about the competitive side of things?

No one would want to hear the detail. But the competition was serious and often stressful. There were two divisions: the 4WD drivers and the racers. In the end, we came a respectable third in our division out of maybe sixty crews so we felt we hadn't wasted our time. But the joy of the event was in the spectacle, the camaraderie, the fascination of the countries we visited that we would never have thought to see otherwise, the cultural learning and especially the lifelong bond made between Chris, Tim and myself.

Our arrival was on the concourse of the Sydney Opera House to another huge crowd. What a relief. A competitors' final dinner was held that night and the final speech was given by a representative of the competitors in honour of the organisers. A murmur ran through the guests as the drivers' representative climbed the rostrum. He had with him a large bottle of whisky. He introduced himself by saying: "I have here a bottle of outstandingly beautiful single malt Scotch whisky. By the time I finish this speech, the bottle will be empty." He proceeded to finish his speech, and the bottle, and four men were required to carry him to his seat. To his enormous credit, he didn't require hospitalisation although I suspect he was AWOL for quite a time thereafter.

What a tale! Anything a bit less ambitious?

How about baking?

Sounds good to me.

Well, you know I love cooking of all kinds. When I was with Mary, I really didn't have much time for the kitchen although I did cook some specials for the kids at weekends, like home-made pastas.

I'd always loved bread and still do. In fact, I would say that if I'm addicted to anything, it's a crunchy, crackly, flavoursome loaf covered in an unhealthy quantity of Gippsland butter.

I experimented with bread baking now and then when I was younger, but my results were poor and the avalanche of information now on the internet about artisanal bread-making wasn't available, and I have to admit my early efforts were poorly researched. Nowadays, having persisted with this mania for so many years, the house feels naked without its freshly cooked loaf.

I've wondered why I like to bake bread. I started well before Covid, so there's nothing occasional about the habit. It's a bit like making pasta, or beer or wine: it's an ancient practice, it connects me with humanity, the results are always satisfying – especially the reveal, when the lid comes off the Dutch oven and there lies the fragrant, hot, toasty, shapely result of your efforts, utterly transformed from the wobbly white dough you placed in it not more than forty or so minutes before. And it tastes so wonderful.

The fact that this interest surprises others is a plus, but it's not the heart of the reason I do it.

I can share some of the secrets, however, from years of attempts.

The first thing you learn is to live with disappointment. It's very hard to turn out loaves well and predictably. There will be many failures. Even now, when I'm well down the baking road, I produce a slightly different result every time: like fingerprints, there's always something about the ambient temperature, or the moisture content of the flour, or the condition of your yeast, or whether it's sunny or raining, that's invisible but makes for change. It's tricky in the way that making good puff pastry, or croissants, or excellent pinot is. You need patience, a plan, attention to detail, a capacity to measure and persistence.

So here is the truth and the way.

You'll need a 7-plus litre cast iron casserole or Dutch oven and an oval or round proofing basket or banneton.

Bread has infinite variety, as Enobarbus said of Cleopatra. But here is how to make a simple white loaf.

You have to use a high-protein hard wheat flour – around 12% protein – which maintains its rise and shape, and delivers good crumb. That means a stretchy bread full of holes, with a hard crust, deep golden colour and long shelf life. Laucke makes a good flour called Wallaby.

You have to use live compressed yeast rather than dried yeast, which you can buy from a bakery if they like you. This needs to be refrigerated but will deliver a more even, stronger rise and better flavours. Try sourdough if you want but for me it wasn't worth the effort.

Use kosher salt if possible.

Don't knead, as so many amateurs do, because it will homogenise your gluten structure and you'll get a crumb that's fine and cake-like. This took me forever to learn because I used a bread-making machine to do my dough mixing.

Take a large stainless-steel bowl, and measure into it exactly 600 grams of flour. Add 1 ½ teaspoons of salt and mix well.

Then take 425 millilitres of lukewarm water and crumble 25 grams of compressed yeast and 2 teaspoons of raw sugar into a vessel containing 100 millilitres of that water. Mix thoroughly and leave aside for 15 minutes while the yeast wakes up and the volume doubles to 200 millilitres.

That, for the scientifically minded, means a total hydration ratio of 72%, around about right for an artisanal loaf.

Make a depression in the flour mix and add the yeast starter, then the remaining 350 millilitres of warm water, and combine the two with a small wooden spoon for a minute or so but not too long.

Leave the mix in the steel bowl under a tea towel. Depending on the ambient temperature, leave to rise for two to three hours and when the dough looks puffy and bubbly, fold it inward three to four times – this will flatten it a bit – and go through the same process one more time after another hour.

Flour your banneton well and then drop in the dough, cover and allow to rise again but not too much otherwise the dough might collapse. Preheat your oven to maximum.

Then line your Dutch oven with baking paper and tip the risen dough onto the baking paper, meaning the underside of the dough in the banneton becomes the top side. Using a very sharp knife or razor, slash the top of the dough evenly. I use a sushi knife which I wet between cuts, which does a good job.

Throw the Dutch oven into your oven with the lid on. Remove the lid after, say, 20 minutes while reducing the oven temperature to 160 degrees, to allow browning and crisping to occur, which should take another 20 minutes. Remove the Dutch oven when the loaf is deep golden in colour and place the loaf on a rack to cool. Remember to use a good pair of oven gloves because the heat will be fierce.

Then attack!

Success is all technique and experimentation but you'll get there if you persist. There are endless variations of flours and more complex steps like dough refrigeration, but launch first and see what happens.

OK! I'd like to go back to your life after law if we can? Let's hear a bit more about that if we can.

Fine. As a lawyer, not only were you hired often as a form of insurance rather than as a creative project contributor, but when you delivered constructive deal proposals, your ideas were either pinched or suppressed by the investment bankers with whom you were usually hired. These were people like Macquarie Bank, JPMorgan and Moelis.

As a result, and also because of the conservative way in which lawyers approached business management, we had a per-hour fee rather than a deal remuneration fee. That also meant that there was little scope for incentive payments. I tried to persuade my firm to take more deal risk in exchange for a success-related pay packet but no one was interested. So, while my earnings would be fine month-to-month, I could never see myself accumulating significant capital to give me a comfortable retirement.

When I arrived at Allens in Sydney as an exchange partner after our 2001 merger, I was, as were the other Melbourne exchange partners, shunned by the somewhat self-regarding Allens partners, which made life drab indeed. It had made sense for me and Donna to go to Sydney because of the intense heat and drama created when Mary and I separated, but Allens in Chifley Tower was no fun at all.

Around twelve months before this I had persuaded my managing partner Tom Poulton to let me establish a part-time business consultancy within the firm, which we called Allens Business Solutions. We focused on a small number of big projects, including the creation of assets suited to acquisition by the Australian superannuation industry, which, since the introduction of compulsory super for Australian workers, had generated a high demand for investments that their rising tide of cash flow could be deposited into. I was lucky to find and recruit another bright young lawyer, Andrew Martin, to join Allens Business Solutions to develop this idea.

To cut a long story short, at the suggestion of my old Sydney mate Peter Carre, I went to the US to visit a Chicago-based industrial property trust that Peter believed might be willing to sell a portfolio of Chicago property into a listed trust vehicle that we would establish in Australia, which we would sell pieces of to Australian institutions and manage at a healthy recurring annual fee.

So, Andrew and I had developed the US property trust partially via Allens Business Solutions. We decided soon that the only way we could progress the deal was to leave Allens and partner with an investment bank and an Australian property company that would be willing to finance the substantial pre-listing costs of the project in return for a slice of the trust management rights.

Knowing that the more conservative end of the partnership was not frantically keen on Allens Business Solutions, I saw that this might be the perfect moment to leave the law and establish a new business where we might be competitive.

So, one wet winter afternoon, I sat down with Tom and did the thing I never thought I would have the courage to do: resign.

This must have been a worrying time!

I was calm about the odds: no better than 50%, or less, chance of success, but as I was rebuilding my life and had Donna by my side, I knew I had to take the chance.

The firm was generous: we were allowed to take away all of the Allens Business Solutions projects for no charge, including our US deal, and we were given twelve months rent-free accommodation in Chifley Tower. I left the firm with virtually nothing – under the partnership deed there was no buy-in and no capital out – so bearing in mind the cost of my divorce, I was exposed to financial death. But that's the nature of risk: there's never anyone to come to your financial funeral but plenty to celebrate your success.

So Arcadis Capital was born. Our US project succeeded after months of grim struggle; we launched and delivered a second Japan real estate trust and then moved into our China phase.

Between 2007 and 2010, Arcadis launched two China projects, the first to raise capital for a private trust for Chinese investment into Australian resources assets, which had been crushed by the 2007–08 Global Financial Crisis, and the second to purchase Chinese commercial property to be injected into an Australian-listed trust and sold to Australian superannuation funds.

The stock market collapse during the Global Financial Crisis threw most Australian resource stocks into the toilet. The junior companies with beautiful deposits, especially in iron ore, were collapsing all over the place for lack of cash, and were willing to issue convertible notes at historic low equity conversion prices to raise money. It seemed obvious that this would be an ideal time to set up a fund aimed at Chinese investors to buy these bargain basement Australian mining convertibles.

I approached Rob Adamson of RFC, a mining consultancy CEO, to partner Arcadis in China in seeking Chinese investors for our trust, and to help in the process of securing a package of prospective convertibles and other equity positions. He agreed, and a joint venture was set up.

We then needed to populate the trust's board with credible mining figures to soothe what we knew would be the reserve of our Chinese investors, because collective investment via trusts was virtually unknown in China then.

I was able to persuade Owen Hegarty, a former Rio colleague and also the MD of the emerging mining group Oxiana, to make himself available, and through a friend I offered Bob Hawke a directorship as well.

I met Bob with Blanche D'Alpuget on the terrace of their mansion looking over Middle Harbour in Sydney, made the offer not believing there was any hope he'd agree, and after a couple of Cubans and much whisky, he accepted. This was a major coup, because Bob had access to anyone in the Beijing bureaucracy at any time and might be able to generate interest for us.

I also saw that Arcadis would be in for a long and expensive fight to win the battle because of the extreme complexity and risk of doing business in China. I had formed a relationship with the large accounting firm KPMG through another friend, David Dunn, who was a senior partner, and he offered to provide our development capital for a share of the deal proceeds. So, Arcadis was hedged, but managing this whole circus was a considerable task.

As it turned out, equity markets recovered quickly post-GFC, and had we managed to convince the Chinese that the investment would succeed, Andrew and I would have been able to feed our families for many generations. But we failed, despite the magnificence of the opportunity, and despite our introduction to the cream of China's investment and bureaucratic community via Bob. I'll never know exactly what happened, but I decided that there were two main reasons. The first was that we didn't know who to bribe and how much. The second was that the individual Chinese state-owned entities that we targeted couldn't bring themselves to co-invest. Ancient enmities and family rivalries probably played a part but no westerner will ever penetrate that veil. One of the KPMG Chinese employees who accompanied us and translated for us, a couple of years later, cloned our idea and our structure, and succeeded. He knew how to manage things the Chinese way, and I suspect he may have sandbagged our efforts in his own interests. How were we to know? But it was the one that got away, a beautiful idea.

The proposed China real estate deal also failed when our partner tried to switch the deal economics we had agreed to late in the day, believing we had no option because by that time a signing in Beijing with Kevin Rudd attending on our side had been agreed. We walked, to some intense squawking by Austrade and DFAT, and just as well we did, because our perfidious counterparty would have made our acquisition hell.

Still, the memories of several visits to Beijing with Bob Hawke remain – including a hilarious game of golf with him alone on the most exclusive army golf course in China, during which Bob excelled himself as a lie-adjuster and arithmetic failure, and pronounced Golda Meir to be the greatest politician of his lifetime. We dined extravagantly every night and Bob regularly demonstrated his unique capacity for alcohol. I would always place Bob next to either Donna or a younger female consultant or bureaucrat. Bob never let us down. He would always be at his gracious best with his companion. We were given access to the leaders of the Communist Party, the government departments and the state-owned enterprises. I doubt that any Australian business group had ever been honoured to that degree. Bob truly was a hero to the Chinese.

I think he liked me, and most of all Donna. The two of them would retire nightly to the smoking room in our hotel for whisky and cigars. I would excuse myself on health grounds to Bob's great pleasure – he then had Donna (in a conversational sense) to himself.

We were invited, some time later, to his eightieth birthday dinner at the Opera House. We sat opposite Paul Keating, who didn't say a word to us all night! A discourteous man. We were close to the last to leave. God bless you, Bob.

Markets for our kinds of products died post-GFC, so we decided to sell Arcadis in 2008 or 2009 to Mirvac, which had agreed to give us a put option in the early days. They wriggled but eventually paid, meaning my life with Donna was financially secure short of a depression.

Andrew and I went our separate ways, happy and sad, he to a brilliant career in asset management at Moelis, and me to my vineyard at Iona. It was a great ride, loads of fun and an example to aspiring young entrepreneurs: if you think you can do it, waste no time; pack your bags and go.

Wanderings

Maybe we do another detour after all that?

Travel? Maybe a bit, although like divorces and slide shows, it bores people fast, doesn't it?

Good idea. Most people who know you are jealous of the amount of travel you've done and the kind of life you led as a diplomat's son. But you continued to explore the world hard and often after you left home.

I did. It was just one aspect of my curiosity. I couldn't stop wanting to know what was over the next hill. Maybe I'll just mention a few of my more entertaining travels, with a few side bars?

OK.

I've told you about my first European experience in Switzerland as a child, and about my life in Singapore. I've also had many trips to the UK, with Mary and Donna and for work.

I've always loved the British Isles, especially northern Scotland and western Ireland. I've drunk whisky at bright midnight in summer with the farmers near Loch Naver twenty miles south of the North Sea Coast, climbed northern Bens (Scottish mountains), dined at Inverlochy Castle, caught mackerel from a small fishing dinghy off the Scottish west coast and eaten haggis in Inverness. With Donna I've visited Campbeltown on the furthest western promontories of Scotland to inspect and taste casks of Springbank single malt whisky that I purchased and stored there, not far from the legendary Mull of Kintyre.

And England of course. The Thames Valley at Henley Regatta, feeling ridiculously privileged as a member of the Stewards Enclosure and Leander Club; tennis at Hurlingham Club; all the theatre, restaurants, bars, sleaze, art, music, cricket and tourist attractions that only London can provide; the hospitality of Donna's London family into which she was drawn as a young nanny; Cornwall to visit the land of my ancestors; dining with successful Aussie expats in their fine new houses in Mayfair; and exploring the UK coastline on board their classic yachts.

I've drunk Guinness in pubs all the way up and down the west coast of Ireland, visited the grave of Yeats, sat in awe and silence in the library of Trinity College Dublin, viewed the Book of Kells illuminated on the Hebridean island of Iona by Irish monks led there by Saint Columba in the sixth century, played golf at Ballybunion, taken cooking lessons at the heavenly Ballymaloe Cookery School, driven around the Ring of Kerry, watched hurling and Irish football matches and revelled with mad Irishmen and women in the pubs of Dublin beside the River Liffey.

I've visited Japan maybe sixty times on business. I had the unbelievable pleasure of running around the Imperial Palace in Tokyo during a winter snowstorm then dining in the main restaurant in the Imperial Hotel on my own whilst the storm continued to batter the windows. I've been taken to the smallest and most famous sushi and tempura bars in Tokyo, stayed at faultless onsens and traditional residences in Kyoto, spent three months living with Donna in an apartment in Chiyoda near the Imperial Palace, travelling every weekend during that time to a new destination on Honshu. I've dined and been entertained traditionally at the Mitsui Trading Company's eighteenth-century Tokyo house, complete with old-style, respectable geishas, and skied in the thistledown powder snow at Niseko in Hokkaido.

With Mary and Michael, I visited Africa in the mid-'80s. We toured in Zimbabwe and Zambia, looked over Victoria Falls, spent two weeks in Hwange National Park watching every conceivable wildlife animal, canoed down the Zambezi, holidayed on a magnificent motor cruiser on Lake Victoria and lived in a friend's house in the ritzy Cape Town suburb of Llandudno just below Table Mountain, and drifted slowly through the Stellenbosch vineyards.

In the late '80s I went trekking in Nepal, around the Annapurna Circuit. We were out for six weeks. We climbed to Annapurna base camp and saw all the legendary Western mountains: Annapurna, Annapurna II, Dhaulagiri, Machhapuchhare.

I completed, in two stages, the 800-kilometre pilgrimage walk known as the Camino de Santiago across northern Spain, the first stage on my own with Donna in support, and the second with my old mate Tom Daffy, again with Donna providing brilliant logistical help.

I was drawn to this because pilgrims had trodden these pathways since the Middle Ages, because I'd always wanted to find out what a long, slow and arduous physical commitment might bring forth, and because the Camino and its pilgrims had been guarded by the Knights Templar in the Middle Ages and this was a chance to see their castles and strongholds. I was also aware that the whole route had been placed on UNESCO's World Heritage List and that we would have the chance to overnight at the world-famous Paradores.

The first leg, to Burgos, was more beautiful, uncrowded and satisfying than the second, where crowds of Camino tourists clogged the route and stretched the hotels and restaurants. The terrain in the west was less friendly too. Galicia is all jagged mountains, peaks and troughs, heat and discomfort.

The best day of all was the very first – the spectacular climb from Saint-Jean-Pied-de-Port in western France to the summit of the Pyrenees, through the pass of Roland and down through soft pine forests into the ancient monastery of Roncesvalles. Never will I forget my first beer with Donna that baking afternoon.

There was a clear spiritual element about the journey for me, even though I undertook it not because I was Catholic or out of some other religious duty. Six weeks of walking thirty kilometres a day provides the chance to think, to meet and befriend men and women from all around the world, to discuss divorces, failed careers, enlightenment, blisters, Spanish food and wine, and to glimpse the eternal. I spent many days walking with members of the Irish Sligo mountaineering club: none of them really knew why they were there either but their ability to consume alcohol was astounding. I regret that most of the friendships that formed then came to nothing – it was a case of ichi go, ichi e. But I remember it all with affection and sense of accomplishment.

As we approached Santiago, I developed shin splints, or shin tendonitis, which was crippling, and I was lucky to have Tom there to get me to the end. I realised that I'd finished the walk in the nick of time – another two or three years and I wouldn't have been able to. One of my problems was that I had allowed myself to become too heavy. When I got back home I decided that after too many years of indulgence a lasting solution was needed. So, over the next nine months, I lost forty kilos, which for reasons that I don't fully understand, has stayed off. In one blow, I removed a problem that had beset my life since birth.

The sense of arrival and relief when, finally, we turned the corner of a narrow lane and there before us was the Santiago Cathedral can't be described. I was exhausted and to have Donna take the wheel on our trip back to France was a blessing. I couldn't have taken another step or have eaten another croqueta.

You must have spent a fair amount of time in France because of your interest in wine?

I did. When my family lived in Switzerland we were in and out of France all the time but mainly the north-east.

Mary and I visited France and Italy two or three times during the '80s as part of longer European trips. The children were young and managing them wasn't always easy, but they were made a fuss of in hotels and restaurants. Even starred places were happy to make them chips and sandwiches – they were attractive and happy kids that everyone warmed to.

I did impose on them a rich diet of cathedrals and vineyards, which they didn't approve of, but forgave me for.

We visited Bordeaux each time. Then, tourists were far fewer, and the grand chateaux were much more willing to provide tours and tastings than they are today.

Having French, and not being English, was a blessing too. Most of the vineyard owners were surprised to meet a large Australian who spoke French well, and who claimed to be a fellow winemaker. I may have burnished my winemaking credentials slightly, but if my hosts suspected anything was amiss they were most polite about it. So, by sitting on the phone in our hotel for an hour or so, I was able to construct almost the ideal itinerary, including Lafite, Palmer, Cos d'Estournel, Margaux, d'Yquem, Léoville-Las Cases, and my favourite, Domaine de Chevalier in Graves, to the south of Bordeaux.

The Chevalier estate is located in a beautiful forest and is bordered on one side by one of the French feeder routes into the main Camino de Santiago. My host on my first visit was the then proprietor, Claude Ricard, a quiet, civilised and enormously knowledgeable man who was also a fine musician and royal tennis player. He walked me through the estate and the cellars for more than an hour and then presented me with a bottle of his red, a gesture that was unheard of at that time, much less now. For a young and rough-around-the edges man such as me, this was an unforgettable compliment.

Someone told me that you owned a house in France at one stage?

I never owned a house there, though I came close to buying one. In 2004 I became aware from Chris Long that a Dutch friend of his had a house in northern Burgundy that she might be willing to lease us for a longish period. Arcadis Capital had just completed its first major transaction, the formation of the Mirvac Industrial Property Trust, and I was busy launching a second project, a Japan office trust, with the Galileo Group. I thought it would be possible for me to do this successfully from France, with a commute to Tokyo when needed.

Donna and I decided this made sense and negotiated the lease of the house for six months, through the winter and spring of 2004. The house was located in the small village of Nicey, some forty kilometres north of Chablis, with an easy hour-long commute to Paris on the TGV rail service.

Our first stay in Nicey was delightful. The house itself was a somewhat run-down maison de maître with two hectares of grounds. It was essentially un-heatable, so that winter was a real challenge, and all the fittings were unreliable, but nothing could spoil the joy of life in rural France. We shopped at the Chablis markets, bought and drank lovely wine for almost nothing, ate baguettes from the local baker, attended to a constant stream of friends and hangers-on who just happened to be in the area, sharpened our French cooking skills and travelled far and wide.

Any interesting tales to tell?

Many could be told of that period but one in particular has always delighted me.

During one of our early visits to the Chablis market, we stopped at the stall of the man who supplied chickens, duck, goose and game birds, some big, some small and almost all illegally poached. The owner asked me where I was from, and when I told him I was Australian, he roared with pleasure and asked whether I played rugby because he was from the south and had been a player himself in the past. I told him about my modest rugby career and he immediately embraced me, held my arm up in the air and announced in an ear-splitting shout that the market was privileged to have a visitor from Australia who would henceforward be known as "Monsieur Wallaby". From then on, he greeted us with "Bonjour, Monsieur Wallaby" from afar every time we visited and always gave us the best of his produce, as did his neighbours.

We inherited a careful and hard-working cleaner, Odette Plait, from the village, who taught us who was who and what was what and supplied us with Bresse chickens. Her husband Dede was our maintenance man, who liked to be paid in cheap rosé, and helped us develop a big kitchen garden.

You said that one of your aims while in France was to get out and about. Deciding where in France to go, well, it's a task, I know – it's a big place. I was on my yacht for fifteen summers in the Med and had the same doubts when choosing my routes and marinas.

I didn't have a yacht like you, Jimmy! We bought a middle-aged, grey Renault Scenic diesel van that was unglamorous but tough and efficient.

Donna did a lot of the driving. She's careful and perceptive but get her on a motorway and down goes the foot. There are speed limits advertised but the French pay no attention to them, believing in Gallic tradition that they're only suggestions, and Donna adopted the custom with pleasure. If I went to sleep on a long leg, I knew that when I did the average speed calculations the result would be hair raising, but not being one to flog a dead horse, I buckled up and hoped for the best.

Our main travel destinations were wine growing areas, including Beaune, the Rhône Valley, the Loire, Vouvray, Sancerre, the Dordogne, Bordeaux, Champagne and Cognac. We would always come home with our van groaning with wine, and over the time we spent in Nicey, we collected around 1,500 bottles. It took me around forty-five minutes to ride my bike from Nicey to the village of Les Riceys on the southern tip of the Champagne appellation. Good champagne could be bought there for around €10 a bottle, so our stocks were considerable, and many an afternoon I rode back with a fine bottle in my backpack.

We did have some trips to the Rhône Valley, Provence, Spain, Switzerland and Italy as well. On one memorable trip to southern Spain our van broke down on our return in a small, hot village called El Molar. We took the van to the local mechanic, who, after much shoulder shrugging, told us that we would need to wait several days for parts to arrive, and that we should book a room in the local hotel.

We had in our crew a crazy New Zealander, Jacqueline Houghton, who decided that the best way to combat the heat would be to strip off to her bra and hot shorts and walk up and down outside the hotel to catch what pitiful breeze there was. Donna, somewhat more conservatively attired, joined her.

It took seconds for news to spread around the young men of the village that there were fine sights to be seen – in her rig, Jackie was more than alluring for young Spanish men and although less provocatively attired, Donna was appreciated as well. They found themselves surrounded by a leering and gesturing crowd of boys.

I was called in by Donna to render assistance and managed to shepherd them back to the pub out of harm's way without incident.

The pub was atrocious, the single restaurant bad and the heat and humidity stifling.

After five days of this we finally got out of Dodge, but to say that these were lost days would be a considerable understatement.

We had six or so summers in Nicey but all good things come to an end. So, with genuine tears in our eyes, we ended that part of our life and came back home happier, wiser and with a fine cellar on board ship.

Sounds to me as though you had just the right amount of time in Nicey, don't you think?

I agree. It was a lovely time in our lives that helped us to bond and from which we learned much. But it was over. I should say I owe Donna much for putting up with my travel to and from Tokyo, which exposed her to boredom and the anxiety of living in a foreign place without the language, and a long way from help if she needed it.

Any other travel highlights to mention?

Too many. But I'll mention just a couple more. China, then Russia.

I first went to China from Hong Kong as a university student under a student union visit plan. This must have been in 1971 or 1972, just after the start of Mao's Cultural Revolution, which devastated China for ten years. It was just a one-day glimpse of Shenzhen across the border. The starting point was the famous Lo Wu railway station, where we could see, I would guess, two or three thousand Chinese men and women all dressed in black and navy Mao suits with high collars, pressed against the station fence, gawking at the tourists as you might look at men from Mars.

We crossed the border from the station into buses that took us on a journey of a couple of hours or so through the countryside to the local waterworks, to a school where we stopped for a concert provided by the students, then on to a Chinese lunch at a local restaurant. I'd been looking forward to a real Chinese meal but it was not to be: the food was mean and poor.

The Shenzhen we toured was just farms. Forty years later it's a brand-new commercial metropolis of around five million people and an example of the amazing feats of development and construction that have propelled China to world leadership.

I saw a lot of China in the '90s as the Asia managing partner of my law firm and as we established our Shanghai office. But I didn't have much contact after that until the Arcadis period that I told you about earlier, which involved maybe fifty visits between 2007 and 2010.

During that period I travelled widely around eastern China including Harbin, Dalian, where I had several near-death experiences with the liquor Maotai, pressed on me by local businessmen who were keen to smash an evil westerner or two, Hebei, Shanghai, Fujian and Guangzhou.

I've decided that I'll never visit China again. Fascinating though it may be, it's now a grim, authoritarian, dirty and risky place. No more.

The other highlight was my trip with Donna to Russia and the Trans-Siberian Railway.

We had always had romantic notions of travelling on this fabled train from Moscow to Vladivostok. In the '60s it was regarded as on a par with the overland hippie trail from Australia to London via the Middle East, which some of my friends had done, although most contracted debilitating diseases like dysentery or typhoid and lived with the consequences for many years. Then, it wasn't a tourist undertaking: you boarded the train with your fellow Russian passengers and bought all of your food, drink and other necessities at stations along the line, and even in the upper classes, occupied grimy seats or tiny cabins that were smelly and uncomfortable.

When I started our research, a company had been established to run tourist trains appropriate for westerners that would provide a more familiar level of comfort, with planned stops along the way during which travellers would be entertained with concerts, home meals, historical tours and decent shopping opportunities. The train was called the Tsar's Gold Trans-Siberian Express and took two and a half weeks. You could opt to go to Vladivostok, or turn south at the Mongolian border and transit Mongolia to Beijing, with a stop in Ulan Bator. The main intermediate stops were Kazan, Irkutsk and Ulan-Ude. We opted for Mongolia. It looked like a fabulous opportunity, of course at a fabulous price.

We launched our expedition in Paris, travelled to St Petersburg for a few days, then took the train to Moscow for a week before boarding.

St Petersburg – formerly Petrograd, then Leningrad – is a northern and freezing city on the Baltic Sea coast founded by Peter the Great, which was Russia's imperial capital, and whose formal architecture follows the Swedish and Finnish in style. It was the centre of the communist October Revolution of 1917 and is regarded as Russia's cultural and spiritual capital. It's full of magnificent Orthodox churches and palaces, many of which we saw. Donna and I pinned our ears back in the restaurants and bars. One of the most impressive evenings was devoted, amidst the protests of our bank manager, to genuinely fine caviar, vodka and blinis. The combination was pure melody and put versions we had tasted outside Russia in deep shade.

It's also the home of the State Hermitage Museum, which houses one of the greatest collections of art in the world, including Black Square by Malevich, believed to be the world's first abstract expressionist picture. I found the Malevich gripping because my main interest in painting is abstraction. My great rowing comrade and art influencer is Paul Guest, who has gathered probably the broadest and finest private Australian abstract impressionist collection, so no surprise that this should have been my aesthetic choice.

We were placed in a European group on the train for excursions, drinking and dining. This included a couple of other Aussies, some Americans, some Brits and some Canadians. It was like being put in a small spacecraft for a journey to another planet. Everything was cramped, noisy and physically difficult to navigate. Despite everyone being thrown together in close proximity, social divisions emerged: you were with the quick kids or the slow kids. Thanks to Donna we were adopted by the quicks, and we met many lovely, bright people who made the long spaces during the day less dull.

Russia is huge and endowed with every commodity and every talent. But we found it fearful, withdrawn, poor and run down. I couldn't help wondering what kind of country it would have been under a democratic, free enterprise system.

The artistic highlights were the concerts we were invited to at local conservatoriums, where young artists barely in their teens would sing or play like seasoned virtuosos. As boxing is for Black Americans, so is music for young Russians: one of the few avenues to the West, and political and financial freedom.

Mongolia was spare, dry and empty. I made a huge error in booking a yurt for an overnight stay during a rest stop. My smiling hosts offered me dinner, which included naturally made yoghurt: horse milk poured into a tray and put out in the sun for days to curdle and dry. I was vomiting convulsively in an hour and on my back immobilised for two days while the train wound its way to Beijing.

Beijing was unbearably crowded, smelly and hot. No need to say more.

I had never been happier with a trip, but never more grateful to clamber onto our plane home.

Johnnie, I'm sure there is a lot of your life's travelogue you've left out, but the point is: there can't be many people who've had the exposure to places and people that you have, and who have integrated all that interest and worldly feedback well into their lives. You're lucky.

I know. Observers might say that I've been over-privileged, but as we agreed earlier, half the task we have on earth is to get to know the place and to stay curious and respectful. I hope I've done that. The fire still burns. Donna and I are in the middle of planning a three-month stay on the island of Syros in Greece. Just to decompress completely, enjoy an ancient civilisation, make some friends, think and swim and write. I'll keep doing this as long as I can. I'm feeling the cold winds of time more now, so I need to take every opportunity.

One thing some others mightn't realise is the quantity of work involved in financing, self-planning and executing a long foreign journey. It's why people choose cruises, managed tours or just don't go. Being a successful and regular foreign traveller is like being, say, a writer: you need stamina, application, flexibility and balance.

Donna and I have done one such upmarket, all-found trip, to Egypt in 2020 with the legendary Abercrombie & Kent. It was a marvellous travel experience. We had private transport, guides, first-class hotels, bespoke itineraries and privileged access to everything. We were discreetly shadowed by police during the entire trip so felt completely safe. It fulfilled our long interest in seeing the ancient world and if that also attracts you, go no further than Egypt: it has the lot. We are still in regular contact with two of our guides, both smart and delightful Egyptian women who in an economy with more opportunity, could have been world-class anything.

Stepping out again, I thought I might ask you to let me have your thoughts on politics and social dialogue in Australia today?

Also a subject that bores people if you go on too long, but I'm happy to say a few words about it.

One of the contemporary problems with political discussion is that, it seems, everyone has been forced into a political tribe or corner and has lost the ability to look at policy without resorting to sledging, shaming or shouting.

While I admire anyone who genuinely tries to advance social justice and inclusivity, these concepts are too often used by advocates to suppress discussion and label opposing views as inherently offensive, and to de-platform worthy individuals without informed and reasonable judgement. In a way, it's secular religion. It's one thing to be virtuous, and another and regrettable thing to signal virtue to gain social approval by claiming moral superiority. Useful debate then ends. This approach derails bipartisan policy formation. It also shallows the scope of the debate and results in increased polarisation. None of that is good.

What would you suggest we do about all that?

My professors at the University of Virginia would always ask, when considering any legal rule, what was the underlying policy: was it fair, did the relevant legislation execute it and what did experience with the application of the rule suggest? You were asked not just to *know* the law, but to understand *why* the law. Only then could you work out where that law stood in the huge forest of other proximate laws, which would be the only certain way in which useful and complete advice could be given.

We were being encouraged to adopt a rational and unbiased approach to any policy question. How abandoned does that idea seem these days? People appear to believe that any policy brought forward by their party is ipso facto valuable, needed and worthy of defending, whereas that is far from true, especially when government can be one of the most enthusiastic virtue signallers.

I have otherwise intelligent and accomplished friends whom I cannot tell that from time to time I read *The Australian* newspaper. I know that if I did they would classify me as deep right and, according to the mindset I described earlier, a lesser and perhaps undesirable person. But I subscribe to *The Economist*, *The Atlantic Monthly* and *The New York Times*, all left-leaning publications; I watch the US *PBS NewsHour* and Al Jazeera, and my primary Australian television news source is SBS. What I seek is completeness and balance, which, in most cases, these friends do not. I find myself able to read an opinion piece by, say, Janet Albrechtsen without being, or turning into, a Nazi!

I consume a lot of ABC material, especially from people like the remarkable Geraldine Doogue and Phillip Adams, but I find that the institution's lefty stance can be a problem. There aren't any significant conservative commentators, there are many more importantly placed female commentators than males, and the correctness agenda is often run too hard. I'd like it to be genuinely neutral but that's unlikely, I fear. I wonder whether it will survive the current reconstruction toward digitalisation and youth orientation as the place we've all known.

Anyway, all we can do is continue to call this out, to persuade good people to go into politics and to support them actively when they do. We can't stay silent.

Can you give me examples of the kinds of political behaviours you find unacceptable?

Take the argument around the First Nations Voice to Parliament constitutional referendum. The government encouraged us to believe that anyone opposing the Voice was reactionary, ungenerous, un-Australian and racist. I find that unfortunate and unworthy of our leadership. It is propaganda and speaks to the ethical uncertainty of the political class.

The reality is that the Albanese government's management of the Voice question was not a success. The government ought to have legislated for it, trialled it, if necessary amended it and then if successful, have entrenched it. It should never have been necessary to entrench it in the constitution as a first step. But if the government had to move to entrenchment, it should have gathered a convention to develop and realise the proposal in detail; that Albanese decided not to do that is what has generated a big part of the electoral suspicion that we saw.

The proposal failed comprehensively, which will set back relations between Indigenous and non-Indigenous Australians for years. I think I understand why the First Nations representatives were so insistent on entrenchment: it would represent unchangeable and complete recognition, justice, contrition for past abuses, a sweeping away of paternalism and a stepping stone toward a treaty involving some kind of sovereignty-sharing. But the existence of widespread opposition to entrenchment wasn't created by the LNP opposition: it was always there and all of the romanticising and pleading by the government was never going to change it.

In the aftermath of the referendum, Donna had a phone conversation with a good, smart lefty friend, who started to trash all no voters as racist, insensitive, ignorant and unworthy. Donna responded by saying that it was unlikely that over sixty per cent of Australians could be thus described, whereupon her friend asked, in anger, how she could continue the conversation any further in light of Donna's comment. The last thing on her mind, it seems, was rational discussion. More appropriate to machine gun the messenger.

Do you have a view yourself about the Voice?

I do. If the government had legislated for it, I would have been a supporter, although I'm not sure whether in the end the body so created would have brought about useful change.

I didn't like the idea of constitutional entrenchment, especially when I didn't know what the body would cost, how it would be constituted, how it would operate in practice, what the impact would be on the day-to-day working of the executive and whether the board of the body would be collaborative or aggressive.

But there is no doubt that First Nations policies across the board need reform because their communities continue to suffer. There needs to be a root-and-branch review of the exact state of disadvantage, current policies – and why in many cases they've failed – what new options are available to improve outcomes, where spending should occur and how to change tack if progress isn't made.

Labor's political exploitation of Brittany Higgins' alleged rape before the May 2022 election was similarly questionable in ethical terms. The alacrity with which Labor jumped on the Brittany bandwagon and showered Morrison and the then government with parliamentary accusations of sexism, misogyny and insensitivity, and the strong possibility of a cover-up, can't be excused.

Anything else?

The tragedy of the comic genius Barry Humphries. He aimed his scything wit at Australian society with precision; his successful attempts to shine light on our common hypocrisies, lies and confections contributed directly to Australia's social growing up, as well as always paralysing us with laughter. I loved the man and mourn that the woke constrictions now drowning us will never again give us the same comic latitude. The acts of the arts brigade blackening his name in his last years is unforgivable. Now he is to be made a Companion of the Order of Australia posthumously! Why not ten years ago? Barry would be howling with laughter at the cowardice of it; if anything proves his point about Australia, that would be it.

I have been a true left-liberal all my life, but I voted for Whitlam, for Hawke and for Keating at every election they contested except when Whitlam's government collapsed and had to be changed. While Tony Smith was in Canberra, I supported him financially and sometimes morally. I believe he was one of the most upright members of any party and by common consent an outstanding speaker.

One of the things that's annoyed me in recent years is political polarisation both in the macro sense and also at the personal level. Common sense and bipartisanship have gone and what are we to replace it with? How can we govern a country successfully when we seem to sit in armed political camps?

That bothers me greatly as well. I regret that I can no longer have a good-natured, intelligent and policy-driven discussion of contemporary political issues with many of my friends. I'm forced to be careful to learn where their politics lie and to manage what I say accordingly: it only takes moments for those kinds of conversations to become strained and dogmatic. Why are political loyalties like football loyalties? Why do people prefer to shout rather than reason? Why is the conservative side of politics pronounced to be inherently sexist, unreliable, incorrect, corrupt and potentially deviant? That may accomplish short-term gains, but what about the long-run future of recruitment to Canberra, of elevating the quality of parliamentarians, of identifying strong, ethical and capable leaders?

Cultures of decency, hard work and fairness take decades to build and days to destroy. The more our parliamentarians sup with the devil ethically, the less chance we have of regaining any semblance of government honesty and capability. I want them to stop. The only thing in the end is good policy implemented in a generous, flexible and clever way that gets under the radar of the signallers.

Does that give you a sense of where I'm at, Jimmy?

I'm much the same: we have a lot of work to do. Most of all we need a leader with integrity, intelligence and personal clout. Is there anything you want to add about your work life after the end of the Arcadis era and your return from France?

You know about our vineyard up the hill and Wild Fire Wines. In a mad fit, mostly mine, Donna and I decided to open a wine bar and restaurant in Warburton, launching the project in early 2019. We did this in partnership with a Dutch couple who owned and managed a fine cheese business in the upper Yarra Valley area. The concept was that we would offer curated wine and cheese pairings that would form the revenue base of the business, and layer a restaurant and fine wine offering on top of that.

The regulatory set-up – with liquor licensing, council permitting, footpath trading controls, refuse disposal, grease trap design, insurance, labour management and so on ad infinitum – was extraordinarily detailed, long-winded and expensive. It took a good year. Then, we opened in March 2020 only to be closed two weeks later for a full twelve months during the first Covid lockdown. We also hired a supposed friend as manager, who we discovered too late was fundamentally unsuitable, and after limping along during the succeeding on/off Covid period, the business died and we called it quits. Not many people realise how tough small business is to launch, much less run profitably. Never again.

And for one reason or another I've always been asked to help with other people's problems, whether they be professional or personal, which I've done willingly without any expectation of reward.

I arranged several divorce settlements and personal insolvencies for friends of Donna. I also guided my old friend Tim Cecil, one of my early wine partners and CEO of Henry Buck, the traditional and prestigious men's outfitter in Collins Street, through a dissolution of the family ownership in the business. The reality was that there was no one left in the family to run it, and after a close shave with insolvency, we managed to find a buyer on reasonable terms just before Covid hit. We would never have sold post-Covid, so we were lucky.

I've looked after my old mates as an investment adviser, confidant, guarantor, rent payer and executor.

I've involved myself with civic affairs in Warburton to a degree: I chaired a group that worked for around five years to secure an upgrade of our mobile telecoms infrastructure. Now we have five bars of reception and excellent 5G broadband, plus the knowledge that our mobile phones will work in floods and bushfires.

What about charitable involvements?

Here comes another quote, from Marcus Aurelius in his *Meditations*:

"Be always doing something serviceable to mankind and let this constant generosity be your only pleasure, not forgetting a due regard to god."

I have always taken this as one of my duties, but I would say that while I've been serviceable when it suited me, I've been less good when it didn't.

Donna and I don't have a disciplined giving program, which we should, but we've been regular contributors to sound institutions and to our friends who've needed help.

From pretty much since the start of my career until around five years ago, I'd served charities in a formal capacity as a board member and sometimes as chair. These included Hanover Welfare Services, dedicated to helping homeless men; the Queen Elizabeth II Silver Jubilee Trust; the Life Education Centre, an anti-drug education body; Brainwave, which provides support and research funding for child cancer victims; the board of the Melbourne Grammar School Foundation; and the Lasallian Foundation, a lay organisation sponsored by the Catholic Lasallian Brotherhood, which funded and sponsored the construction and operation of schools and orphanages in Sri Lanka, PNG, Vietnam, Laos, Pakistan and India. This last organisation had to be wound up in 2018 on my instruction because of the paedophilia scandal in the Catholic Church. The church lied to my board consistently about its exposure to these problems and we were forced to take action when the scale of the disaster became known.

That must have been a tough time for you.

It was. I can't recall having been as disappointed. The Catholic Church will never recover from those stains.

Johnnie, I sense we might be getting close to the end of our journey, and I want to tell you how much I've enjoyed the ride and how grateful I've been for being able to share pieces of your life that not many others might have. I hope what we've spoken about

helps in writing the story of your life and that the intended audience is respectful of the effort involved.

Well Jim, I hope so, although it will be what it is. And anyway, I might have edged away stage left by then.

Can I ask you how you're managing life, how you're managing ageing and your health at the moment? I'm not in a great place myself. I didn't tell you, but I've got some issues to deal with.

Like what?

I've got lung cancer. I'm in remission after chemo at the moment but it's not looking great.

I'm seriously sorry, Jimmy.

It just goes to show how much of a lottery life is, doesn't it. I've had a great time in my life, and I've been mighty lucky, so no complaint. But I'm a bit like Woody Allen, who said he didn't mind the idea of dying but he just didn't want to be there when it happened. And I did take a lot from myself when you think about my lifestyle.

I don't have anything like that on the horizon but at our age it could be tomorrow. Everyone says just make the most of it while you can, and I do, but the shadow stalks you and you can't help looking around too often to work out when it's going to be on top of you.

My dear mate Peter Newman, partner in wine, writer, poet, dilletante, bushman, thespian, is in hospital as we speak, stricken by a huge coronary, brain dead and on life support. His puff of white smoke has been blown away. We find it almost impossible to accept that such a thing could happen to us at any hour. We must, every minute of every day, thank the universe for giving us life, beauty, honour, imagination and compassion. Vale Peter, I grieve for you, and myself. I'm too close to your back to be comfortable.

Despite all of that I'm happy. Donna is so strong and so supportive. She's scared about my future but we've done a good job of ignoring it and getting on with life, immersing ourselves in friends, family, travel, reading, the property, my pro-bono work, my music, everything really.

I don't think about ageing too much. I've got my head up, my shoulders back, I'm looking at life in the eye, I know I'll be looked after if I get really crook. The next major transition will be moving to Melbourne but that's a couple of years away.

I lean back and go quiet for a minute.

"I think that might be it, Jim."

"Maybe it is."

"I want you to know how grateful I am for your time and your kindness. You've always been important to me. I'm sorry I haven't had the sense to tell you that before. Maybe it's because we've always believed we'd never die! We should say hello to each other a bit more while we can."

"I've loved the chat, Johnnie. You're a man I always admired and wanted to get closer to. I don't think you've told me everything but you've told enough for a good story."

"We really are solitary in this universe in the end, aren't we?"

"We are. But I can't tell you how happy I am that you're connected, loved and content. It's been a long road for you and I wish you well and a ton of luck for the future."

"Back to you, Jim. Thanks for your life, and for your kindness."

We drift back to the kitchen and the fire to share a last cup of tea. Jim gathers his stuff and I walk him to his car. We embrace and promise each other that we'll speak soon. I hope we do.

Epilogue

My mate James Marr died of raging lung cancer around fifteen years ago, long before this story was even an idea. I didn't have the courage to visit him in his last days. I had been with my father when he died not long before and the experience was so terrible that I refused to go through it again. The shame and sadness of that will never go away.

As well as being solitary, this universe is random and cruel. I feel lucky to have been a survivor but also completely guilty for having had so much more good life than Jim.

My times with him in the cold surf at Lorne made my life when I was growing up. When I get sad, I think of his face and his laugh and the two foaming pots of beer on the bar of the Pacific Hotel, and when I do, the world seems a little brighter.

Scribblings

I thought I might include with this book a few scraps of writing from different times in my life to illustrate perhaps more directly my interests, my state of mind and the way I looked at the world.

There are diary excerpts, poems, blogs and a couple of speeches I was invited to make in honour of old friends on notable occasions.

Here they are, in no order, in keeping with the rest of this.

For the Love of Wine

(Written for and published by *Reflektor Art Magazine*, 2019)

The moments of my greatest delight are on winter pruning afternoons, when I'm bent over my vines, cold and stiff, puzzling over how I can shape a wild burst of unruly canes into a spare and beautiful form that will bring forth abundant and delicious fruit.

Minds and hands that are disciplined and hard-working learn to solve the spatial and biological dilemmas: which cane is the best placed and most robust? Which will strike and fruit most consistently and cleanly? Which may have been diseased and carry hidden weakness? Which will encourage the most promising vine profile in the season after next, and the one after that?

To see a well-shaped vineyard after pruning is to see a blend of imagination, effort, skill and hope. So many aren't that way. The journey from vine to bottle begins with this creative effort and rewards come only when it is present. A finely-pruned vineyard was once described to me, by one who knows these things, as looking like a regiment of the Napoleonic army marching to Russia in glittering battle dress. Romantic perhaps, but next time you see a good vineyard late on a sunny winter afternoon, you'll know what he meant.

There is much else to do, of course, before good wine is safely in bottle and slumbering in the cellar. But usually, if the vigneron is a good and persistent craftsman in winter, the chances are he will be a good shepherd for the remainder of the journey.

These jottings will be driven by the same idea: to present readers with knowledge and opinion about wine that has been made in this spirit, and without compromise.

The wine industry is bitterly competitive and, as in similar commercial fields, those with fewer scruples than others will cut corners, mislead and use 'enhancers' of all kinds to generate short-term advantages. We'll tell you only about wines, people and vineyards that we know and can vouch for as honest.

I hope this will be a pleasurable addition to the knowledge of those who already are touched by the madness of wine collection and cellaring; and as an understandable and helpful guide to those who are just embarking on their journey in wine.

I have long been interested in Heathcote as a growing and winemaking area. I used to drive from Melbourne to Echuca regularly in the 1970s, and one day in around 1978 a sign appeared on the highway announcing the opening of the Jasper Hill winery by Ron Laughton. I turned up his drive immediately and received a courteous tasting from Ron, and left with a boot full of his shiraz, which matured into some of the most delicious wine in my cellar. I was tremendously surprised that this dry, dusty and hot area contained microclimates that would deliver such quality. Now, of course, Jasper Hill is eminent, rare and expensive, but Ron's successes, with the other pioneers, launched the Heathcote area as one of the premier Shiraz and Viognier producing areas in the world.

One of the best and most reasonably priced examples of Heathcote Shiraz I've tried is from one of the original producers, Hennings Vineyards. This is Hennings "Croquet" Shiraz from the 2016 vintage, $22/bottle. Mid-weight, concentrated and classic Heathcote aroma-blue and black fruits, dust, cedar and spice, long, sweet fruit in the mouth with fine tannins. A bargain at this price. Go to:

https://www.henningsvineyard.com/

There are many other Heathcote wineries now, but I've bought fruit and made wine from the Shiraz produced by Norbert Baumgartner from Mia Valley Estate; it has developed wonderfully in the bottle and while a slightly more dense wine than the Hennings, it has a finesse and perfume that is exceptional. Norbert's Shiraz is available in vintages going back to 2008 at least, from $32–36/bottle, and that kind of age is necessary for his wine. Dark, highly complex and perfumed aroma; beautifully structured, long and fine flavour. More expensive but worth it for the quality and maturity.

http://www.miavalleyestate.com.au/

I'm also a big fan of the Chenin Blanc white wine variety. This grape is cultivated most extensively in the Loire Valley south of Paris, and is used to produce Vouvray, which is made in essentially two styles, semi-sweet and dry. Vouvray is an astonishingly long-lived wine; it begins its life as a fresh, lightly aromatic herbal style, and as it matures, acquires nutty, oatmeal and vanillin characters while maintaining its acid line and much of its freshness. My wife Donna bought a few bottles from the 1947 vintage the last time we were in France (to commemorate my birthday, I have to admit), and it is still a very good drink. No Australian white would have survived anything like that long in decent shape.

Chenin Blanc used to be grown in Australia as a workhorse variety to fill flagons and then containers of "Chateau Cardboard". It was irrigated hard and over-cropped.

Now, there have been plantings by serious makers in good areas, and some of the results have been gratifying. Voyager Estate from Margaret River is such a maker. The Loire is a much cooler place, but Voyager's Chenin is excellent despite the WA warmth, like the Chardonnay, although it is less taut and the fruit is more ample and tropical. It has been released as part of the Voyager "Estate" range with a small amount of residual sugar in imitation of its French counterpart. It's still too early to know whether it will have a long life, but even young, it's well worth having in your cellar as a counterpoint to the racks of Chardonnay and Riesling you've gathered! At $20/bottle, well worth a try. Go to:

https://www.voyagerestate.com.au/

Beechworth is a small and lovely old gold-mining town located around 40 km east of Wangaratta and a similar distance south of Wodonga. It sits in the foothills of the Great Dividing Range at 560 m above sea level, so enjoys a temperate climate during the vine growing season. It is 22 km west of Yackandandah, home of one of Australia's premier folk music festival.

Here, some of the greatest Chardonnay, Pinot Noir and Shiraz in the country is grown. The most familiar name to most is Giaconda, now a by-word in quality and to be purchased at a commensurately high price.

One of the best producers is Castagna, which exports to high quality outlets all over the world. The vineyard is located on granitic soils overlying clay, and produces fruit of great concentration, austerity and purity. Although I am not a believer in some of the more extreme biodynamic growing principles, the winemaker Julian Castagna is, and the results speak for themselves.

The Castagna "Genesis" Syrah is one of my favourites. The wine (with aromas of violets, berries, liquorice and spice) bolts out of the glass and the flavours are to match. Often not the case in highly promoted wine. Complex, long, upright and balanced. Quite delicious. Castagna also makes a limited range of wines from classic Italian varieties including Nebbiolo, the grape of Barolo and Barbaresco.

The Genesis 2015 is available on-line at $75/bottle. I would buy it before Grange any day. Go to:

https://www.castagna.com.au

The final area into which I'd like to wander today is Leongatha, a wine growing centre in South Gippsland around 140 km south-east of Melbourne.

Gippsland is typically green and rolling, with deep soils and lush pastures. Not surprisingly, it is a dairy stronghold.

Vines have been planted around the town for many years, but its reputation as a fine wine region has been shot forward by the success of Philip Jones at Bass Philip in making some very fine Chardonnay and Pinot Noir. Philip has emphasised close-planted vines to moderate the vine vigour imparted by the deep red, rich soils, low cropping, biodynamics and minimal intervention.

A Leongatha vineyard making wine of a similar quality, although more conventionally (and perhaps more reliably) is Bellvale. Their wines are a fraction of the price of Bass Philip and, to my palate, detailed, expressive of variety and terroir and lovely. The proprietor and winemaker is John Ellis, a former military and airline pilot originally from New York. I declare my interest immediately: John is a good friend! But as a result I know he is a great professional and deeply honest in his approach to his vines and winemaking craft.

One of my favourites of his is Bellvale "Quercus Vineyard" 2017 Pinot Noir. It is fresh, bright, sappy, energetic and complete. One of the great Australian Pinots. $32.50/ bottle in case lots. Go to:

http://www.bellvalewine.com.au

I'm very happy to reply to email questions and comments.
Look forward to chatting with you!

John Harry
Partner and Winemaker
Wild Fire Wines
www.wildfirewines.com.au
(0419) 596 404

Blogsite Excerpt: Visit to Normandy, 2016

The 2016 adventures of John and Donna

Back to London, Then France

Sunday 19 June:
A short flight back to Heathrow. Robbed by yet another London cabbie for the fare to the Kings Road flat we rustled up at short notice on Airbnb-another beautie. After downing some more chemistry for her bad back, Donna was able to make the trip for dinner with Richard and Lizzie Brown, which was loud, funny and joyful.

Much of the chat was about Brexit. Even though the family were saying that the "stay" vote would win comfortably, I got the sense that most of them wanted to vote "go" even though they knew it made no sense.

If only I'd placed a bet on the outcome and shorted Sterling!!

Monday 20 June:
Donna and I went our separate ways on a drizzly and dank morning to look for this and that-in my case to visit Harrods and Peter Jones to find some more trousers and shirts. Harrods was a zoo. The menswear department was just a collection of fancy boutiques spread out over a couple of floors, designed for a quick visit by wealthy Arabs and Russians looking for a brand fix. Definitely not for a plus-sized Aussie looking for a deep range of sizes, prices and qualities! The first depressing glance from the first bored attendant said it all. I dislike being scrutinized by anyone, much less shop attendants. No wonder men invented tailors. How things have changed – this once great institution is just a tourist trap.

The famed food hall was worse. I bought "triple smoked Shropshire ham" (like sweaty leather) and sushi (disgracefully dry and stale) at a staggering price. Maybe it was just my bad luck, or maybe my advancing years, but the scent of rip-off was everywhere and I was delighted to hit the pavement.

Our great friend Hilary White invited me to attend a private wine tasting this evening at the home of Ann Tupker, whom Donna and I knew from previous visits. Ann runs a small wine importation and distribution business and is an MW-a "Master of Wine"-a very hard-to-gain award for deep knowledge of wine and the wine business.

I'm always wary of functions like this. I find being squashed in a small un-air-conditioned space in summer with a large number of people I don't know to be a real trial. On the credit side, the range of wines (twenty reds and twenty whites) was diverse and interesting and Hilary as always was attentive and friendly; on the debit side, as expected, the heat and humidity rose to red-alert levels as the air circulation dropped to zero. Still, it was fun.

After the tasting we strolled around the corner to a small and good Italian restaurant with Hilary and her husband Adrian, and an Irish friend Tim Blakeley. Tim is a splendid and sympathetic man, who despite his complete conviviality, wears the puzzlement and resignation of someone whose relationships with women have always confounded him. He invited me to have a nightcap after dinner. To my shame, I declined. I have to try harder not to let in the old man.

Tuesday 21 June:
Quiet day.

I visited Abbey Road Studios to see pay my respects to the place where the Beatles recorded most of their music, including their last Album, called Abbey Road, with the photo of the famous pedestrian crossing on the cover. Going the wrong way. It's been a long time, I guess.

I had a look around the shop, and took photos of the graffiti, which everyone does. I sat on a dusty ledge outside the studio and watched the teenagers take photos of each other imitating the mournful walk of the broken-up band over the crossing, and tried to gather my thoughts about when the Beatles meant to me and my life.

I wasn't expecting my great regret. The Beatles crashed into my life in the early sixties on a cheap transistor radio as I was hiking on a remote trail in Tasmania. I knew instantly that here was something brand new, unexpected, happy, thrilling. The Beatles drove my friendships, my tastes in music and fashion, my decision to learn the guitar, my decision to join a band, my understanding of cool, my realisation that if four untrained, unruly boys were capable of making the greatest and most durable and original contribution to any musical genre, anything was possible in my own life, that convention didn't matter, that beauty could be carved forever out of the ordinary if you had the talent and the impudence.

And yet, what was left? Two of the Fabs dead; a band ruptured so long before its time; personal tragedies, bitterness, betrayal, convention (Sir Paul?); and me, a sworn believer and spiritual friend, with so little time left to contemplate and understand this musical wonder.

But the works in all their brilliance remain. There are new, crystalline and live remixes of the Beatles classics now available that John and George never heard-it doesn't get sadder than that. I've bought them all but most days I find that listening to them is too hard. I console myself with the thought that I'm one of a rapidly diminishing band of children of the sixties who was there and who understands what happened, who received the blessing and the message.

There are always the books.

Takeaway dinner with Nicholas and Wynn Brown at the Kings Road. A short but happy evening.

Wednesday 22 June:
Lovely Hilary arranged tickets for us today to see one of the Wimbledon warm-up tennis tournaments at the Hurlingham Club with a group of her friends.

Donna was still resting her back and wasn't able to come.

Hurlingham is a large, green and spotless London institution, sitting on the banks of the Thames south of Chelsea. We arrived at noon and set up shop in a wonderfully breezy marquee on the club lawns. I've been to Henley Royal Regatta many times and the form here was similar; several bottles of English champagne (not bad at all) to calm down the frenetically vibrating social antennae of the guests; white and red wine with the salmon, salads and strawberries, to release the intimacy, laughter and gentle profanities; loo stops all around; then into the stands for a couple of exhibition matches on a gorgeous, brand-new lawn surface between the chosen Wimbledon competitors. No question about their quality–Berdich, Gasquet included. I felt very lucky.

Donna is improving but has a fair way to go before she's ready for the long train journey.

Another dinner at home.

Thursday 23 June:

Another rest day for Donna. She has found a strong, determined and expensive Dutch physio in the Kings Road to look at her back. There is progress but we know from past experiences that Donna needs to hasten slowly, which she finds it hard to do.

I set out via Uber to Covent Garden to find laptop chargers which I carelessly left behind in Portugal. The huge Apple shop facing the square is a gorgeous, icy monument to consumerism: provide things that solve the problems of ordinary people perfectly in the age of instant communication, and stand back and watch the tidal waves of cash roll in.

I stopped in at the National Portrait Gallery for a quick visit, then on through a packed Trafalgar Square till I bagged a taxi back to the apartment.

After lunch I visited the Imperial war museum in South London. It was rebuilt only recently into a fresh and modern "communication" centre full of sound, video, "interactive" exhibits, "human interest stories" and smart lighting that while making some of the information more accessible, nonetheless seemed to diminish the horror, the blood, the grime and the tragic dignity of the fighting men.

Tonight we dined for the last time with our London family at Didier's Earl's Court restaurant. Now just post-Brexit, there was much to discuss. Long may these friendships continue.

Friday 24 June:
To St Pancreas mid-morning to catch the fast train to Paris. This was crammed with boozy gangs of soccer fans going to Paris the last week of the European soccer Championship. Donna was not completely over her back, and the commotion and aromas on the train didn't improve her mood.

This was to blacken completely as we entered our Paris Airbnb apartment on the Seine in St Germain. The place, and everything in it, stank of stale tobacco, stale food and rubbish. It was too late to relocate that afternoon, so we fled to the Pompidou for a couple of hours of relief, then dined at a local pasta restaurant at outrageous tourist prices.

Saturday 25 June:
The next morning we checked in at a lovely hotel north up the hill, called L'Hôtel de L'Abbeye. We were reminded again of the reason why we were following the Airbnb path-our room was the size of a small campervan @ 650 Euros a night. After a brief visit to the Pompidou and St Sulpice, we dined well at a restaurant just around the corner near the Luxembourg Gardens, ruminated over the tumultuous day with some fine Graham's port in the lounge and hit the sack.

By checkout time the following morning we had secured a new Air BnB apartment in a quiet street on the Isle St Louis, and were deeply relieved to find that it was operated by a wealthy American by a pleasant and patient American friend in Paris. We had moved from disaster to ideal in less than 24 hours.

This part of Paris is why people come to France-perfectly positioned, peaceful, full of pretty restaurants with hearty menus whose waiters have the right mix of competence and insolence, to remind diners of their inferiority while eventually presenting them with the goods.

Sunday 26 June:
Our move to the Isle St Louis was calm. The apartment, complete with our meet-and-greet friend Tania from New York, was perfect and before long we were seated in sun dappled comfort at the bistro over the road. There were buskers, pimps, tourists, dogs, ladies of high fashion, bouquinistes, priests, bicycles, river boats, artists and all the other paraphernalia of a fine Parisian afternoon-our hearts at last began to sing. Candle lit dinner at home.

Monday 27 June:
Today was Louvre Day. We had booked tickets on line because, our website told us, it would be faster getting in. Our "pre-booked" queue was twice the length of the walk-up queue. It began to rain but we managed to hustle inside before the deluge. What greeted us was a scene from the Inferno. I first came here in the 60s, when you bought your ticket, strolled in and could get a view of anything easily. This was like being on the London tube at peak hour-or for footy lovers, at the base of the first pack to form at the G after the bounce at the Grand Final. There must have been at least 250,000 visitors all milling, elbowing, swearing, belching and sweating. This made navigation impossible because all the signs were obscured by the throng, the guidebooks were in micro type and the attendants appeared to be on strong doses of narcotics. Donna and I found a seat, wrested a cold coffee from a tired waiter at an even more tired "cafe", looked at each other and headed for the exits.

When in doubt head through the Tuileries for the Orangerie Museum and marvel at the Monet murals from Giverny. We did, and they were as wildly beautiful and mysterious as ever. Two special exhibitions were also on show: works from the collection of Paul Guillaume, a famous collector, gallerist and art sponsor of the late 19th and early 20th Century; and a portrayal of the life and time of Guillaume Apollinaire, an important French poet, playwright and art critic.

Italian dinner on the Isle-homely but delicious and-amazingly-not too expensive. I think the Maître took a shine to Donna – in our family this has often proved an advantage.

Tuesday 28 June:
Today we cabbed it up to the Australian Embassy near the Eiffel Tower to vote (easy) and to meet an old friend of Donna's, with whom we enjoyed a very satisfactory coffee and strawberry crepe. After a stroll around the Tower and across the Seine to the Trocadero, we headed back to the apartment for the remains of our foie gras and cheeses, which I attempted to walk off by visiting Notre Dame, the Pantheon and a money changer for some small $US bills we were going to need on the Trans-Siberian. The attempt was a failure, although I did enjoy the walk, which passed the church of St Etienne du Mont, where lie the alleged remains of the patron saint of Paris, St Genevieve. Inside the Pantheon was an exhibition of photographs taken by numerous photographers of every single monument in France built in honour of the combatants in WW1 and WW2, of which there were scores of thousands. I'm not sure what this was meant to achieve, although it did succeed in being exceptionally boring.

Wednesday 29 June:
Donna and I had planned to spend three days in Normandy visiting the D Day battlefields but her back was still a problem so we decided that I would go to Normandy solo and that she would rest and poke around Paris unencumbered by me.

I collected my hire car not far from St Sulpice at (naturally) rush hour. It took me a nightmarish 90 minutes to clear Paris but the remainder of the journey to Trouville-sur-Mer was a joy-light traffic, green and gently rolling hills and a perfectly behaved GPS. My Airbnb apartment was obscurely located but I found it eventually at around 4pm and once again it was spotless and central. I went out to see the town and pick up some essentials for the house. Trouville is one of a series of towns along the Atlantic coast which were inhabited by wealthy and smart Belle Epoque Parisians in summer, and where they built many quite spectacular beach-side mansions in vaguely art-nouveau style. It is still an important trading and fishing town but has pretty much lost its old cachet in favour of Nice, Cannes and St Tropez. I walked a few kilometres of the wide but faintly dirty beach before being driven back by the quite lusty rain and wind.

I went out to dinner at a smart-looking bistro just opposite the beach and enjoyed one of the best meals of my life, which included Atlantic oysters as big as your hat, flounder, baguette and frites to die for, the famous local cider, apple pie drowning in thick local yellow double cream with a half bottle of Montrachet. There are times when life can be good.

It won't surprise readers to learn that I revisited this extraordinary place the next night, and the night after that.

Thursday 30 June:
I was collected at 9am sharp by my guides Murielle and Frederic to begin our tour of the American D Day sector, with the British/Canadian sector to follow tomorrow.

Fred and Murielle had driven down to Trouville from St Quentin, at least three hours away. Our first day was to be dedicated to the "American Sector" that runs from Colleville-sur-Mer, just behind the landing at Omaha Beach by the US 29th and First Infantry Divisions, Westward to Utah Beach. Omaha was famously the site of the bloodiest reception on D Day, these units suffering 3000-odd casualties in the first hours of fighting.

The Americans have constructed at Colleville, and maintain in pristine condition, the most beautiful memorial and cemetery on the whole Normandy coast. The main British cemetery, also a most beautiful War Graves Commission site, is at Bayeux, which Montgomery reached on D Day from the British sector beaches of Juno, led by Canadian forces, and Sword and Gold, led by the English.

We arrived at Omaha on a drizzly and dark morning. Looking at the enormous, windswept beach and the huge surf, it wasn't hard to appreciate the immensity and complexity of the Allied undertaking.

After visiting the Colleville memorial and cemetery, we drove slowly around the sector, visiting many of the intact defensive gun emplacements, the memorial at the Pointe du Hoc which the US Rangers bravely scaled to extinguish a dangerous series of gun emplacements only to find that the cannon had been removed inland only hours earlier, and the site of the famous engagement at Brecourt Manor by "E" (Easy) Company of the 2nd Battalion, 506th Parachute Infantry regiment of the 101st US Airborne Division, known as the "Screaming Eagles". The Company has become one of the most famous in US Army not only on D Day but in many other engagements during the invasion including in Holland and in the Ardennes. It was the subject of the popular TV series "Band of Brothers".

We attempted to reach Utah and St Mere Eglise, but we were disappointed to find that the area was entirely blocked because of the departure of a sector of the Tour de France from St Mere the next day. Life has to go on!

There are dozens of memorials and museums both public and private throughout the US sector, a few of which we stopped at.

We completed our visit at Arromanches, the main port on the coast where a fuel pipeline laid across the Channel reached and supplied all of the Allied armies, and the main "Mulberry" floating harbour complex was installed, large parts of which remain buried in the beach to this day.

Friday 1 July:
Today we began our tour at Bayeux, went on to Juno/Gold/Sword and finished by visiting the site of the landings at the Pegasus Bridge on the Caen Canal near the Village of Benouville. The intention of the landing was to capture and block the two bridges across the Canal to prevent German reinforcements from reaching the battlefields further West. The British succeeded in landing several troop gliders with great precision only metres from the Bridge itself, and taking and defending the bridge until

reinforcements arrived. We visited the large and well-stocked Museum and other exhibits.

On the whole I found the American sector better preserved and cared for that the British, although this is not surprising given the enormous number of American ex-servicemen and tourists who pour through the area during the summer months.

When visiting war sites and cemeteries I am always deeply sad for those politicians, administrators and servicemen and women alike, who were swept up in these terrible wars; nothing provides a justification for the colossal carnage and waste; but I was glad for the opportunity, at last, to pay my respects to the brave ones who fought in this campaign, and to listen to the rustling of their spirits, still so clearly audible from the beaches and hedgerows that are still as they were on June 6, 1944.

There is much more to be said about Normandy, but not for my impatient readers. For those who are interested, find a copy of Antony Beevor's "D Day-The Battle for Normandy"-an austere but wonderful account of those times.

Last email to my dying mate Chris Dane, 2022

Chris

You're the first of my brothers to leave and I miss you.

Your door wasn't open to me much in recent times but you had your reasons and that was you: you decided how your life would be and that was that. I knew you were there even if the phone didn't go that often.

Chris Dane: kind, loyal, profane, irreverent, loud, fair, complex, irascible, industrious, courageous, honest, loveable. Who taught me that water can be as flat as a shit carter's hat and what syphoning the lizard meant. Who as my stroke took me to the promised land one translucent afternoon in April nearly sixty years ago on a sparkling Barwon River; who gave me respect and tolerated a mountain of reverses with calm and dignity; who knew the meaning of misunderstanding and intolerance and who was a good and thoughtful father. Who could walk with anyone. Who could execute a sledge magnificently. Who made me laugh harder than anyone else and worked like a lunatic. Is there anyone else like that?

You were a hard bloke to know and be close to but you were loved unconditionally by many. You were by me and always will be.

All the best, mate. Peace at last.

John

Poem for Donna 11/2019

Girl with Lightning in her Eyes

Did you have the luck to meet
As you walked in tears along her street
The girl with lightning in her eyes

Did her smile blind you
Her wisdom beguile you
Her goodness confront you
Her vision transform you
Her knowledge confound you
Her confidence shock you
Her vision force you

To think of the nature of man and of time
To grieve for your unforgiven crime
To wonder if it's always too late
To change the engraving of anyone's fate
On this life with no anchor
On this place with no truth
this lament with no end

Did you see her iron way
Did you hear her softly say
Lightning strike would come today

Did her honour amaze you
Did her welcome displace you
Did her kindness support you
Did her loyalty sway you
Did her honesty shake you
Did her clarity pierce you
Did her vision disarm you

You can face the light or turn away
You can choose to come another day
But stop here, look, and join the wise
And meet the girl with lightning in her eyes

Reflection on the Camino de Santiago

Green Square, Requejo, 8 June 2017

A kind friend said enter, for here you will find
in this small green square of paradise
many questions; and if you look and listen well, many answers
that in the long pilgrimage that brought you here
may not be found.

This garden has grown up, she said, spare but wild and full,
at the foot of this ancient church wall.
The church is one in whose name great but also terrible things have been
done; it is not at peace; it is a thing and a place from which generosity,
compassion, modesty, curiosity and love have slowly crept away.

Look around you and consider: this garden, and this house,
that are not five steps from the altar from which the keepers
have claimed all knowledge and obedience and have broken lives,
owe everything to memory, respect, kindness, trust, loyalty and love.

Some benevolence has thrown seed at the foot of this wall;
The strength and beauty of its growth is the truth.
The birdsong, clear light, roar of bees, intensity of bloom and irresistible
existential joy will fill you with awe and hope.

I give you this place without reservation; for the short time you are here,
open yourself to my green square and believe in the possibilities of
the other path that you have entered here today.

Speech in honour of Paul Guest, QC, OAM on his 80th Birthday

Paul Guest: 80th Birthday

Paul, that I'm standing here must mean that somehow I passed the audition. I've got no idea why, but who cares: I've got you where I want you.

I had a feeling I should send my notes to you for review, but having often lost the battle with your red pen, I followed Oscar Wilde's advice, and I lay down till the feeling went away.

You're a hard man to summarise. You're a kaleidoscope: every time I look at you, your life reforms and reveals something new and surprising.

This is no eulogy; Paul's life is still in full flood despite the advice of his mates to rest on his rowing laurels, to stop his art auction battles, and to quit challenging the speed cameras. He broke the world ergometer record for his age group just a few days ago. He sometimes describes his life as becoming less full than it was. Sounds like bullshit to me.

This also isn't an occasion on which flowery praise will do. Paul hates insincerity with venom: For him it's the truth or nothing.

We're here because we're a kind of tribe and one of the oldest tribal rituals is the marking out of senior and great members at special times.

Paul is such a person, and this a special time. He stands out in the forest of our history not because of his formidable CV, but because of his singular and magnificent character.

I first saw Paul in 1964, when his Victorian crew drifted into the staging one shimmering, summer Saturday. I was a green schoolboy oarsman whose life changed in that moment. It was as though eight battle-weary Roman Centurions had appeared on the Yarra bank, bronzed, hard and intent. I remember Terry Davies, in the stroke seat. No oarsman has ever had such arms. I remember Paul: lean, elegant, dark, striking: almost from another world. I decided right then that I wanted to go to the party.

How could I have known that five years later, he and I would have rowed together in the same Kings Cup crew, and won easily, and beautifully.

The arc of Paul's Rowing life has been majestic.

I won't list his selections and wins: that's now part of rowing folklore.

The question in my mind is, rather, where he fits in the ranks of Australian oarsmen. The environment of his era was hard: poor equipment, variable coaching, no national squad system, less international competition, constant politics, and you had to work.

In my mind, Paul is the athletic and competitive equal of James Tomkins, the finest oarsman of the modern era. Those two stand side by side on my podium as the best in our sport's history.

Paul is now a life member of Rowing Australia, which is the closest thing to a peerage that rowing offers. I think we should now call him Lord Guest of Princes Bridge.

He was chosen by Banks Rowing Club to be their President. There is no greater compliment from one's comrades.

A Paul Guest rowing medal has been struck at Wesley to recognize outstanding student oarsmen and women, which will exist for as long as does the school.

The Rowing community admires him not just for his performances but for what he's given back to the sport.

Paul has every talent. He's a brilliant athlete who works harder than anyone else; he's a relentless competitor; he was a superb sledger of other crews; he's smart; he's loyal to his friends; he's the man everyone wants to be next to in battle. I waited for years for Paul to take a light stroke, and he never did.

He judges people quickly and fairly, into good blokes and rats. There's never any grey. I once saw him reduce a rat who dodged his shout in a pub to tears, in a couple of sentences. Justice was done. Hard sometimes, but unfair never.

There are many stories I could tell you about Paul.

All you need to know is that he loves excellence; he's seriously attracted to mischief; he'll fight for you, shed tears for you, say wise things to you and share his fallibility with you; he loves many and is much loved in return; he looks after those less fortunate; he's immersed in books, music, art, the law, food and the bush, he buys my wine; and he collects friends from every corner of the world: eccentrics, athletes, painters, winemakers, adventurers, priests, philosophers and a constellation of others, all because their honesty and lack of pretence resonate with his.

He's a life Governor of the Bendigo Art Gallery; a rare honour that shows the respect in which his artistic choices are held.

And yet he often judges himself harshly, and he can be vulnerable to criticism and occasionally, I suspect, to the black dog. His abilities and his charisma are so outrageous and his personal stature so imposing that he can inspire jealousy from others. His slight tendency to speak his mind robustly could be part in this.

It's all just one part of his humanity, and his complexity.

Life has softened and tempered him, a little, and he accepts and manages a body that won't do everything he wants; but always quietly and always with dignity.

We trust and rely on people like Paul instinctively and without proper acknowledgement. To me, he's like a double bass in an orchestra: part of the foundation of his friends' lives, undemanding but fundamental. Long may the music play.

Paul is acknowledged as a living legend of the Bar. His colleagues admired him deeply for his skills and commitment. He was the go-to man on questions of Bar ethics, which speaks volumes. He advocated sound legal policy growth in his field. He carried the same qualities into his arduous and important career on the bench and was much praised for it.

The speeches made at his induction as a judge, from the great and good of the legal world, covered 18 pages; those at his departure ceremony, from the even more great and more good, swelled to fully 22 pages; they were either very sad to see him go, or very happy.

What sings from those speeches, though, when the ceremony is cut away, are two things: everyone was deeply relieved to welcome someone so human; and everyone knew that here was someone they could trust to deal well with the emotional and technical mountains a family court judge would face.

Paul can't help himself helping others. He is a patron to too many artists; he is always working for charities. He educates poor children; and now he's in the process of giving away one of the most important abstract art collections in Australia. He was the honorary chairman of the selection appeals tribunal of Rowing Australia and there he provided wisdom and gave dignity to many young competitors.

Most of us know that Paul's family life hasn't always been a walk down a rose-filled lane. Because of his talents, the demands on his time have been extreme, and he would admit, as I willingly do in relation to myself, that he would like to have spent more time with his siblings and his delightful children and grandchildren, had the universe been differently constructed.

But Paul's capacity to love and to want good for others is vast; his door is always open to anyone who wants to renew or repair a friendship; the fact that you might need to slam him between the eyes with a mallet to get his attention shouldn't matter; but kick the door open now, because, like it or not, most of us now live in what Robert Menzies called "Afternoon Light".

So, all this, and he is still surprised by his achievements, and he's one of the most modest, curious, loyal, creative, entertaining and approachable men I know.

He has the love and support of Janette, without whom today would not have happened: if a woman of such quality can love him, then some of what I've said must be true. Thanks, Janette, for bringing this perfect occasion to life.

Nowadays, many young men are uncertain about what it means to be male. They're regularly fed the preposterous idea that masculinity is toxic, and they often lack wise mentoring.

Paul shows the way: note well young men: aspire to his values, and your lives and our society will be the better.

Our admiration for this man is complete. We find it hard to believe that one life could have contained so much achievement and richness.

By any definition, Paul's life has been a great one, and his fire **still** burns. Afternoon light is calm and invites rest and reflection. Perhaps, finally, Paul, you'll allow it to seduce you, even a touch, into a light application of the brakes. You don't need to worry about anyone emulating your life, mate: you are, and you will always be, one of a kind.

Paul, we extend our most sincere congratulations to you on your 80th birthday; we thank you for your life, your friendship and your character, and we wish you flat water, a tail wind and the stream behind you in your many coming years.

It is my huge honour to ask you all to be upstanding to drink to the birthday health of my brother Paul Guest.

Eulogy for my NSW rowing mate Peter Dickson 2008

Peter Dickson

I offer a memory or two of Peter, because Alison asked.

I'm unworthy to speak about a life that spoke for itself. But this is the last time we'll remember, together, the great oak of a man that Peter was. So we must praise him in the loudest voice we can muster. Peter shouted for us more loudly than we ever shouted for him; I don't mean his voice, which could have dug the Harbour Tunnel; I mean that he was a man who asked little and gave much. Each one of us would be proud to have such an epitaph. Few will.

Peter was a rare man who, in the life of his friends was like the earth. He was powerful, kind, honest and humble. He was incapable of malice. He was hurt deeply when it came his way and could never understand why anyone would want to be cruel. His first instinct was to protect; his last instinct was to harm. He had a bottomless capacity for love and trust. He truly was a person of substance.

Like the earth, the comfort and strength he provided was something we got used to. It's only when the earth isn't there any more that we understand what it meant.

The quality of his life shone in the manner of his death. Peter knew what was happening to him and there was not a tear, not a complaint, not a murmur. He copped it sweet.

I was a fellow oarsman. I competed against him in only two King's Cups, because he retired too early at only 23. He was a prodigious man; huge, rock-hard and depressingly confident. I'll always remember him because in 1967, New South Wales and my first ever Vic crew were level at about the halfway mark. It was then that I first heard the expression "pissant". It was part of the longer expression "OK boys, let's get these Vic pissants", which emerged, with the usual vibrancy, from the five seat. The Vics lost by four lengths and we didn't know what had hit us. The next year he beat me by ten feet to win the right to go to the Mexico Olympics. I was actually fairly happy to hear that he'd retired after that, and funnily enough the Vics started to win again.

I've often thought about winning crews, especially how cruel it is that they cross the line at the height of their power and glory, only to die at that moment, in the sense that the crew will never race that way again. But I reckon there's something beautiful about that too: it can never be the same again so the winning somehow has that much more value.

I feel a bit the same about you, Pete. You've crossed the line a winner and I can tell you the win was powerful and the win was glorious. And you're dead now but we'll always remember you, you light blue pissant, with awe and with love and with gratitude.

John Harry
Sydney
6 pm
27 June 2008

Poem for Donna 2009

Princess

Her smile dances dazzling from
the heart of some transparent pool
of joy and lingers open for
an instant or a lifetime. It is

then that you must show her
if you want the quickly spinning
strobelight flash to blind you
for that moment or forever.

When the light blast hits, get ready.
You will think you know what's happening
but you won't, until you realise
it's too late, that you've been captured

by a mind that's here one moment
then there before you know it,
by a heart that gives itself
to everyone and thing completely.

In her life she's given more
to friends and tramps and dogs and graves
than she will ever see returned,
and more than she believes she's earned.

No one else would love us as
she does, or be as constant as
she is; how can a person who
is only little, love like you?

Well done Princess, you make us proud
You drive us all to have a crack.
Right! You love us, we'll love you back!

JH | Surry Hills | January 2009

Song Lyrics, 2025: a Meditation on Loss

She came upon me as a summer storm
As I stood dreaming reckless
The day was dead and I was worn
My labour always endless

Her eyes spoke loud, with me she said
You'll venture now and always
To lands unknown and full of dread
Cross every road and byway

Why me why me well you should know
I've wife and home awaiting
I cannot be with you and owe
My life to your creating

Her eyes struck lightning in my soul
Her tempest overcame me
Do not resist, be not so bold
Don't think you can deny me

My life then fell into her arms
And years of wandering over
Lands near and far, forever charmed
My life it was to hold her

We sat beside a raging sea
Alone one misty morning
The time has come she said to me
To say that I'm for going
My time with you has been a joy
But mountains are for crossing

Tomorrow I must be away
New times I must be lost in

I said you'll always be my love
I cannot now deny you
Remember me and the blue above
Where one day I will see you.

Remember me and the blue above
Where one day I will see you.

Sir Frederick Holder KCMG and his Daughter and Portraitist Rhoda Holder

Biographical Details

Speaker, 9 May 1901 to 23 November 1903; 2 March 1904 to 5 November 1906; 20 February 1907 to 23 July 1909
Free Trade Party, 1901 to 1903
Protectionist Party, 1903 to 1906
Anti-Socialist Party, 1906 to 1909

Frederick Holder (1850-1909) was the first Speaker of the Australian Parliament.[1] During his Speakership, he was elected and twice re-elected, unopposed. It would be over 100 years before another Speaker matched this record.

Holder was born in Happy Valley, South Australia. He was educated by his father before attending state schools, followed by the Collegiate School of St Peter. Holder's early professional history was varied, being headmaster of the Burra Public School, a store manager, town clerk, proprietor of the *Burra Record* newspaper and mayor of Burra. In 1877 he married Julia Maria Stephens, with whom he shared Wesleyan convictions. They had eight children.

Holder was the Member for Burra in the SA House of Assembly from 1887 to 1901. Most notably he became Premier (and Treasurer) of SA in 1892, but his term only lasted four months. He was elected a delegate to the 1897 Australasian Federal Convention and, through this, drove his belief of free trade and universal adult suffrage and was instrumental in SA becoming the first Australian colony in which women could vote. Holder again became Premier (and Treasurer) in 1899. When Premier, his Government established libraries in country towns, introduced standard time across SA and completed the Bundaleer and Barossa water schemes.

He moved to federal Parliament in 1901 as a Member for SA (and, later, Wakefield), where he was elected Speaker. As Australia's first Speaker, he had the difficult task of adapting standing orders from both the colonial parliaments and the Westminster Parliament to the new federal arena, which by all accounts he did impartially and decisively.

His contributions were not limited to his role as Speaker. The 1903 report of the Joint Library Committee (of which he was chairman) became a blueprint for the eventual National Library of Australia. He was knighted in 1902.

Holder's regard for his own health was not as high as his level of influence and advocacy. In the early hours of 23 July 1909, after an all-night sitting, he shifted from the Speaker's chair onto a seat on the front bench and uttered his final words – 'Dreadful, dreadful!' – before collapsing, still in his Speaker's wig and gown. He died of a cerebral haemorrhage later that afternoon, still in Parliament House, Melbourne, without regaining consciousness. He received a state funeral in Adelaide. The Canberra suburb of Holder is named in his honour.

Rhoda Holder (1880–1925) was born in Burra, South Australia. Her early talent for art was shown when in 1895 she won a prize for drawing from the Board of Governors of the Public Library of SA. Holder studied at the School of Design, Painting and Technical Art – now part of the University of South Australia – from 1898 to 1900. From 1907, she began teaching private classes in drawing, painting, and china painting at a studio in the Adelaide Commercial Chambers. Her portraits, including one of her father, were exhibited at galleries in Melbourne and Adelaide, and her china paintings at the Melbourne Exhibition of Women's Work. In September 1912 she responded to an advertisement seeking expressions of interest from artists interested in painting portraits for the HMC. Holder's request to be commissioned to paint her father's portrait was unsuccessful, the Committee instead choosing George AJ Webb. This portrait of Sir Frederick Holder was donated to the HMC in 1955 by the Holder family.

Acknowledgements

I began thinking about this memoir during a trip Donna and I made to Egypt in 2019. Our collision with that civilisation was at once so surprising, so rich and so shocking that I found myself asking how much poorer our civilisation would have been without the determination of so many men and women to uncover all its secrets, and to record their knowledge in a permanent way. I decided then and there to create a personal record for my family, my friends and anyone else who might be interested. The first tentative pages were typed on the Nile voyage from Luxor to Cairo.

I owe an enormous debt to Donna for her encouragement, her wise and just advice, her willingness to part with me for many writing retreats and for her patience with the publishing process.

I owe a similar debt to my sister Virginia Woolley, whose neutral and smart commentary especially around my relationship with my father ensured that old frustrations were sensitively managed and due credit was given where needed.

My daughter Pip, a highly accomplished writer herself, has given me strong support at every turn; she was the one who introduced me to the indomitable and incomparable Jess Mudditt, from whose kindness, experience and administrative elan the project has benefited enormously. I'm also indebted to Peter and Heather Newman, who took an unexpected interest in what I had to say; to Susan Mackie, who convinced me that there was a story to tell and I had the skill to tell it; to Leanne Greig, for her willingness to read a long manuscript and her honest appraisal; and finally to Karen Comer, Penny Carroll and Meg English for their editorial, proofing and publishing support. I'd be surprised if a more kind and skilled group of women existed anywhere.

And, as it is customary to say, this is all my work and the buck stops with me.

About the Author

Born in Washington DC to an accomplished diplomat, John Harry spent his formative years in Geneva and Singapore before the family moved to Melbourne in 1957, where he has lived and worked ever since.

A law graduate from Melbourne University, John completed his Master of Laws at the University of Virginia through the ITT International Fellowship Program. He began his career with the Rio Tinto mining group, later becoming a partner at prominent law firm Allens, where he represented major corporations and state governments.

Throughout his life, John has made substantial contributions to charitable and community causes, supporting organisations such as the NotFair Art Foundation and the Life Education Centre. John's passion for rowing – as a competitor, coach, administrator and fundraiser – was sparked during his university days, and he has successfully represented both Victoria and Australia.

John now lives on his small Warburton farm in Victoria with his wife Donna. He is frequently visited by his three children – including award-winning children's author Pip Harry – and five grandchildren. Active in the wine industry as a partner in Wild Fire Wines in the Yarra Ranges, John is an avid traveler, musician, photographer, cook, winemaker, brewer and vintage car crank.

Talking of Michaelangelo is John's first book – it is a reflection on, and an attempt to understand, the exciting and puzzling whirlwind that has been his life.

www.ingramcontent.com/pod-product-compliance
Lightning Source LLC
Chambersburg PA
CBHW061228070526
44584CB00030B/4031